With the First Aid Nursing Yeomanry

With the First Aid Nursing Yeomanry

Two Accounts of the F.A.N.Y.'s
During the First World War

Fanny Goes to War

Pat Beauchamp

A Nurse at the War

Grace McDougall

LEONAUR

With the First Aid Nursing Yeomanry
Two Accounts of the F.A.N.Y.'s During the First World War
Fanny Goes to War
by Pat Beauchamp
A Nurse at the War
by Grace McDougall

FIRST EDITION

First published under the titles
Fanny Goes to War
and
A Nurse at the War

Leonaur is an imprint
of Oakpast Ltd

ISBN: 978-1-78282-269-1 (hardcover)
ISBN: 978-1-78282-270-7 (softcover)

http://www.leonaur.com

Contents

Fanny Goes to War

Contents

To
T.H.

Introduction

I eagerly avail myself of the author's invitation to write a foreword to her book, as it gives me an opportunity of expressing something of the admiration, of the wonder, of the intense brotherly sympathy and affection—almost adoration—which has from time to time overwhelmed me when witnessing the work of our women during the Great War.

They have been in situations where, five short years ago, no one would ever have thought of finding them. They have witnessed and taken active part in scenes nerve-racking and heart-rending beyond the power of description. Often it has been my duty to watch car-load after car-load of severely wounded being dumped into the reception marquees of a Casualty Clearing Station. There they would be placed in long rows awaiting their turn, and there, amid the groans of the wounded and the loud gaspings of the gassed, at the mere approach of a sister there would be a perceptible change and every conscious eye would brighten as with a ray of fresh hope. In the resuscitation and *moribund* marquees, nothing was more pathetic than to see "Sister," with her notebook, stooping over some dying lad, catching his last messages to his loved ones.

Women worked amid such scenes for long hours day after day, amid scenes as no mere man could long endure, and yet their nerves held out; it may be because they were inspired by the nature of their work. I have seen them, too, continue that work under intermittent shelling and bombing, repeated day after day and night after night, and it was the rarest thing to find one whose nerves gave way. I have seen others rescue wounded from falling houses, and drive their cars boldly into streets with bricks and debris flying.

I have also, alas! seen them grievously wounded; and on one occasion, killed, and found their comrades continuing their work in the actual presence of their dead.

The free homes of Britain little realise what our war women have been through, or what an undischarged debt is owing to them.

How few now realise to what a large extent they were responsible for the fighting spirit, for the morale, for the tenacity which won the war! The feeling, the knowledge that their women were at hand to succour and to tend them when they fell raised the fighting spirit of the men and made them brave and confident.

The above qualities are well exemplified by the conduct and bearing of our authoress herself, who, when grievously injured, never lost her head or her consciousness, but through half an hour sat quietly on the roadside beside the wreck of her car and the mangled remains of her late companion. Rumour has it that she asked for and smoked a cigarette.

Such heroism in a young girl strongly appealed to the imagination of our French and Belgian Allies, and two rows of medals bedeck her khaki jacket.

Other natural qualities of our race, which largely helped to win the war, are brought out very vividly, although unconsciously, in this book, *e.g.* the spirit of cheerfulness; the power to forget danger and hardship; the faculty of seeing the humorous side of things; of making the best of things; the spirit of comradeship which sweetened life.

These qualities were nowhere more evident than among the F.A.N.Y. Their *esprit-de-corps,* their gaiety, their discipline, their smartness and devotion when duty called were infectious, almost an inspiration to those who witnessed them.

Throughout the war the "Fannys" were renowned for their resourcefulness. They were always ready to take on any and every job, from starting up a frozen car to nursing a bad typhoid case, and they rose to the occasion every time.

H.N. Thompson, K.C.M.G., C.B., D.S.O.,

Major-General.

Director of Medical Services, British Army of the Rhine

Assistant Director Medical Services, 2nd Division, 1914; *ditto* 48th Division, 1915; Deputy-Director Medical Services, VI Corps, May 1915 to July 1917; Director Medical Services, First Army, July 1917 to April 1919.

CHAPTER 1

In Camp Before the War

The First Aid Nursing Yeomanry was founded in 1910 and now numbers roughly about four hundred voluntary members.

It was originally intended to supplement the R.A.M.C. in field work, stretcher bearing, ambulance driving, etc.—its duties being more or less embodied in the title.

An essential point was that each member should be able to ride bareback or otherwise, as much difficulty had been found in transporting nurses from one place to another on the *veldt* in the South African War. Men had often died through lack of attention, as the country was too rough to permit of anything but a saddle horse to pass.

The First Aid Nursing Yeomanry was on active service soon after war was declared and, though it is not universally known, they were the pioneers of all the women's corps subsequently working in France.

Before they had been out very long they were affectionately known as the F.A.N.Y.'s, to all and sundry, and in an incredibly short space of time had units working with the British, French, and Belgian Armies in the field.

It was in the Autumn of 1913 that, picking up the *Mirror* one day, I saw a snapshot of a girl astride on horseback leaping a fence in a khaki uniform and *topee*. Underneath was merely the line "Women Yeomanry in Camp," and nothing more. "That," said I, pointing out the photo to a friend, "is the sort of show I'd like to belong to: I'm sick of ambling round the row on a park hack. It would be a rag to go into camp with a lot of other girls. I'm going to write to the Mirror for particulars straight away."

I did so; but got no satisfaction at all, as the note accompanying the photo had been mislaid. However, they did inform me there was such a corps in existence, but beyond that they could give me no particulars.

I spent weeks making enquiries on all sides. "Oh, yes, certainly there was a Girls' Yeomanry Corps." "Where can I join it?" I would ask breathlessly. "Ah, that I can't say," would be the invariable reply.

The more obstacles I met with only made me the more determined to persevere. I went out of my way to ask all sorts of possible and impossible people on the off-chance that they might know; but it was a long time before I could run it to earth. "Deeds not words" seemed to be their motto.

One night at a small dance my partner told me he had just joined the Surrey Yeomanry; that brought the subject up once more and I confided all my troubles to him. Joy of joys! He had actually seen some of the corps riding in Hounslow Barracks. It was plain sailing from that moment, and I hastened to write to the adjutant of the said barracks to obtain full particulars.

Within a few days I received a reply and a week later met the C.O. of the F.A.N.Y.'s, for an interview.

To my delight I heard the corps was shortly going into camp, and I was invited to go down for a weekend to see how I liked it before I officially became a member. When the day arrived my excitement, as I stepped into the train at Waterloo, knew no bounds. Here I was at last en route for the elusive Yeomanry Camp!

Arrived at Brookwood, I chartered an ancient fly and in about twenty minutes or so espied the camp in a field some distance from the road along which we were driving. "'Ard up for a job I should say!" said my cabby, nodding jocosely towards the khaki figures working busily in the distance. I ignored this sally as I dismissed him and set off across the fields with my suitcase.

There was a large mess tent, a store tent, some half dozen or more bell tents, a smoky, but serviceable-looking, field kitchen, and at the end of the field were tethered the horses! As I drew nearer, I felt horribly shy and was glad I had selected my very plainest suit and hat, as several pairs of eyes looked up from polishing bits and bridles to scan me from top to toe.

I was shown into the mess tent, where I was told to wait for the C.O., and in the meantime made friends with "Castor," the corps' bull-dog and mascot, who was lying in a clothes-basket with a bandaged paw as the result of an argument with a regimental pal at Bisley.

A sudden diversion was caused by a severe thunderstorm which literally broke right over the camp. I heard the order ring out "To the horse-lines!" and watched (through a convenient hole in the canvas) several "troopers" flying helter-skelter down the field.

To everyone's disappointment, however, those old skins never turned a hair; there was not even the suggestion of a stampede. I cautiously pushed my suitcase under the mess table in the hope of keeping it dry, for the rain was coming down in torrents, and in places poured through the canvas roof in small rivulets. (Even in peace-time comfort in the F.A.N.Y. Camp was at a minimum!)

They all trooped in presently, very wet and jolly, and Lieutenant Ashley Smith (McDougal) introduced me as a probable recruit. When the storm was over she kindly lent me an old uniform, and I was made to feel quite at home by being handed about thirty knives and asked to rub them in the earth to get them clean. The cooks loved new recruits!

Feeling just then was running very high over the Irish question. I learnt a contingent had been offered and accepted, in case of hostilities, and that the C.O. had even been over to Belfast to arrange about stables and housing!

One enthusiast asked me breathlessly (it was Cole-Hamilton) "Which side are you on?"

I'm afraid I knew nothing much about either and shamelessly countered it by asking, "Which are you?"

"Ulster, of course," she replied.

"I'm with you," said I, "it's all the same to me so long as I'm there for the show."

I thoroughly enjoyed that weekend and, of course, joined the corps. In July of that year we had great fun in the long summer camp at Pirbright.

Work was varied, sometimes we rode out with the regiments stationed at Bisley on their field days and looked after any casualties. (We had a horse ambulance in those days which followed on these occasions and was regarded as rather a dud job.) Other days some were detailed for work at the camp hospital near by to help the R.A.M.C. men, others to exercise the horses, clean the officers' boots and belts, etc., and, added to these duties, was all the everyday work of the camp, the grooming and watering of the horses, etc. Each one groomed her own mount, but in some cases one was shared between two girls. "Grooming time is the only time when I appreciate having half a horse," one of these remarked cheerily to me. That hissing noise so

17

beloved of grooms is extraordinarily hard to acquire—personally, I needed all the breath I had to cope at all!

The afternoons were spent doing stretcher drill: having lectures on first aid and nursing from a R.A.M.C. sergeant-major, and, when it was very hot, enjoying a splash in the tarpaulin-lined swimming bath the soldiers had kindly made for us. Rides usually took place in the evenings, and when bedtime came the weary troopers were only too ready to turn in! Our beds were on the floor and of the "biscuit" variety, being three square *paillasse* arrangements looking like giant reproductions of the now too well known army "tooth breakers." We had brown army blankets, and it was no uncommon thing to find black earth beetles and earwigs crawling among them! After months of active service these details appear small, but in the summer of 1914 they were real terrors. Before leaving the tents in the morning each "biscuit" had to be neatly piled on the other and all the blankets folded, and then we had to sally forth to learn the orders of the day, who was to be orderly to our two officers, who was to water the horses, etc., etc., and by the time it was eight a.m. we had already done a hard day's work.

One particular day stands out in my memory as being a specially strenuous one. The morning's work was over, and the afternoon was set aside for practising for the yearly sports. The rescue race was by far the most thrilling, its object being to save anyone from the enemy who had been left on the field without means of transport. There was a good deal of discussion as to who were to be the rescued and who the rescuers. Sergeant Wicks explained to all and sundry that her horse objected strongly to anyone sitting on its tail and that it always bucked on these occasions. No one seemed particularly anxious to be saved on that steed, and my heart sank as her eye alighted on me. Being a new member I felt it was probably a test, and when the inevitable question was asked I murmured faintly I'd be delighted. I made my way to the far end of the field with the others fervently hoping I shouldn't land on my head.

At a given command the rescuers galloped up, wheeled round, and, slipping the near foot from the stirrup, left it for the rescued to jump up by. I was soon up and sitting directly behind the saddle with one foot in the stirrup and a hand in Sergeant Wicks' belt. (Those of you who know how slight she is can imagine my feeling of security!) Off we set with every hope of reaching the post first, and I was just settling down to enjoy myself when going over a little dip in the field two terrific bucks landed us high in the air! Luckily I fell "soft," but as I picked myself up I couldn't help wondering whether in some cases falling into the enemy's hand might not be the lesser evil! I spent the next ten minutes catching the "Bronco!" After that, we retired to our mess for tea, on the old Union Jack, very ready for it after our efforts.

We had just turned in that night and drawn up the army blankets, excessively scratchy they were too, when the bugle sounded for everyone to turn out. (This was rather a favourite stunt of the C.O.'s.) Luckily it was a bright moonlight night, and we learnt we were to make for a certain hill, beyond Bisley, carrying with us stretchers and a tent for an advanced dressing station. Subdued groans greeted this piece of news, but we were soon lined up in groups of four—two in front, two behind, and with two stretchers between the four. These were carried on our shoulders for a certain distance, and at the command "Change stretchers!" they were slipped down by our sides. This stunt had to be executed very neatly and with precision, and woe betide anyone who bungled it.

It was ten o'clock when we reached Bisley Camp, and I remember to this day the surprised look on the sentry's face, in the moonlight, as we marched through. It was always a continual source of wonderment to them that girls should do anything so much like hard work for so-called amusement. That march seemed interminable—but singing and whistling as we went along helped us tremendously. Little did we think how this training would stand us in good stead during the long days on active service that followed. At last a halt was called, and luckily at this point there was a nice dry ditch into which we quickly flopped with our backs to the hedge and our feet on the road. It made an ideal armchair!

We resumed the march, and striking off the road came to a rough clearing where the tent was already being erected by an advance party. We were lined up and divided into groups, some as stretcher bearers, some as "wounded," some as nurses to help the "doctor," etc. The wounded were given slips of paper, on which their particular "wound" was described, and told to go off and make themselves scarce, till they were found and carried in (a coveted job). When they had selected nice soft dry spots they lay down and had a quiet well-earned nap until the stretcher bearers discovered them. Occasionally they were hard to find, and a panting bearer would call out "I say, wounded, give a groan!" and they were located. First Aid bandages were applied to

19

the "wound" and, if necessary, *impromptu* splints made from the trees near by. The patient was then placed on the stretcher and taken back to the "dressing station."

"I'm slipping off the stretcher at this angle," she would occasionally complain.

"Shut up," the panting stretcher bearers would reply, "you're unconscious!"

When all were brought in, places were changed, and the stretcher bearers became the wounded and *vice versa*. We got rather tired of this pastime about 12.30 but there was still another wounded to be brought in. She had chosen the bottom of a heathery slope and took some finding. It was the C.O. She feigned delirium and threw her arms about in a wild manner. The poor bearers were feeling too exhausted to appreciate this piece of acting, and heather is extremely slippery stuff. When we had struggled back with her the *soi-disant* doctor asked for the diagnosis. "Drunk and disorderly," replied one of them, stepping smartly forward and saluting! This somewhat broke up the proceedings, and *lèse majesté* was excused on the grounds that it was too dark to recognise it was the C.O. The tent pegs were pulled up and the tent pulled down and we all thankfully tramped back to camp to sleep the sleep of the just till the reveille sounded to herald another day.

CHAPTER 2

First Impressions

The last chapter was devoted to the F.A.N.Y.'s in camp before the war, but from now onwards will be chronicled facts that befell them on active service.

When war broke out in August 1914 Lieutenant Ashley Smith lost no time in offering the corps' services to the War Office. To our intense disappointment these were refused. However, F.A.N.Y.'s are not easily daunted. The Belgian Army, at that time, had no organised medical corps in the field, and informed us they would be extremely grateful if we would take over a Hospital for them. Lieutenant Smith left for Antwerp in September 1914, and had arranged to take a house there for a hospital when the town fell; her flight to Ghent where she stayed to the last with a dying English officer, until the Germans arrived, and her subsequent escape to Holland have been told elsewhere. (A F.A.N.Y. in France—Nursing Adventures.) Suffice it to say we were delighted to see her safely back among us again in October; and on the last day of that month the first contingent of F.A.N.Y.'s left for active service, hardly any of them over twenty-one.

I was unfortunately not able to join them until January 1915; and never did time drag so slowly as in those intervening months. I spent the time in attending lectures and hospital, driving a car and generally picking up every bit of useful information I could. The day arrived at last and Coley and I were, with the exception of the Queen of the Belgians (travelling *incognito*) and her lady-in-waiting, the only women on board.

The hospital we had given us was for Belgian Tommies, and called Lamarck, and had been a convent school before the war. There were fifty beds for "*blessés*" and fifty for typhoid patients, which at that period no other hospital in the place would take. It was an extremely

21

virulent type of pneumonic typhoid. These cases were in a building apart from the main hospital and across the yard. Dominating both buildings was the cathedral of Notre Dame, with its beautiful East window facing our yard.

The top floor of the main building was a priceless room and reserved for us. Curtained off at the far end were the beds of the chauffeurs who had to sleep on the premises while the rest were billeted in the town; the other end resolved itself into a big untidy, but oh so jolly, sitting room. Packing cases were made into seats and piles of extra blankets were covered and made into "tumpties," while round the stove stood the interminable clothes horses airing the shirts and sheets, etc., which Lieutenant Franklin brooded over with a watchful eye! It was in this room we all congregated at ten o'clock every morning for twenty precious minutes during which we had tea and biscuits, read our letters, swanked to other wards about the bad cases we had got in, and generally talked shop and gossiped. There was an advanced dressing station at Oostkerke where three of the girls worked in turn, and we also took turns to go up to the trenches on the Yser at night, with fresh clothes for the men and bandages and dressings for those who had been wounded.

At one time we were billeted in a fresh house every three nights which, as the reader may imagine in those "moving" times, had its disadvantages. After a time, as a great favour, an empty shop was allowed us as a permanency. It rejoiced in the name of *"Le Bon Génie"* and was at the corner of a street, the shop window extending along the two sides. It was this "shop window" we used as a dormitory, after pasting the lower panes with brown paper. When they first heard at home that we "slept in a shop window" they were mildly startled. We were so short of beds that the night nurses tumbled into ours as soon as they were vacated in the morning, so there was never much fear of suffering from a damp one.

Our patients were soldiers of the Belgian line and cavalry regiments and at first I was put in a *blessé* ward. I had originally gone out with the idea of being one of the chauffeurs; but we were so short of nurses that I willingly went into the wards instead, where we worked under trained sisters. The men were so jolly and patient and full of gratitude to the English "Miskes" (which was an affectionate diminutive of "Miss"). It was a sad day when we had to clear the beds to make ready for fresh cases. I remember going down to the Gare Maritime one day before the Hospital ship left for Cherbourg, where they were all taken. Never shall I forget the sight. In those days passenger ships had been hastily converted into hospital ships and the accommodation was very different from that of today. All the cases from my ward were "stretchers" and indeed hardly fit to be moved. I went down the companion way, and what a scene met my eyes. The floor of the saloon was packed with stretchers all as close together as possible. It seemed terrible to believe that every one of those men was seriously wounded. The stretchers were so close together it was impossible to try and move among them, so I stayed on the bottom rung of the ladder and threw the cigarettes to the different men who were well enough to smoke them. The discomfort they endured must have been terrible, for from a letter I subsequently received I learnt they were three days on the journey. In those days when the Germans were marching on Calais, it was up to the medical authorities to pass the wounded through as quickly as possible.

Often the men could only speak Flemish, but I did not find much difficulty in understanding it. If you speak German with a broad Cumberland accent I assure you you can make yourself understood quite easily! It was worth while trying anyway, and it did one's heart good to see how their faces lighted up.

There were some famous characters in the hospital, one of them being Jefké, the orderly in Ward 1, who at times could be tender as a woman, at others a veritable clown keeping the men in fits of laughter, then as suddenly lapsing into a profound melancholy and reading a horrible little greasy prayer book assuring us most solemnly that his one idea in life was to enter the Church. Though he stole jam right and left his heart was in the right place, for the object of his depredations was always some extra tasty dish for a specially bad *blessé*. He had the longest of eyelashes, and his expression when caught would be so comical it was impossible to be angry with him.

Another famous *"impayable"* was the coffin-cart man who came on occasions to drive the men to their last resting place. The coffin cart was a melancholy looking vehicle resembling in appearance a dilapidated old crow, as much as anything, or a large bird of prey with its torn black canvas sides that flapped mournfully like huge wings in the wind as Pierre drove it along the streets. I could never repress a shiver when I saw it flapping along. The driver was far from being a sorry individual with his crisp black moustaches *bien frisés* and his merry eye. He explained to me in a burst of confidence that his *métier* in peace times was that of a trick cyclist on the Halls. What a contrast from his

23

present job. He promised to borrow a bicycle on the morrow and give an exhibition for our benefit in the yard. He did so, and was certainly no mean performer. The only day I ever saw him really downcast was when he came to bid goodbye. "What, Pierre," said I, "you don't mean to say you are leaving us?"

"Yes, Miske, for punishment—I will explain how it arrived. Look you, to give pleasure to my young lady I took her for a joy-ride, a very little one, on the coffin cart, and on returning behold we were caught, *voilà*, and now I go to the trenches!"

I could not help laughing, he looked so downcast, and the idea of his best girl enjoying a ride in that lugubrious car struck me as being the funniest thing I had heard for some time.

We were a never-failing source of wonderment to the French inhabitants of the town. Our manly Yeomanry uniform filled them with awe and admiration. I overheard a chemist saying to one of his clients as we were passing out of his shop, "Truly, until one hears their voices, one would say they were men."

"There's a compliment for us," said I, to Struttie. "I didn't know we had manly faces until this moment."

After some time when work was not at such a high pressure, two of us went out riding in turns on the sands with one of the commandants. Belgian military saddles took some getting used to with the peak in front and the still higher one behind, not to mention the excessive slipperiness of the surface. His favourite pastime on the return ride was to play follow my leader up and down the sand dunes, and it was his great delight to go streaking up the very highest, with the sand crumbling and slipping behind him, and we perforce had to follow and lie almost flat on the horse's backs as we descended the "precipice" the other side. We felt English honour was at stake and with our hearts in our mouths (at least mine was!) followed at all costs.

If we were off duty in the evening we hurried back to the "shop window" buying eggs *en route* and anything else we fancied for supper; then we undressed hastily and thoroughly enjoyed our picnic meal instead of having it in the hospital kitchen, with the sanded floor and the medley of Belgian cooks in the background and the banging of saucepans as an accompaniment. Two of the girls kept their billet off the Grand Place as a permanency. It was in a funny old-fashioned house in a dark street known universally as "the dugout"—*Madame* was fat and capable, with a large heart. The French people at first were rather at a loss to place the English "Mees" socially and one day two of us looked in to ask *Madame's* advice on how to cook something. She turned to us in astonishment. "How now, you know not how to cook a thing simple as that? Who then makes the 'cuisine' for you at home? Surely not *Madame* your mother when there are young girls such as you in the house?" We gazed at her dumbly while she sniffed in disgust. "Such a thing is unheard of in my country," she continued wrathfully. "I wonder you have not shame at your age to confess such ignorance."

"What would she say," said my friend to me when she had gone, "if I told her we have two cooks at home?"

This house of Madame's was built in such a way that some of the bedrooms jutted out over the shops in the narrow little streets. Thompson and Struttie who had a room there were over a Café Chantant known as the "*Bijou*"—a high class place of entertainment! Sunday night was a gala performance and I was often asked to a "scrambled-egg" supper during which, with forks suspended in mid air, we listened breathlessly to the sounds of revelry beneath. Some of the performers had extremely good voices and we could almost, but not quite, hear the words (perhaps it was just as well). What ripping tunes they had! I can remember one especially when, during the chorus, all the audience beat time with their feet and joined in. We were evolving wild schemes of disguising ourselves as *poilus* and going in a body to witness the show, but unfortunately it was one of those things that is "not done" in the best circles!

CHAPTER 3

The Journey Up to the Front

Soon my turn came to go up to the trenches. The day had at last arrived! We were not due to go actually into the trenches till after dark in case of drawing fire, but we set off early, as we had some distance to go and stores to deliver at dressing stations. Two of the trained nurses, Sister Lampen and Joynson, were of the party, and two F.A.N.Y.'s; the rest of the good old "Mors" ambulance was filled with sacks of shirts, mufflers, and socks, together with the indispensable first-aid chests and packets of extra dressings in case of need.

Our first visit was made to the Belgian Headquarters in the town for our *laisser passers*, without which we would not be allowed to pass the sentries at the barriers. We were also given the *mots du jour* or passwords for the day, the latter of which came into operation only when we were in the zone of fire. I will describe what happened in detail, as it was a very fair sample of the average day up at the front. The road along which we travelled was, of course, lined with the ubiquitous poplar tree, placed at regular intervals as far as the eye could see. The country was flat to a degree, with cleverly hidden entrenchments at intervals, for this was the famous main road to Calais along which the *Kaiser* so ardently longed to march.

Barriers occurred frequently placed slantwise across the roads, where sentries stood with fixed bayonets, and through which no one could pass unless the *laisser passer* was produced. Some of those barriers were quite tricky affairs to drive through in a big ambulance, and reminded me of a gymkhana! It was quite usual in those days to be stopped by a soldier waiting on the road, who, with a gallant bow and salute, asked your permission to "mount behind" and have a lift to so and so. In fact, if you were on foot and wanted to get anywhere quickly it was always safe to rely on a military car or ambulance coming along, and then simply wave frantically and ask for a lift. Very much a case of share and share alike.

We passed many regiments riding along, and very gay they looked with their small cocked caps and tassels that dangled jauntily over one eye (this was before they got into khaki). The regiments were either French or Belgian, for no British were in that sector at this time. Soon we arrived at the picturesque entry into Dunkirk, with its drawbridge and medieval towers and grey city wall; here our passes were again examined, and there was a long queue of cars waiting to get through as we drew up. Once "across the Rubicon" we sped through the town and in time came to Furnes with its quaint old market place. Already the place was showing signs of wear and tear. Shell holes in some of the roofs and a good many broken panes, together with the general air of desertion, all combined to make us feel we were near the actual fighting line. We learnt that bombs had been dropped there only that morning. (This was early in 1915, and since then the place has been reduced to almost complete ruin.) We sped on, and could see one of the famous coastal forts on the horizon. So different from what one had always imagined a fort would look like. "A green hill far away," seems best to describe it, I think. It wasn't till one looked hard that one could see small dark splotches that indicated where the cannon were.

A Belgian whom we were "lifting" ("lorry jumping" is now the correct term!) pointed out to us a huge factory, now in English hands, which had been owned before the war by a German. Under cover of the so-called "factory" he had built a secret gun emplacement for a large gun, to train on this same fort and demolish it when the occasion arose. At this point we saw the first English soldiers that day in motor boats on the canal, and what a smile of welcome they gave us!

Presently we came to lines of Belgian Motor transport drawn up at the sides of the road, car after car, waiting patiently to get on. Without exaggeration this line was a mile in length, and we simply had to crawl past, as there was barely room for a large ambulance on that narrow and excessively muddy road. The drivers were all in excellent spirits, and nodded and smiled as we passed—occasionally there was an officer's car sandwiched in between, and those within gravely saluted.

About this time a very cheery Belgian artilleryman who was exchanging to another regiment, came on board and kept us highly amused. Souvenirs were the aim and end of existence just then, and he promised us shell heads galore when he came down the line. On leaving the car, as a token of his extreme gratitude, he pressed his artillery cap into our hands saying he would have no further need of it in his new regiment, and would we accept it as a souvenir!

The roads in Belgium need some explaining for those who have not had the opportunity to see them. Firstly there is the *pavé*, and a very popular picture with us after that day was one which came out in the Sketch of a Tommy in a lorry asking a haughty French dragoon to "Alley off the bloomin' *pavee—vite*." Well, this famous *pavé* consists of cobbles about six inches square, and these extend across the road to about the width of a large cart—On either side there is mud—with a capital M, such as one doesn't often see—thick and clayey and of a peculiarly gluey substance, and in some places quite a foot deep. You can imagine the feeling at the back of your spine as you are squeezing past another car. If you aren't extremely careful plop go the side wheels off the "bloomin' *pavee*" into the mud beyond and it takes half the Belgian Army to help to heave you on to the "straight and narrow" path once more.

It was just about this time we heard our first really heavy firing and it gave us a queer thrill to hear the constant boom-boom of the guns like a continuous thunderstorm. We began to feel fearfully hungry, and stopped beside a high bank flanking a canal and not far from a small *café*. Bunny and I went to get some hot water. It was a tumble-down place enough, and as we pushed the door open (on which, by the way, was the notice in French, "During the bombardment one enters by the side door") we found the room full of men drinking coffee and smoking. I bashfully made my way towards one of the oldest women I have ever seen and asked her in a low voice for some hot water. As luck would have it she was deaf as a post, and the whole room listened in interested silence as with scarlet face I yelled out my demands in my best French. We returned triumphantly to the waiting ambulance and had a very jolly lunch to the now louder accompaniment of the guns. The passing soldiers took a great interest in us and called out whatever English words they knew, the most popular being "Goodnight."

We soon started on our way again, and at this point there was actually a bend in the road. Just before we came to it there was a whistling, sobbing sound in the air and then an explosion somewhere ahead of us. We all shrank instinctively, and I glanced sideways at my companion, hoping she hadn't noticed, to find that she was looking at me, and we both laughed without explaining.

As we turned the corner, the usual flat expanse of country greeted our eyes, and a solitary red tiled farmhouse on the right attracted our attention, in front of which was a group of soldiers. On drawing near we saw that this was the spot where the shell had landed and that there were casualties. We drew up and got down hastily, taking dressings with us. The sight that met my eyes is one I shall never forget, and, in fact, cannot describe. Four men had just been blown to pieces—I leave the details to your imagination, but it gave me a sudden shock to realise that a few minutes earlier those remains had been living men walking along the road laughing and talking.

The soldiers, French, standing looking on, seemed more or less dazed. While they assured us we could do nothing, the body of a fifth soldier who had been hit on the head by a piece of the same shell, and instantaneously killed, was being borne on a stretcher into the farm. It all seemed curiously unreal.

One of the men silently handed me a bit of the shell, which was still warm. It was just a chance that we had not stopped opposite that farm for lunch, as we assuredly would have done had it not been hidden beyond the bend in the road. The noise of firing was now very loud, and though the sun was shining brightly on the farm, the road we were destined to follow was sombre looking with a lowering sky overhead. Another shell came over and burst in front of us to the right. For an instant I felt in an awful funk, and my one idea was to flee from that sinister spot as fast as I could. We seemed to be going right for it, "looking for trouble," in fact, as the Tommies would say, and it gave one rather a funny sinking feeling in one's tummy! A shell might come whizzing along so easily just as the last one had done. Someone at that moment said "Let's go back," and with that all my fears vanished in a moment as if by magic.

"Rather not, this is what we've come for," said a F.A.N.Y., "hurry up and get in, it's no use staying here," and soon we were whizzing along that road again and making straight for the steady boom-boom, and from then onwards a spirit of subdued excitement filled us all. Stray shells burst at intervals, and it seemed not unlikely they were potting at us from Dixmude. We passed houses looking more and more dilapidated and the road got muddier and muddier. Finally we arrived at the village of Ramscapelle. It was like passing through a village of the dead—not a house left whole, few walls standing, and furniture lying about haphazard. We proceeded along the one main street of the village until we came to a house with green shutters which had been previously described to us as the Belgian headquarters. It was in a better state than the others, and a small flag indicated we had arrived at our destination.

CHAPTER 4

Behind the Trenches

We got out and leaped the mud from the *pavé* to the doorstep, and an orderly came forward and conducted us to a sitting room at the rear where Major R. welcomed us, and immediately ordered coffee. We were greatly impressed by the calm way in which he looked at things. He pointed with pride to a gaily coloured print from the one and only "*Vie*" (what would the dugouts at the front have done without "*La Vie*" and Kirchner?), which covered a newly made shell hole in the wall. He also showed us places where shrapnel was embedded; and from the window we saw a huge hole in the back garden made by a "Black Maria." Beside it was a grave headed by a little rough wooden cross and surmounted by one of those gay tasselled caps we had seen early that morning, though it seemed more like last week, so much had happened since then.

As it was only possible to go into the trenches at dusk we still had some time to spare, and after drinking everybody's health in some excellent benedictine, Major R. suggested we should make a tour of inspection of the village. "The bombardment is over for the day," he added, "so you need have no fear." I went out wondering at his certainty that the Boche would not bombard again that afternoon. It transpired later that they did so regularly at the same time every afternoon as part of the day's work! There did come a time, however, when they changed the programme, but that was later, on another visit.

We made for the church which had according to custom been shelled more than the houses. The large crucifix was lying with arms outstretched on a pile of wreckage, the body pitted with shrapnel. The *curé* accompanied us, and it was all the poor old man could do to keep from breaking down as he led us mournfully through that devastated cemetery. Some of the graves, even those with large slabs over them, had been shelled to such an extent that the stone coffins beneath could clearly be seen, half opened, with rotting grave-clothes, and in others even the skeletons had been disinterred. New graves, roughly fashioned like the one we had seen in the back garden at headquarters, were dotted all over the place. Somehow they were not so sinister as those old heavily slabbed ones disturbed after years of peace. The *curé* took me into the church, the walls of which were still standing, and begged me to take a photo of a special statue (this was before cameras were tabooed), which I did. I had to take a "time" as the light was so bad, and quite by luck it came out splendidly and I was able to send him a copy.

It was all most depressing and I was jolly glad to get away from the place. On the way back we saw a battery of *sept-cinqs* (French seventy-fives) cleverly hidden by branches. They had just been moved up into these new positions. Of course the booming of the guns went on all the time and we were told Nieuport was having its daily "ration." We had several other places to go to to deliver hospital stores; also two advanced dressing stations to visit, so we pushed off, promising Major R. to be back at 6.30.

We had to go in the direction of Dixmude, then in German occupation, and the mud at this point was too awful for words, while at intervals there were huge shell holes full of water looking like small circular ponds. Luckily for us they were never right in the middle of the road, but always a little to one side or the other, and just left us enough pavé to squeeze past on, which was really very thoughtful of the Boche!

The country looked indescribably desolate; but funnily enough there were a lot of birds flying about, mostly in flocks. Two little partridges quietly strutted across the road and seemed quite unperturbed!

Further on we came across a dead horse, the first of many. It had been hit in the flank by a shell. It was a sad sight; the poor creature was just left lying by the side of the road, and I shall never forget it. The crows had already taken out its eyes. I must say that that sight affected me much more than the men I had seen earlier in the day. There was no one then to bury horses.

We came to the little *poste de secours* and the officer told us they had been heavily shelled that morning and he sent out an orderly to dig up some of the fuse-tops that had fallen in the field beyond. He gave us as souvenirs three lovely shell heads that had fused at the wrong time. Everything seemed strangely unreal, and I wondered at times if I was awake. He was delighted with the hospital stores we had brought and showed us his small dressing station, from which all the wounded had been removed after the bombardment was over. We then went on to another at Caeskerke within sight of Dixmude, the ruins of which could plainly be seen. I found it hard to realise that this was really the much talked of "front." One half expected to see rows and rows of regiments instead of everything being hidden away. Except for the extreme desolation and continual sound of firing we might have been anywhere.

We were held up by a sentry further on, and he demanded the mot de jour. I leant out of the car (it always has to be whispered) and murmured "Gustave" in a low voice into his ear. "Non, Mademoiselle," he said sadly, "pas ça."

"Does he mean it isn't his own Christian name?" I asked myself. Still it was the name we had been given at the État Major as the pass word. I repeated it again with the same result. "I assure you the colonel himself at C—— gave it to me," I added desperately. He still shook his head, and then I remembered that some days they had names of people and others the names of places, and perhaps I had been given the wrong one. "Paris" I hazarded. He again shook his head, and I decided to be firm and in a voice of conviction said, "Allons, c'est 'Arras,' alors."

He looked doubtful, and said, "Perhaps with the English it is that today."

He was giving me a loophole and I responded with fervour, "Yes, yes, assuredly it is 'Arras' with the English," and he waved us past. I thought regretfully how easily a German spy might bluff the sentry in a similar manner.

Time being precious I salved my conscience about it as we drew up in Pervyse and decided to make tea. I saw a movement among the ruins and there, peeping round one of the walls, was a ragged hungry looking infant about eight years of age. We made towards him, but he fled, and picking our way over the ruins we actually found a family in residence in a miserable hovel behind the one-time Hôtel de Ville. There was an old couple, man and wife, and a flock of ragged children, the remnants of different families which had been wiped out. They only spoke Flemish and I brought out the few sentences I knew, whereupon the old dame seized my arm and poured out such a flow of words that I was quite at a loss to know what she meant. I did gather, however, that she had a niece of sixteen in the inner room, who spoke French, and that she would go and fetch her. The niece appeared at this moment and was dragged forward; all she would say, however, was "*Tiens, tiens!*" to whatever we asked her, so we came to the conclusion that was the limit to her knowledge of French, very non-committal and not frightfully encouraging. So with much bowing and smiling we departed on our way, after distributing the remainder of our buns among the group of wide-eyed hungry looking children who watched us off. The old man had stayed in his corner the whole time muttering to himself. His brain seemed to be affected, which was not much wonder considering what he had been through, poor old thing!

On our way back to Ramscapelle we had the bad luck to slip off the "bloomin' *pavee*" while passing an ammunition wagon; a thing I had been dreading all along. I got out on the foot board and stepped, in the panic of the moment, into the mud. I thought I was never going to "touch bottom." I did finally, and the mud was well above my knees. The passing soldiers were greatly amused and pulled me to shore, and then, stepping into the slough with a grand indifference, soon got the car up again. The evening was drawing in, and the land all round had been flooded. As the sun set, the most glorious lights appeared, casting purple shadows over the water: It seemed hard to believe we were so near the trenches, but there on the road were the men filing silently along on their way to enter them as soon as dusk fell. They had large packs of straw on their backs which we learnt was to ensure their having a dry place to sit in; and when I saw the trenches later on I was not surprised at the precaution.

Mysterious "Star-lights" presently made their appearance over the German trenches, gleamed for a moment, and then went out leaving the landscape very dark and drear. We hurried on back to Ramscapelle, sentries popping up at intervals to enquire our business. Floods stretched on either side of the road as far as the eye could see. We were obliged to crawl at a snail's pace as it grew darker. Of course no lights of any sort were allowed, and the lines of soldiers passing along silently to their posts in the trenches seemed unending; we were glad when we drew up once again at the Headquarters in Ramscapelle.

Major R. hastened out and told us that his own men who had been in the trenches for four days were just coming out for a rest, and he wished we could spare some of our woollies for them. We of course gladly assented, so he lined them up in the street littered with *débris* in front of the Headquarters. We each had a sack of things and started at different ends of the line, giving every man a pair of socks, a muffler or scarf, whichever he most wanted. In nearly every case it was socks; and how glad and grateful they were to get them! It struck me as rather funny when I noticed cards in the half-light affixed to the latter, texts (sometimes appropriate, but more often not) and verses of poetry. I thought of the kind hands that had knitted them in far away England and wondered if the knitters had ever imagined their things would be given out like this, to rows of mud-stained men standing amid shell-riddled houses on a dark and muddy road, their words of thanks half-drowned in the thunder of war.

CHAPTER 5

In the Trenches

Major R., who is a great admirer of things English, suddenly gave the command to his men, and out of compliment to us "It's a long way to Tipararee" rang out. The pronunciation of the words was most odd and we listened in wonder; the major's chest however positively swelled with pride, for he had taught them himself! We assured him, tactfully, the result was most successful.

We returned to the headquarters and sorted out stores for the trenches. The major at that moment received a telephone message to say a farm in the Nieuport direction was being attacked. We looked up from our work and saw the shells bursting like fireworks, the noise of course was deafening. We soon got accustomed to it and besides had too much to do to bother. When all was ready, we were given our instructions—we were to keep together till we had passed through the village when the doctor would be there to meet us and, with a guide, conduct us to the trenches; we were all to proceed twenty paces one after the other, no word was to be spoken, and if a Verey light showed up we were to drop down flat. I hoped fervently it might not be in a foot of mud!

Off we set, and I must say my heart was pounding pretty hard. It was rather nervy work once we were beyond the town, straining our eyes through the darkness to follow the figure ahead. Occasionally a sentry popped up from apparently nowhere. A whispered word and then on we went again. I really can't say how far we walked like this; it seemed positively miles. Suddenly a light flared in the sky, illuminating the surrounding country in an eerie glare. It didn't take me many minutes, needless to say, to drop flat! Luckily it was *pavé*, but I would have welcomed mud rather than be left standing silhouetted within sight of the German trenches on that shell-riddled road. Finally we saw a long black line running at right angles, and the guide in front motioned me to stop while he went on ahead.

I had time to look round and examine the place as well as I could and also to put down my bundle of woollies that had become extremely heavy. These trenches were built against a railway bank (the railway lines had long since been destroyed or torn up), and just beyond ran the famous Yser and the inundations which had helped to stem the German advance. I was touched on the shoulder at this point, and clambered down into the trench along a very slippery plank. The men looked very surprised to see us, and their little dug-outs were like large rabbit hutches. I crawled into one on my hands and knees as the door was very low. The two occupants had a small brazier burning. Straw was on the floor—the straw we had previously seen on the men's backs—and you should have seen their faces brighten at the sight of a new pair of socks. We pushed on, as it was getting late. I shall never forget that trench—it was the second line—the first line consisting of "listening posts" somewhere in that watery waste beyond, where the men wore waders reaching well above their knees. We squelched along a narrow strip of plank with the trenches on one side and a sort of cesspool on the other—no wonder they got typhoid, and I prayed I mightn't slip.

We could walk upright further on without our heads showing, which was a comfort, as it is extremely tiring to walk for long in a stooping position. Through an observation hole in the parapet we looked right out across the inundations to where the famous "*Ferme Violette,*" which had changed hands so often and was at present German, could plainly be seen. Dark objects were pointed out to us sticking up in the water which the sergeant cheerfully observed, holding his nose the meanwhile, were *sales Boches!* We hurried on to a bigger dugout and helped the doctor with several *blessés* injured that afternoon, and later we helped to remove them back to the village and thence to a field hospital. Just then we began bombarding with the 75's. which we had seen earlier on. The row was deafening—first a terrific bang, then a swizzing through the air with a sound like a sob, and then a plop at the other end where it had exploded—somewhere.

At first, as with all newcomers in the firing line, we ducked our heads as the shells went over, to a roar of delight from the men, but in time we gave that up. During this bombardment we went on distributing our woollies all along the line, and I thought my head would split at any moment, the noise was so great. I asked one of the officers, during a pause, why the Germans weren't replying, and he said we had just got the range of one of their positions by 'phone, and as these guns we were employing had just been brought up, the Boche would not waste any shells until they thought they had our range.

Presently we came to the officer's dugout, and, would you believe it, he had small windows with lace curtains! They were the size of pocket handkerchiefs; still the fact remains, they were curtains. He showed us two bits of a shell that had burst above the day before and made the roof collapse, but since then the damage had been remedied by a stout beam. He was a merry little man with twinkling eyes and very proud of his little house.

Our things began to give out at this point and we were not at the end of the line by any means. It was heart breaking to hear one man say, "*Une paire de chaussettes, Mees, je vous en prie; il y a trois mois depuis que j'en ai eu.*" (A pair of socks, miss, I beseech you, it's three months since I had any). I gave him my scarf, which was all I had left, and could only turn sorrowfully away. He put it on immediately, cheerfully accepting the substitute.

We were forced to make our *adieux* at this point, as there was no reason for us to continue along the line. We promised to bring more things the next night and start at the point where we had left off. I thought regretfully it would be some days before my turn came round again.

The same care had to be observed on the return journey, and we could only speak in the softest of whispers. The bombardment had now died away as suddenly as it had begun. The men turned from their posts to whisper "*Bon soir, bonne chance,*" or else "*Dieu vous bénisse.*" The silence after that ear-splitting din was positively uncanny: it made one feel one wanted to shout or whistle, or do something wild; anything to break it. One almost wished the Germans would retaliate! That silent monster only such a little way from us seemed just waiting to spring. We crawled one by one out of the trenches on to the road, and began the perilous journey homewards with the *blessés*, knowing that at any moment the Germans might begin bombarding.

As we were resting the captain of the battery joined us, and in the semi-darkness I saw he was offering me a bunch of snowdrops! It certainly was an odd moment to receive a bouquet, but somehow at the time it did not seem to be particularly out of place, and I tucked them into the belt of my tunic and treasured them for days afterwards— snowdrops that had flowered regardless of war in the garden of some cottage long since destroyed.

Arrived once more at headquarters we were pressed to a *petit verre* of some very hot and raw liqueur, but nevertheless very warming, and very good. I felt I agreed with the Irish coachman who at his first taste declared "The shtuff was made in Hiven but the Divil himself invinted the glasses!" We had got terribly cold in the trenches. After taking leave of our kind hosts we set off for the hospital.

It was now about 1.30 a.m., and we were stopped no less than seventeen times on our way back. As it was my job to lean out and whisper into the sentry's "pearly," I got rather exasperated. By the time I'd passed the seventeenth "Gustave," I felt I'd risk even a bayonet to be allowed to snooze without interruption. The *blessés* were deposited in hospital and the car, once rid of its wounded load, sped through the night back to Lamarck, and I wondered sleepily if my first visit to the trenches was a reality or only a dream.

CHAPTER 6

The Typhoid Wards

When I first came to hospital I had been put as V.A.D. in Ward 1, on the surgical side, and at ten o'clock had heard "shop" (which by the way was strictly debarred, but nevertheless formed the one and only topic of conversation), from nurses and sisters in the Typhoid Wards, but had never actually been there myself. As previously explained the three Typhoid Wards—rooms leading one out of the other on the ground floor—were in a separate building joined only by some outhouses to the main portion, thus forming three sides of the paved yard.

The east end of the cathedral with its beautiful windows completed the square, and in the evenings it was very restful to hear the muffled sounds of the old organ floating up through the darkness.

Sister Wicks asked me one day to go through these wards with her. It must be remembered that at this early period there were no regular typhoid hospitals; and in fact ours was the only hospital in the place that would take them in, the others having refused. Our beds were therefore always full, and the typhoid staff was looked on as the hardest worked in the hospital, and always tried to make us feel that they were the only ones who did any real work!

It was difficult to imagine these hollow-cheeked men with glittering eyes and claw-like hands were the men who had stemmed the German rush at Liége. Some were delirious, others merely plucking at the sheets with their wasted fingers, and everywhere the sisters and nurses were hurrying to and fro to alleviate their sufferings as much as possible. I shall always see the man in bed sixteen to this day. He was extremely fair, with blue eyes and a light beard. I started when I first saw him, he looked so like some of the pictures of Christ one sees; and there was an unearthly light in his eyes. He was delirious and seemed very ill. The sister told me he had come down with a splendid fighting record, and was one of the worst cases of pneumonic typhoid in the ward.

My heart ached for him, and instinctively I shivered, for somehow he did not seem to belong to this world any longer. We passed on to Ward 3, where I was presented to *"Le Petit Sergent,"* a little bit of a man, so cheery and bright, who had made a marvellous recovery, but was not yet well enough to be moved. Everywhere was that peculiar smell which seems inseparable from typhoid wards in spite, or perhaps because of, the many disinfectants. We left by the door at the end of Salle 3 and once in the sunlight again, I heaved a sigh of relief; for frankly I thought the three typhoid *salles* the most depressing places on earth. They were dark, haunting, and altogether horrible.

"Well," said Sergeant Wicks cheerfully, "what do you think of the typhoid wards? Splendid aren't they? You should have seen them at first." As I made no reply, she rattled gaily on, "Well, I hope you will find the work interesting when you come to us as a pro. tomorrow."

I gasped. "Am I to leave the *blessés*, then?" was all I could feebly ask.

"Why, yes, didn't they tell you?"—and she was off before I could say anything more.

★★★★★★

When one goes to work in France one can't pick and choose, and the next morning saw me in the typhoid wards which soon I learnt to love, and which I found so interesting that I hardly left them from that time onwards, except for "trench duty."

I was in Salle 1 at first—the less serious cases—and life seemed one eternal rush of getting "feeds" for the different patients, "doing mouths," and making "Bengers." All the boiling and heating was done in one big stove in Salle 2. Each time I passed No. 16 I tried not to look at him, but I always ended in doing so, and each time he seemed to be thinner and more ethereal looking. He literally went to skin and bone. He must have been such a splendid man, I longed for him to get better, but one morning when I passed, the bed was empty and a nurse was disinfecting the iron bedstead. For one moment I thought he had been moved. "Where—What?" I asked, disjointedly of the nurse.

"Died in the night," she said briefly. "Don't look like that," and she went on with her work. No. 16 had somehow got on my mind, I suppose because it was the first bad typhoid case I had seen, and from the first I had taken such an interest in him. One gets accustomed to these things in time, but I never forgot that first shock. In the afternoons the men's temperatures rose alarmingly, and most of the time was spent in "blanket-bathing" which is about the most back-aching pastime there is; but how the patients loved to feel the cool sponges passing over their feverish limbs. They were so grateful and, though often too ill to speak, would smile their thanks, and one felt it was worth all the backaches in the world.

It was such a virulent type of typhoid. Although we had been in-oculated, we were obliged to gargle several times during the day, and even then we always had more or less of a "typy" throat.

Our gallant sergeant, Sister Wicks, who had organised and run the whole of the three *salles* since November '14, suddenly developed para-typhoid, and with great difficulty was persuaded to go to bed. Fortunately she did not have it badly, and in her convalescent stage I was sent to look after her up at the "shop window." I was anxious to get her something really appetising for lunch, and presently heard one of the famous fish wives calling out in the street. I ran out and bargained with her, for of course she would have been vastly disap-pointed if I had given her the original price she asked. At last I re-turned triumphant with two nice looking little "Merlans," too small to cut their heads off, I decided. I had never coped with fish before, so after holding them for some time under the tap till they seemed clean enough, put them on to fry in butter. I duly took them in on a tray to Wicks, and I'm sure they looked very tasty.

"Have you cleaned them?" she asked suspiciously.

"Yes, of course I have," I replied.

She examined them. "May I ask what you did?" she said.

"I held them under the tap," I told her, "there didn't seem anything more to be done," I added lamely.

How she laughed—I thought she was never going to stop—and I stood there patiently waiting to hear the joke. She explained at length and said, "No, take them away; you've made me feel ever so much bet-ter, but I'll have eggs instead, thank you."

I went off grumbling, "How on earth was I to know anyway they kept their tummies behind their ears!"

That fish story went all over the hospital.

Nursing in the typhoids was relieved by turns up to the trenches behind Dixmude, which we looked forward to tremendously, but as they were practically—with slight variations in the matter of shelling and bombardments—a repetition of my first experience, there is no object in recounting them here.

The typhoid doctor—"Scrubby," by name; so called because of the inability of his chin to make up its mind if it would have a beard or not—was very amusing, without of course meaning to be. He liked to write the reports of the patients in the sister's book himself, and was very proud of his English, and this is what occasionally appeared:

Patient No. 12. "If the man sleep, let him sleep."

Patient No. 13. "To have red win (wine) in the spoonful."

Patient No. 14. "If the man have a temper (i.e. temperature) reduce him with the sponges." And he was once heard to remark with reference to a flat tyre: "That tube is contrary to the swelling state!"

So far, I have made no mention of the men orderlies, who I must say were absolute bricks. There was Pierre, an alert little Bruxellois, who was in a bank before the war and kept his widowed mother. He was in constant fear as to her safety, for she had been left in their little house and had no time to escape. He was well-educated and most interesting, and oh, so gentle with the men. Then there was Louis, Ziské, and Charlké, a big hefty Walloon who had been the butcher on a White Star liner before the war, all excellent workers.

About this time I went on night duty and liked it very much. One was much freer for one thing, and the sisters immediately became more human (especially when they relied on the pros. to cook the midnight supper!), and further there were no remarks or reflections about the defects of the "untrained unit" who "imagined they knew everything after four months of war." (With reference to cooking, I might here mention that since the fish episode Mrs. Betton and I were on more than speaking terms!)

There were several very bad cases in Salle 2. One especially sister feared would not pull through. I prayed he might live, but it was not to be. She was right—one night about 2 a.m. he became rapidly worse and perforation set in. The dreadful part was that he was so horribly conscious all the time. "Miske," he asked, "think you that I shall see my wife and five children again?" Before I could reply, he continued, "They were there *là bas* in the little house so happy when I left them in 1914—My God," and he became agitated. "If it were not permitted that I return? Do you think I am going to die, Miske?"

"You must try and keep the patient from getting excited," said the calm voice of the sister, who did not speak French. He died about an hour later. It was terrible.

"Why must they go through so much suffering?" I wondered miserably. If they are to die, why can't it happen at once?"

This was the first typhoid death I had actually witnessed. In the morning the sinister coffin cart flapped into the yard and bore him off to his last resting place. What, I wondered, happened to his wife and five children?

When I became more experienced I could tell if patients were going to recover or not; and how often in the latter case I prayed that it might be over quickly; but no, the fell disease had to take its course; and even the sisters said they had never seen such awful cases.

CHAPTER 7

The Zeppelin Raid

Once while on night duty I got up to go to a concert in the town at the theatre in aid of the Orphelins de la Guerre. I must say when the Frenchman makes up his mind to have a charity concern he does it properly, and with any luck it begins at 2.30 and goes on till about 9 or possibly 10 p.m.

This was the first we had attended and they subsequently became quite a feature of the place. It was held on a Sunday, and the entire population turned out *colimenté* and *endimanché* to a degree. The French and Belgian uniforms were extraordinarily smart, and the Belgian guides in their tasselled caps, cheery breeches, and hunting-green tunics added colour to the scene.

The mayor of the town opened the performance with a long speech, the purport of which I forget, but it lasted one hour and ten minutes, and then the performance began. There were several intervals during which the entire audience left the *salle* and perambulated along the wide corridors round the building to greet their friends, and drink champagne out of large flat glasses, served at fabulous prices by fair ladies of the town clad in smart muslin dresses. The French governor-general, covered with stars and orders, was there in state with his *aides-de-camp*, and the Belgian general *ditto*, and everyone shook hands and talked at once. Heasy and I stood and watched the scene fascinated.

Tea seemed to be an unheard of beverage. Presently we espied an Englishman, very large and very tall, talking to a group of French people. I remark on the fact because in those days there were no English anywhere near us, and to see a staff car passing through the town was quite an event. We were glad, as he was the only Englishman there, that our people had chosen the largest and tallest representative they could find. Presently he turned, and looked as surprised to see two khaki-clad English girls in solar topees (the pre-war F.A.N.Y. headgear), as I think we were to see him.

The intervals lasted for half an hour, and I came to the conclusion they were as much, if not more, part of the entertainment as the concert itself.

It was still going strong when we left at 7 p.m. to go on duty, and the faithful "Flossie" (our Ford) bore us swiftly back to hospital and typhoids.

On the night of March 18th, 1915, we had our second Zeppelin raid, when the hospital had a narrow escape. (The first one occurred on 23rd February, wiping out an entire family near the "Shop-window.") I was still on night duty and, crossing over to Typhoids with some dressings, noticed how velvety the sky looked, with not a star to be seen.

We always had two orderlies on at night, and at 12 o'clock one of them was supposed to go over to the kitchen and have his supper, and when he came back at 12.30 the other went. On this particular occasion they had both gone together, sister had also gone over at 12 to supper, so I was left absolutely alone with the fifty patients.

None of the men at that time were particularly bad, except No. 23, who was delirious and showed a marked inclination to try and get out of bed. I had just tucked him in safely for the twentieth time when at 12.30 I heard the throb of an engine. Aeroplanes were always flying about all day, so I did not think much of it. I half fancied it might be Sidney Pickles, the airman, who had been to the Hospital several times and was keen on stunt flying. This throbbing sounded much louder though than any aeroplane, and hastily lowering what lights we had, with a final tuck to No. 23, I ran to the door to ascertain if there was cause for alarm. The noise was terrific and sounded like no engine I had ever heard in my life. I gazed into the purple darkness and felt sure that I must see the thing, it seemed actually over my head.

The expanse of sky to be seen from the yard was not very great, but suddenly in the space between the surgical side and the cathedral I could just discern an inky shadow, whale-like in shape, with one small twinkling light like a wicked eye. The machine was travelling pretty fast and fairly low down, and by its bulk I knew it to be a Zeppelin. I tore back into the ward where most of the men were awake, and found myself saying, "*Ce n'est rien, ce n'est qu'un Zeppelin*" ("It's nothing—only a Zeppelin"), which on second thoughts I came to the

45

conclusion was not as reassuring as I meant it to be. By this time the others were on their way back across the yard, and I turned to give 23 another tuck up.

Such a long time elapsed before any firing occurred; it seemed to me when I first looked out into the yard I must be the only person who had heard the Zepp. What were the sentinels doing, I wondered? The explanation I heard later from a French gunnery lieutenant. The man who had the key to the ammunitions for the anti-aircraft guns was not at his post, and was subsequently discovered in a drunken sleep—probably the work of German spies—at all events he was shot at dawn the following day. In such manner does France deal with her sons who fail her. As soon as the Zepp. had passed over, the firing burst forth in full vigour to die away presently. So far, apparently, no bombs had been dropped. I suggested to Pierre we should relight one or two lamps, as it was awkward stumbling about in complete darkness. "*Non, non*, Miske, he will return," he said with conviction.

Apparently, though, all seemed quiet; and sister suggested that after all the excitement, I should make my way across the yard to get some supper. Pierre came with me, and at that moment a dull explosion occurred. It was a bomb. The Zeppelin was still there. The guns again blazed away, the row was terrific. Star shells were thrown up to try and locate the Zepp., and the sky was full of showering lights, blue, green, and pink. Four searchlights were playing, shrapnel was bursting, and a motor machine gun let off volleys from sheer excitement, the sharp tut-tut-tut adding to the general confusion. In the pauses the elusive Zepp. could be heard buzzing like some gigantic angry bee. I wouldn't have missed it for anything. It looked like a fireworks display, and the row was increasing each minute. Every Frenchman in the neighbourhood let off his rifle with gusto.

Just then we heard an extraordinary rushing noise in the air, like steam being let off from a railway engine. A terrific bang ensued, and then a flare. It was an incendiary bomb and was just outside the Hospital radius. I was glad to be in the open, one felt it would be better to be killed outside than indoors. If the noise was bad before, it now became deafening. Pierre suggested the cave, a murky cellar by the gate, but it seemed safer to stay where we were, leaning in the shadow against the walls of Notre Dame. Very foolish, I grant you, but early in 1915 the dangers of falling shrapnel, etc., were not so well known. These events happened in a few seconds. Suddenly Pierre pointed skywards. "He is there, up high," he cried excitedly. I looked, but a blinding light seemed to fill all space, the yard was lit up and I remember wondering if the people in the Zepp. would see us in our white overalls.

The rushing sound was directly over our heads; there was a crash, the very walls against which we were leaning rocked, and to show what one's mind does at those moments, I remember thinking that when the cathedral toppled over it would just fit nicely into the Hospital square. Instinctively I put my head down sheltering it as best I could with my arms, while bricks, mortar, and slates rained on, and all around, us. There was a heavy thud just in front of us, and when the dust had cleared away I saw it was a coping from the cathedral, 2 feet by 4! Notre Dame had remained standing, but the bomb had completely smashed in the roof of the chapel, against the walls of which we were leaning! It was only due to their extreme thickness that we were saved, and also to the fact that we were under the protection of the wall. Had we been further out the coping would assuredly have landed on us or else we should have been hit by the shrapnel contained in the bombs, for the wall opposite was pitted with it. The dust was suffocating, and I heard Pierre saying, "Come away, *Mademoiselle*." Though it takes so long to describe, only a few minutes had elapsed since leaving to cross the yard. The beautiful East window of the cathedral was shivered to atoms, and likewise every window in the Hospital. All our watches had stopped.

Crashing over broken glass to the surgical side, we pantingly asked if everyone was safe. We met Porter coming down the stairs, a stream of blood flowing from a cut on her forehead. I hastily got some dressings for it. Luckily it was only a flesh wound, and not serious. Besides the night nurses at the hospital, the chauffeurs and housekeeper slept in the far end of the big room at the top of the building. They had not been awakened (so accustomed were they to din and noise), until the crash of the bomb on the cathedral, and it was by the glass being blown in on to their stretcher beds that Porter had been cut; otherwise no one else was hurt.

I plunged through the *débris* back to the typhoids, wondering how 23 had got on, or rather got out, and, would you believe it, his delirium had gone and he was sleeping quietly like a child! The only bit of good the Boche ever did I fancy, for the shock seemed to cure him and he got well from that moment.

The others were in an awful mess, and practically every man's bed was full of broken glass. You can imagine what it meant getting this out when the patients were suffering from typhoid, and had to be moved as little as possible! One boy in Salle 5 had a flower pot from the windowsill above fixed on his head! Beyond being slightly dazed, and of course covered with mould, he was none the worse; and those who were well enough enjoyed his discomfiture immensely.

Going into Salle 3 where there were shouts of laughter (the convalescents were sent to that room) I saw a funny sight. One little man, who was particularly fussy and grumpy (and very unpopular with the other men in consequence), slept near the stove, which was an old-fashioned coal one with a pipe leading up to the ceiling. The concussion had shaken this to such an extent that accumulations of soot had come down and covered him from head to foot, and he was as black as a nigger! His expression of disgust was beyond description, and he was led through the other two wards on exhibition, where he was greeted with yells of delight. It was just as well, as it relieved the tension. It can't be pleasant to be ill in bed and covered with bits of broken glass and mortar, not to mention the uncertainty of whether the walls are going to fall in or not.

"Ah," said the little sergeant to me, "I have never had fear as I had last night."

"One is better in the trenches than in your hospital, Miske," chimed in another. "At least one can defend oneself."

One orderly—a new one whom I strongly suspected of being an *embusqué*—was unearthed in our rounds from under one of the beds, and came in for a lot of sarcasm, to the great joy of the patients who had all behaved splendidly. With the exception of Pierre and the porter on the surgical side, every man jack of them, including the adjutant, had fled to the cave. A subsequent order came out soon after which amused us very much:—In the event of future air raids the *infirmiers* (orderlies) were to fly to the cave with the convalescents while the *très malades* were to be left to the care of the *Mees anglaises!*

It took us till exactly 7 a.m. to get those three wards in anything like order, working without stopping. "Uncle," who had dressed hurriedly and come up to the Hospital from his hotel to see if he could be of any use, brought a very welcome bowl of Ivelcon about 2.30, which just made all the difference, as I had had nothing since 7 the night before. It's surprising how hungry Zeppelin raids make one!

An extract from the account which appeared in *The Daily Chronicle* the following morning was as follows:—

One bomb fell on Notre Dame Cathedral piercing the vault of

one of the chapels on the right transept and wreaking irreparable damage to the beautiful old glass of its gothic windows. This same bomb, which must have been of considerable size, sent *débris* flying into the courtyard of the Lamarcq Hospital full of Belgian wounded being tended by English nurses.

Altogether these Yeomanry nurses behaved admirably, for all the menfolk with the exception of the doorkeeper" (and Pierre, please), "fled for refuge to the cellars, and the women were left. In the neighbourhood one hears nothing but praise of these courageous Englishwomen. Another bomb fell on a railway carriage in which a number of mechanics—refugees from Lille—were sleeping, as they had no homes of their own. The effect of the bomb on these unfortunate men was terrible. They were all more or less mutilated; and heads, hands, and feet were torn off. Then flames broke out on top of this carriage and in a moment the whole was one huge conflagration.

As the Zeppelin drew off, its occupants had the sinister satisfaction of leaving behind them a great glare which reddened the sky for a full hour in contrast with the total blackness of the town.

Chris took out "Flossie," and was on the scene of this last disaster as soon as she could get into her clothes after being so roughly awakened by the splinters of glass.

When the day staff arrived from the "Shop-window," what a sight met their eyes! The poor old place looked as if it had had a night of it, and as we sat down to breakfast in the kitchen we shivered in the icy blasts that blew in gusts across the room, for of course the weather had made up its mind to be decidedly wintry just to improve matters. It took weeks to get those windows repaired, as there was a run on what glaziers the town possessed. The next night our plight in typhoids was not one to be envied—Army blankets had been stretched inadequately across the windows and the beds pulled out of the way of draughts as much as possible, but do what we could the place was like an icehouse; the snow filtered softly through the flapping blankets, and how we cursed the Hun! At 3 a.m. one of the patients had a relapse and died.

Chapter 8

Concerning Baths, "Jolie Annette," "Marie-Margot" and "St. Inglevert"

After this event I was sent back for a time to the *blessés* graves on the surgical side on day duty. All who had been on duty that memorable night had had a pretty considerable shock. It was like leaving one world and stepping into another, so complete was the change from typhoids.

The faithful Jefké was still there stealing jam for the patients, spending a riotous Saturday night *au cinéma*, going to Mass next morning, and then presenting himself in the ward again looking as if butter would not melt in his mouth!

A new assistant orderly was there as well. A pious looking individual in specs. He worked as if manual labour pained him, and was always studying out of a musty little book. He was desperately keen to learn English and spoke it on every possible occasion; was intensely stupid as an orderly and obstinate as a mule. He was trying in the extreme. One day he told me he was intended for higher things and would soon be a priest in the Church. Sister Lampen, who was so quick and thorough herself, found him particularly tiresome, and used to refer to him as her "cross" in life! One day she called him to account, and, in an exasperated voice said, "What are you supposed to be doing here, Louis, anyway? Are you an orderly or aren't you?"

"Mees," he replied piously, rolling his eyes upwards, "I am learning to be a father!"

I gave a shriek of delight and hastened up to tea in the top room with the news. We were continually having what was known as *alertes*, that the Germans were advancing on the town. We had boxes ready in all the wards with a list on the lid indicating what particular dressings, etc., went in each. None of the *alertes*, however, materialized. We heard later it was only due to a company of the gallant Buffs throwing themselves into the breach that the road to Calais had been saved.

There were several exciting days spent up at our Dressing Station at Hoogstadt, and one day to our delight we heard that three of the F.A.N.Y.'s, who had been in the trenches during a particularly bad bombardment, were to be presented with the Order of Leopold II. A daily paper giving an account of this dressing station headed it, in their enthusiasm, "Ten days without a change of clothes. Brave Yeomanry Nurses!"

It was a coveted job to post the letters and then go down to the Quay to watch the packet come in from England. The letters, by the way, were posted in the guard's van of a stationary train where Belgian soldiers sorted and despatched them. I used to wonder vaguely if the train rushed off in the night delivering them.

There was a charm and fascination about meeting that incoming boat; the rattle of chains, the clang as the gangway was fixed, the strange cries of the French sailors, the clicking of the bayonets as the cordon formed round the fussy passport officer, and lastly the excitement of watching to see if there was a spy on board. The *Walmer Castle* and the *Canterbury* were the two little packets employed, and they have certainly seen life since the war began. Great was our excitement if we caught sight of Field Marshal French on his way to G.H.Q., or King Albert, his tall form stooping slightly under the cares of State, as he stepped into his waiting car to be whirled northwards to La Panne.

The big Englishman (accompanied by a little man disguised in very plain clothes as a private detective) also scanned every passenger closely as he stepped on French soil, and we turned away disgustedly as each was able to furnish the necessary proof that he was on lawful business. "Come, Struttie, we must fly," and back we hurried over the bridge, past the lighthouse, across the Place d'Armes, up the Rue de la Rivière and so to hospital once more.

When things became more settled, definite off times were arranged. Up to then sisters and nurses had worked practically all day and every day, so great was the rush. We experienced some difficulty in having baths, as there were none up at the "Shop." Dr. Cools from the Gare Centrale told us some had been fitted in a train down there, and permission was obtained for us to use them. But first we were obliged to present ourselves to the commandant (for the railway shed there had been turned into an Hôpital de Passage, where the men waited on stretchers till they were collected each morning by ambulances for the different hospitals), and ask him to be kind enough to furnish a *Bon pour un bain* (a bath pass)! When I first went to the *bureau* at the *gare* and saw this commandant in his elegant tight-fitting navy blue uniform, with pointed grey beard and general air of importance, I felt that to ask him for a "bath ticket" was quite the last thing on earth! He saw my hesitation, and in the most natural manner in the world said with a bow, "*Mademoiselle* has probably come for *un bon?*" I assented gratefully, was handed the pass and fled. It requires some courage to face four officials in order to have a bath.

Arrived at the said train, one climbed up a step-ladder in to a truck divided into four partitions, and Ziské, a deaf old Flamand, carried buckets of boiling water from the engine and we added what cold we wanted ourselves. You will therefore see that when anyone asked you what you were doing in your free time that day and you said you were "going to have a bath," it was understood that it meant the whole afternoon would be taken up.

At first we noticed the French people seemed a little stiff in their manner and rather on the defensive. We wondered for some time what could be the reason, and chatting one day with *Madame* at the dugout I mentioned the fact to her.

"See you, *Mademoiselle*, it is like this," she explained, "you others, the English, had this town many years ago, and these unlettered ones, who read never the papers and know nothing, think you will take possession of the town once again." Needless to say in time this impression wore off and they became most friendly.

The Place d'Armes was a typical French marketplace and very picturesque. At one corner of the square stood the town hall with a turret and a very pretty Carillon called "Jolie Annette," since smashed by a shell. I asked an old shopkeeper why the Carillon should be called by that name and he told me that in 1600 a well-to-do *commerçant* of the town had built the turret and promised a Carillon only on the condition that it should be a line from a song sung by a fair lady called "*Jolie Annette*," performing at a music hall or Café Chantant in the town at that time. The inhabitants protested, but he refused to give the Carillon unless he could have his own way, which he ultimately did. Can't you imagine the outraged feelings of the good burghers? "*Que voulez-vous, Mademoiselle*," the old man continued, shrugging his shoulders, "*Jolie Annette ne chante pas mal, hein?*" and I agreed with him.

I thought it was rather a nice story, and I often wondered, when

52

I heard that little song tinkling out, exactly what *"Jolie Annette"* really looked like, and I quite made up my mind on the subject. Of course she had long side curls, a slim waist, lots of ribbons, a very full skirt, white stockings, and a pair of little black shoes, and last but not least, a very bewitching smile. It is sad to think that a shell has silenced her after all these years, and I hope so much that someone will restore the Carillon so that she can sing her little song once again.

In one corner of the square was a house (now turned into a furniture shop) where one of the F.A.N.Y.'s greatgrandmothers had stayed when fleeing with the Huguenots to England. They had finally set off across the Channel in rowing boats. Some sportsmen!

Market days on Saturdays were great events, and little booths filled up the whole place, and what bargains one could make! We bought all the available flowers to make the wards as bright as possible. In the afternoons when there was not much to do except cut dressings, I often sat quietly at my table and listened to the discussions which went on in the ward. The Belgian soldier loves an argument.

One day half in French, and half in Flemish, they were discussing what course they would pursue if they found a wounded German on the battlefield. *"Tuez-le comme un lapin,"* cried one. *"Faut les zigouiller tous,"* cried another (almost untranslatable slang, but meaning more or less "choke the lot"). *"Ba, non, sauvez-le p'is qu'il est blessé,"* cried a third to which several agreed. This discussion waxed furious till finally I was called on to arbitrate. One boy was rapidly working himself into a fever over the question. He was out to kill any Boche under any conditions, and I don't blame him. This was his story:

In the little village where he came from, the Germans on entering had treated the inhabitants most brutally. He was with his old father and mother and young brother of eight—(It was August 1914 and his class had not yet been called up). Some Germans marched into the little cottage and shaking the old woman roughly by the arm demanded something to drink. His mother was very deaf and slow in her movements and took some time to understand. "Ha," cried one brute, "we will teach you to walk more quickly," and without more ado he ran his sword through her poor old body. The old man sprang forward, too late to save her, and met with the same fate. The little brother had been hastily hidden in an empty cistern as they came in.

"Thus, *Mademoiselle*," the boy ended, "I have seen killed before my eyes my own father and mother; my little brother for all I know is also dead. I have yet to find out. I myself was taken prisoner, but luckily three days later managed to escape and join our army; do you therefore blame me, Miske, if I wish to kill as many of the swine as possible?" He sank back literally purple in the face with rage, and a murmur of sympathy went round the ward. His wound was not a serious one, for which I was thankful, or he might have done some harm.

One evening I was wandering through the "Place d'Armes" when some violins in a music shop caught my eye. I went in and thus became acquainted with the family Tétar, consisting of an old father and his two daughters. They were exceedingly friendly and allowed me to try all the violins they had. At last I chose a little "Mirecourt" with a very nice tone, which I hired and subsequently bought.

In time Monsieur Tétar became very talkative, and even offered to play accompaniments for me. He had an organ in a large room above the shop cram full of old instruments, but in the end he seemed to think it might show a want of respect to *Madame* his late wife (now dead two years), so the accompanying never came off. For the same reason his daughter, who he said "in the times" had played the violin well, had never touched her instrument since the funeral.

★★★★★★

There was one special song we heard very often rising up from the Café Chantant, in the room at the dug-out. When I went round there to have supper with them we listened to it entranced. It was a priceless tune, very catching and with lots of go; I can hear it now. I was determined to try and get a copy, and went to see Monsieur Tétar about it one day. I told him we did not know the name, but this was the tune and hummed it accordingly. A French officer looking over some music in a corner became convulsed and hurriedly ducked his head into the pages, and I began to wonder if it was quite the thing to ask for.

Monsieur Tétar appeared to be somewhat scandalized, and exclaimed, "I know it, Mademoiselle, that song calls itself *Marie-Margot la Cantinière*, but it is, let me assure you, of a certainty not for the young girls!" No persuasion on my part could produce it, so our acquaintance with the fair Marie-Margot went no further than the tune.

The extreme gratitude of the patients was very touching. When they left for Convalescent homes, other hospitals, or to return to the trenches, we received shoals of post cards and letters of thanks. When they came on leave they never failed to come back and look up the particular Miske who had tended them, and as often as not brought a souvenir of some sort from *là bas*.

One man to whom I had sent a parcel wrote me the following letter. I might add that in hospital he knew no English at all and had taught himself in the trenches from a dictionary. This was his letter:

My Lady (*Madame*), The beautiful package is safely arrived. I thank you profoundly from all my heart. The shawl (muffler) is at my neck and the good socks are at my feet as I write. Like that one has well warmth.

We go to make some *café* also out of the package, this evening in our house in the trenches, for which I thank you again one thousand times.

Receive, my lady, the most distinguished sentiments on the part of your devoted

Jean Prompler,
1st Batt. Infanterie,
12th line Regiment.

I remember my first joyride so well. "Uncle" took Porter and myself up to St. Inglevert with some stores for our small convalescent home, of which more *anon*.

Before proceeding further, I must here explain who "Uncle" was. He joined the corps in 1914 in response to an advertisement from us in the *Times* for a driver and ambulance, and was accepted immediately. He was over military age, and had had his Mors car converted into an ambulance for work at the front, and went up to headquarters one day to make final arrangements. There, to his intense surprise, he discovered that the "First Aid Nursing Yeomanry" was a woman's, and not a man's show as he had at first supposed.

He was so amused he laughed all the way down the Earls Court Road!

He bought his own petrol from the Belgian *Parc d'Automobiles*, and, when he was not driving wounded, took as many of the staff for joyrides as he could.

The blow in the fresh air was appreciated by us perhaps more than he knew, especially after a hard morning in the typhoid wards.

The day in question was bright and fine and the air, when once we had left the town and passed the inevitable barriers, was clear and invigorating, like champagne. We soon arrived at St. Inglevert, which consisted of a little church, an *estaminet*, one or two cottages, the *curé's* house, and a little farm with parish room attached. The latter was now used as a convalescent home for our typhoid patients until they were strong enough to take the long journey to the big camp in the South of France. The home was run by two of the F.A.N.Y.s for a fortnight at a time. It was no uncommon sight to see them on the roads taking the patients out "in crocodile" for their daily walk! Many were the curious glances cast from the occupants of passing cars at the two khaki-clad English girls, walking behind a string of sick-looking men in uniform. Probably they drove on feeling it was another of the unsolved mysteries of the war!

We found Bunny struggling with the stove in the tiny kitchen, where she soon coaxed the kettle to boil and gave us a cup of tea. Before our return journey to hospital we were introduced to the *curé* of St. Inglevert, who was half Irish and half French. He spoke English well and gave a great deal of assistance in running the home, besides being both witty and amusing.

We visited the men who were having tea in their "refectory" under Cicely's supervision, and once more returned to work at Lamarck.

Chapter 9

Typhoids Again, and Paris in 1915

I was on night duty once more in the typhoid wards with Sister Moring when we had our third bad Zeppelin raid, which was described in the papers as "the biggest attempted since the beginning of the war." It certainly was a wonderful sight.

The *tocsin* was rung in the Place d'Armes about 11.30 p.m. followed by heavy gunfire from our now more numerous defences. Almost simultaneously bomb explosions could be heard. We hastily wrapped up what patients were well enough to move, and the orderlies carried them to the *cave*. Returning across the yard one of them called out that there were three Zeppelins this time, but though the searchlights were playing, we saw no sign of them, and presently the "all clear" was sounded.

We had just got the patients from the cave back into bed again when half an hour later a second alarm was heard. Our feelings on hearing this could only be described as "terse," a favourite F.A.N.Y. expression. If only the brutes would leave Hospitals alone instead of upsetting the patients like this.

The sky presented a wonderful spectacle. Half a dozen searchlights were playing, and shells were continually bursting in mid-air with a dull roar. On our way back from the *cave* where we had again deposited the patients, the searchlights suddenly focussed all three Zeppelins. There they were like huge silver cigars gleaming against the stars. They looked so splendid I couldn't help wishing I was up in one. It seemed impossible to connect death-dealing bombs with those floating silver shapes. Shrapnel burst all round them, and then the Zepps. seemed suddenly to become alive, and they answered with machine guns, and the patter of bullets and shrapnel could be heard all around. The commander of one of the Zepps. apparently fearing his airship might be hit, must have given the order for all the bombs to be heaved overboard at once, for suddenly twenty-one fell simultaneously! You can imagine what a sight it was to see those golden balls of fire falling through the air from the silver airship. They fell in a field just outside the town near a little village called Les Barraques, the total bag being five cows!

In spite of the three Zeppelins the Huns only succeeded in killing a baby and an old lady. At last they were successfully driven off, and we settled down hoping our excitements were over for the night, but no, at 3.30 a.m. the *tocsin* again rang out a third alarm! This was getting beyond a joke. The air duel recommenced, bombs were dropped, but fortunately no serious casualties occurred. Luckily at that time none of the patients were in a serious condition, so we felt that for once the Hun had been fairly considerate. It was surprising to find the comparatively little damage the town had suffered. We had several others after this, but they are not worth recording here.

One patient we had at that time was a Dutchman who had joined the Belgian Army in 1914. He was a very droll fellow, and told me he was the clown at one of the Antwerp Theatres and kept the people amused while the scenes were being changed. I can quite believe this, for shouts of laughter could always be heard in his vicinity. He was very good at imitating animals, and I discovered later that among other accomplishments he was also a ventriloquist. Sister and I, when the necessary feeds had been given, used to sit in two deck chairs with a screen shading the light, near the stove in the middle ward, until the next were due.

One night I heard a cat mewing. It seemed to be almost under my chair, I got up and looked everywhere. Yes, there it was again, but this time coming from under one of the men's beds. It was a piteous mew, and I was determined to find it. I spent a quarter of an hour on tiptoe looking everywhere. It was not till I heard a stifled chuckle from the bed next the Dutchman's that I suspected anything, and then, determined they should get no rise out of me, sat down quietly in my chair again. Though that cat mewed for the next ten minutes I never turned an eyelash!

I liked night duty very much, there was something exhilarating about it, probably because I was new to it, and probably also because I slept like a top in the daytime (when I didn't get up, breathe it quietly, to steal out for rides on the sands!). I liked the walk across the yard with the gaunt old cathedral showing black against the purple sky, its poor East window now tied up with sacking.

One night about 1 a.m. I came in from supper in my flat soft felt slippers, and from sheer joy of living executed, quite noiselessly, a few steps for sister's benefit down the middle of the ward! It was a great temptation, and needless to say not appreciated by sister as much as I had hoped. I heard subdued clapping from the clown's bed, and there was the wretch wide awake (he was not unlike Morton to look at), sitting up in bed and grinning with joy!

The next morning as I was going off duty he called me over to him. "He, Miske Kinike," he said, in his funny half Dutch, half Flemish, "if after the war you desire something to do I will arrange that you appear with me before the curtain goes up, at the Antwerp Theatre!" He made the offer in all seriousness, and realising this, I replied I would certainly think the proposition over, and fled across to have breakfast and tell them my future had been arranged for most suitably.

The rolls, the long French kind, were brought each morning in "Flossie," by the day staff on their way up from the "shop" referred to in a F.A.N.Y. alphabet as

R's for the 'Roll-call'"—*a terrible fag*—
"Fetching six yards of bread, done up in a bag!

The other meals were provided by the Belgians and supplemented to a great extent by us. I am quite convinced we often ate good old horse. One day, when prowling round the shops to get something fresh for the night staff's supper, I went into a butcher's. The good lady came forward to ask me what I wished. I told her; and she smiled agreeably, saying, "Impossible, *Mademoiselle*, since long time we have only horse here for sale!" I got out of that shop with speed.

The orderlies on night duty, on the surgical side, were a lazy lot and slept the whole night through, more often than not on the floor of the kitchen. One night the incomparable "Jefké," who was worse than most, was fast asleep in a dark spot near the big stove, when I went to get some hot water. He was practically invisible, so I narrowly missed stepping on his head, and, as it was, collapsed over him, breaking the tea-pot. Cicely, the ever witty, quickly parodied one of the *Ruthless Rhymes*, and said:—

Pat who trod on Jefké's face
(He was fast asleep, so let her,)
Put the pieces back in place,
Saying, 'Don't you think he looks much better'?

(I can't vouch for the truth of the last line.)

One day when up at the front we attended part of a concert given by the Observation Balloon Section in a barn, candles stuck in bottles the only illuminations; we were however obliged to leave early to go on to the trenches. Outside in the moonlight, which was almost as light as day, we found the men busy sharpening their bayonets.

Another day up at Bourbourg, where we had gone for a ride, on a precious afternoon off, we saw the first camouflaged field hospital run by Millicent, Duchess of Sutherland, for the Belgians—the tents were weird and wonderful to behold, and certainly defied detection from a distance.

Heasy and I were walking down the rue one afternoon, which was the Bond Street of this town, when the private detective aforementioned came up and asked to see our identification cards. These we were always supposed to carry about with us wherever we went. Besides the hospital stamp and several others, it contained a passport photo and signature. Of course we had left them in another pocket, and in spite of protestations on our part we were requested to proceed to the citadel or return to hospital to be identified. To our mortification we were followed at a few yards by the detective and a soldier! Never have I felt such an inclination to take to my heels. As luck would have it, tea was in progress in the top room, and they all came down *en masse* to see the two "spies." The only comfort we got, as they all talked and laughed at our expense, was to hear one of the detectives softly murmuring to himself, "Has anyone heard of the Suffragette movement here?"

We learnt later that Boche spies disguised in our uniform had been seen in the vicinity of the trenches. That the Boche took an interest in our corps we knew, for, in pre-war days, we had continually received applications from German girls who wished to become members. Needless to say they were never accepted.

The first English troops began to filter into the town about this time, and important "red hats" with brassards bearing the device "L. of C." walked about the place as if indeed they had bought every stone.

Great were our surmises as to what "L. of C." actually stood for, one suggestion being "Lords of Creation," and another, "Lords of Calais"! It was comparatively disappointing to find out it only stood for "Lines of Communication."

English people have a strange manner of treating their compatriots when they meet in a foreign country. You would imagine that under the circumstances they would waive ceremony and greet one another in passing, but no, such is not the case. If they happen to pass in the same street they either look haughtily at each other, with apparently the utmost dislike, or else they gaze ahead with unseeing eyes.

We rather resented this "invasion," as we called it, and felt we could no longer flit freely across the Place d'Armes in caps and aprons as heretofore.

In June of 1915, my first leave, after six months' work, was due. Instead of going to England I went to friends in Paris. The journey was an adventure in itself and took fourteen hours, a distance that in peace time takes four or five. We stopped at every station and very often in between. When this occurred, heads appeared at every window to find out the reason. "*Qu' est ce qu'il y'a?*" everyone cried at once. It was invariably either that a troop train was passing up the line and we must wait for it to go by, or else part of the engine had fallen off. In the case of the former, the train was looked for with breathless interest and handkerchiefs waved frantically, to be used later to wipe away a furtive tear for those brave *poilus* or "Tommees" who were going to fight for *la belle France* and might never return.

If it was the engine that collapsed, the passengers, with a resigned expression, returned to their seats, saying placidly: "*C'est la guerre, que voulez-vous*," and no one grumbled or made any other comment. With a grunt and a snort we moved on again, only to stop a little further up the line. I came to the conclusion that that rotten engine must be tied together with string. No one seemed to mind or worry. "He will arrive" they said optimistically, and talked of other things. At every station fascinating-looking *infirmières* from the French Red Cross, clad in white from top to toe, stepped into the carriage jingling little white tin boxes. "*Messieurs, Mesdames*, pour *les blessés, s'il vous plaît*," they begged, and everyone fumbled without a murmur in their pockets. I began with 5 *francs*, but by the time I'd reached Paris I was giving ha' pennies.

At Amiens a dainty Parisienne stepped into the compartment. She was clad in a navy blue *tailleur* with a very smart pair of high navy blue kid boots and small navy blue silk hat. The other occupants of the carriage consisted of a well-to-do old gentleman in mufti, who, I decided, was a *commerçant de vin*, and two French officers, very spick and span, obviously going on leave. *La petite dame bien mise*, as I christened her, sat in the opposite corner to me, and the following conversation took place. I give it in English to save translation:

After a little general conversation between the officers and the old *commerçant* the latter suddenly burst out with:—"Ha, what I would like well to know is, do the Scotch soldiers wear the pantalons or do they not?" Everyone became instantly alert. I could see *la petite dame bien mise* was dying to say something. The two French officers addressed shrugged their shoulders expressive of ignorance in the matter. After further discussion, unable to contain herself any longer, *la petite dame* leant forward and addressing herself to the *commerçant*, said, "*Monsieur*, I assure you that they do not!"

The whole carriage "sat up and took notice," and the old *commerçant*, shaking his finger at her said:

"*Madame*, if you will permit me to ask, that is, if it is not indiscreet, how is it that you are in a position to know?"

The officers were enjoying themselves immensely. *La petite dame* hastened to explain. "*Monsieur*, it is that my window at Amiens she overlooks the ground where these Scotch ones play the football, and then a good little puff of wind and one sees, but of course," she concluded virtuously, "I have not regarded, *Monsieur*."

They all roared delightedly, and the old *commerçant* said something to the effect of not believing a word. "Be quiet, *Monsieur*, I pray of you," she entreated, "there is an English young girl in the corner and she will of a certainty be shocked."

"*Bah, non*," replied the old *commerçant*, "the English never understand much of any language but their own" (I hid discreetly behind my paper).

As we neared Paris there was another stop before the train went over the temporary bridge that had been erected over the Oise. We could still see the other that had been blown up by the French in order to stem the German advance on Paris in August 1914. This shattered bridge brought it home to me how very near to Paris the Boche had been.

As I stepped out of the Gare du Nord all the people were looking skywards at two Taubes which had just dropped several bombs. Some welcome, I thought to myself!

Paris in war time at that period (June, 1915) wore rather the appearance of a deserted city. Every third shop had notices on the doors to the effect that the owners were absent at the war. Others were being run by the old fathers and mothers long since retired, who had come up from the country to "carry on." My friend told me that when she had returned to Paris in haste from the country, at the beginning of the war, there was not a taxi available, as they were all being used to rush the soldiers out to the Battle of the Marne. Fancy taxi-ing to a battlefield!

The Parisians were very interested to see a girl dressed in khaki, and discussed each item of my uniform in the Métro quite loudly, evidently under the same impression as the old *commerçant!* My field boots took their fancy most. *"Mon Dieu!"* they would exclaim. "Look then, she wears the big boots like a man. It is *chic* that, *hein?"*

In one place, an old curiosity shop in the Quartier St. Germain, the woman was so thrilled to hear I was an *infirmière* she insisted on me keeping an old Roman lamp I was looking at as a souvenir, because her mother had been one in 1870. War has its compensations.

I also discovered a Monsieur Jollivet at Neuilly, a job-master who had a few horses left, among them a little English mare which I rode. We went in the Bois nearly every morning and sometimes along the race course at Longchamps, the latter very overgrown. "Ah, *Mademoiselle,*" he would exclaim, "if it was only in the ordinary times, how different would all this look, and how *Mademoiselle* would amuse herself at the races!"

One day walking along near the *Observatoire* an old nun stopped me, and in broken English asked how the war was progressing. (The people in the shops did too, as if I had come straight from G.H.Q.!) She then went on to tell me that she was Scotch, but had never been home for thirty-five years! I could hardly believe it, as she talked English just as a Frenchwoman might. She knew nothing at all as to the true position of affairs, and asked me to come in to the convent to tea one day, which I did.

They all clustered round me when I went, asking if I had met their relation so-and-so, who was fighting at the front. They were frightfully disappointed when I said "No, I had not."

I went to their little chapel afterwards, and later on, the Reverend Mother, who was so old she had to be supported on each side by two nuns, came to a window and gave me her blessing. My Scotch friend before I left pressed a little oxidized silver medal of the Virgin into my hand, which she assured me would keep me in safety. I treasured it after that as a sort of charm and always had it with me.

A few days later I was introduced to Warneford, V.C., the man who had brought down the first Zeppelin. He had just come to Paris to receive the *Légion d'Honneur* and the *Croix de Guerre*, and was being *fêted* and spoilt by everybody. He promised towards the end of the week, when he had worked off some of his engagements, to take me up—strictly against all rules of course—for a short flight. I met him on the Monday, I think, and on the Wednesday he crashed while making a trial flight, and died after from his injuries, in hospital. It seemed impossible to believe when first I heard of it—he was so full of life and high spirits.

We went to Versailles one day. The loneliness and general air of desertion that overhang the place seemed more intensified by the war than ever. The grass had grown very long, the air was sultry, and not a ripple stirred the calm surface of the lake. It seemed somehow very like the palace of a Sleeping Beauty. I wondered if the ghost of Marie Antoinette ever revisited the Trianon or flitted up and down the wooden steps of the miniature farm where she had played at being a dairymaid?

As we wended our way back in the evening, the incessant croaking of the frogs in the big lake was the only sound that broke the stillness. There was something sinister about it as if they were croaking "We are the only creatures who now live in this beautiful place, and it is we, with our ugly voices and bodies, who have triumphed over the beautiful vain ladies who threw pebbles at us long ago from the terraces."—We turned away, and the croaking seemed to become more triumphant and echoed in our ears long after we had left the vicinity.

At night, in Paris, aeroplanes flew round and round the city on scout duty switching on lights at intervals that made them look like travelling stars. They often woke one up, and the noise of the engines was so loud it seemed sometimes as if they must fly straight through one's window. I used to love to get up early and go down to "Les Halles," the French Covent Garden, and come back with literally armfuls of roses of all shades of delicate pink, white, and cream. Tante Rose (the only name I ever knew her by) was a widow, and the aunt of my friend. She was one of the *vieille noblesse* and had a charming house in Passy, and was as interesting to listen to as a book. She asked me one day if I would care to go with her to a Memorial Service at the Sacré-Coeur. Looking out of her windows we could see the church dominating Paris from the heights of Montmartre, the mosque-like appearance of its architecture gleaming white against the sky.

At that moment the dying rays of the sun lit up the golden cross surmounting it, and presently the whole building became a delicate rose pink and seemed almost to float above the city, all blue in the haze of the evening below. It was wonderful, and a picture I shall always carry in my mind. I replied I would love to go, and on the following day we toiled up the dazzling white steps. The service was, I think, the most impressive I have ever attended. Crowds flocked to it, all or nearly all in that uniform of deep-mourning incomparably chic, incomparably French, and gaining daily in popularity. Long before the service began the place was packed to suffocation. Tante Rose looked proudly round and whispered to me, "Ah, my little one, you see here those who have given their all for France." Indeed it seemed so on looking round at those white-faced women; and how I wished that some of the people in England, who had not been touched by the war, or who at that time (June, 1915) hardly realised there even was one, could have been present.

During another visit to Tante Rose's I heard the following story from an *infirmière*. A wounded German was brought to one of the French hospitals. In the bed adjoining lay a *zouave* who had had his leg amputated. The Boche asked for a drink of hot water, the hottest obtainable. When the nurse brought it to him he took the glass, and without a word threw the scalding contents in her face! The *zouave* who had witnessed this brutal act, with a snarl of rage, leapt from his bed on to the German's and throttled him to death there and then. The other *blessés* sat up in bed and cheered. "It is thus," she continued calmly, "that our brave soldiers avenge us from these brutes." I looked at her as she sat there so dainty in her white uniform, quite undismayed by what had taken place. It was just another of those little incidents that go to show the spirit of the French nation.

Some American friends of mine took me over their hospital for French soldiers at Neuilly. It was most beautifully equipped from top to bottom, and I was especially interested in the dental department where they fitted men with false jaws, etc. Every comfort was provided, and some of the patients were lying out on balconies under large umbrellas, smiling happily at all who passed. I sighed when I thought of the makeshifts we had *là bas* at Lamarck.

I also went to a sort of review held in the Bois of an Ambulance Volant (ambulance unit to accompany a battalion), given and driven by Americans. They also had a field operating theatre. These drivers were all voluntary workers, and were Yale and Harvard men who had come over to see what the "show" was really like. Some of them later joined the French Army, and one the famous "Foreign Legion," and others went back to the U.S.A. to make shells.

It was very interesting to hear about the "Foreign Legion." In peace time most of the people who join it are either fleeing from justice, or they have no more interest in life and don't care what becomes of them. It is composed of dare-devils of all nationalities, and the discipline is of the severest. They are therefore among the most fearless fighters in the world, and always put in a tight place on the French front. There is one man at the enlisting *dépôt* who is a wonderful being, and can size up a new recruit at a glance. He is known as "*Le Sphinx*." You must give him your real name and reason for joining the Legion, and in exchange he gives you a number by which henceforth you are known. He knows the secrets of all the Legion, and they are never divulged to a living soul; he never forgets, nor do they ever pass his lips. One of the most cherished souvenirs I have is a plain brass button with the inscription "*Légion Étrangère*" printed round it in raised letters.

As early as June, 1915, the French were showing what relics they had brought back from the battlefields. No better place than the "*Invalides*," with Napoleon's tomb towering above, could have been chosen for their display. Part of the courtyard was taken up by captured guns, and in two separate corners a "Taube," and a German scout machine, with black crosses on their wings, were tethered like captured birds. There the widows, leading their little sons by the hand, came dry-eyed to show young France what their fathers had died in capturing for the glory of *La Patrie*.

"Dost thou know, *Maman*," I heard one mite saying, "I would like well to mount astride that cannon there," indicating a huge 7.4, but the woman only smiled the saddest smile I have ever seen, and drew him over to gaze at the silvery remains of the Zeppelin that had been brought down on the Marne.

The rooms leading off the corridors above were all filled with souvenirs and helmets, and in another, the captured flags of some of the most famous Prussian Regiments were spread out in all their glory of gold and silver embroideries and tassels.

We went on to see Napoleon's tomb, which made an impression on me which I shall never forget. The sun was just in the right quarter. As we entered the building, the ante-room seemed purposely darkened to form the most complete contrast with the inner; where the sun, streaming through the wonderful glass windows, shone with a steady shaft of blue light, almost ethereal in colouring, down into the tomb where the great emperor slept.

CHAPTER 10

Concerning a Concert, Canteen Work, Housekeeping, the English Convoy, and Goodbye Lamarck

When I returned to the hospital the "English Invasion" of the town was an accomplished fact, and the Casino had been taken over as a hospital for our men. In the rush after Festubert, we were very proud to be called upon to assist for the time-being in transporting wounded, as the British Red Cross ambulances had more than they could cope with. This was the first official driving we did and was to lead to greater things.

The heat that summer was terrific, so five of us clubbed together and rented a *châlet* on the beach, which was christened The Filbert. We bathed in our off time (when the jelly fish permitted, for, whenever it got extra warm, a whole plague of them infested the sea, and hot vinegar was the only cure for their stinging bites; of course we only found this out well on into the jelly-fish season!). We gave tea parties and supper parties there, weather and work permitting, and it proved the greatest boon to us after long hours in hospital.

As we were never free to use it in the morning we lent it to some friends, and one day a fearful catastrophe happened. Fresh water was as hard to get as in a desert, and the only way to procure any was to bribe French urchins to carry it in large tin jugs from a spring near the Casino. These people, one of whom was the big Englishman, after running up from the sea used the water they saw in the jugs to wash the sand off (after all, quite a natural proceeding) and then, in all ignorance of their fearful crime, virtuously filled them up again, but from the sea!

That afternoon Lowson happened to be giving a rather swell and diplomatic tea party. Gaily she filled the kettle and set it on the stove and then made the tea. The matron of the hospital took a sip and the colonel *ditto*, and then they both put their cups down—(I was not present, but as my friends committed the crime, you may be sure I heard all about it, and feel as if I had been). Of course the generally numerous French urchins were nowhere in sight, and everyone went home from that salt-water tea party with a terrible thirst!

A Remount Camp was established at Fort Neuillay. It was an interesting fact that the last time the fort had been used was by English troops when that part of the coast was ours. One of the officers there possessed a beagle called "Flanders." She was one of the survivors of that famous pack taken over in 1914 that so staggered our allies. One glorious "half-day" off duty, riding across some fields we started a beautiful hare. Besides "Flanders" there was a terrier and a French dog of uncertain breed, and in two seconds the "pack" was in full cry after "puss," who gave us the run of our lives. Unfortunately the hunt did not end there, as some French farmers, not accustomed to the rare sight of half a couple and two mongrels hot after a hare scudding across their fields, lodged a complaint! When the owner of the beagle was called up by the colonel for an explanation he explained himself in this wise.

"It was like this, Sir, the beagle got away after the hare, and we thought it best to follow up to bring her back. You see, Sir, don't you?"

"Yes, I do see," said the colonel, with a twinkle. "Well, don't let it happen again, or she must be destroyed."

A Y.M.C.A. was also established, and Mr. Sitters, the organiser, begged us to get up a concert party and amuse the men. In those days Lena Ashwell's parties were quite unknown, and the men often had to rely on themselves for entertainment. Our free time was very precious, and we were often so tired it was a great undertaking to organise rehearsals, but this Sergt. Wicks did, and very soon we had quite a good show going.

One day Mr. Sitters obtained passes for us to go far up into the English lines, and for days beforehand rehearsals were held in the oddest places. Up to the last minute we were on duty in the wards, and all those who could gave a helping hand to get us off—seven in all, as more could not be spared. It was pouring with rain, but we did not mind. We had had such a rush to get ready and collect such properties as we needed that, as often happens on these occasions, we were all in the highest spirits and the show was bound to go well.

We sped along in the ambulance, "Uncle" driving, and picking up Mr. Sitters *en route*. Our only pauses were at the barriers of the town, and on we went again. We had been doing a good 35 and had slowed up to pass some vehicles going over a bridge, when the pin came out of the steering rod. If we had not slowed up I can't imagine there would have been much of the concert party left to perform!

We pulled up and began to look for it, hoping, as it had just happened, we might see it lying on the road. Luckily for us at that moment an English officer drove up and stopped to see if he could be of any help. He heard where we were bound for, and, as time was getting on, instantly suggested we should borrow his car and driver and he would wait until it came back. Mr. Sitters was only too delighted to accept the offer as it was getting so late.

He suggested that four of us should get into the officer's car and go ahead with him and begin the show, leaving the others to follow. We were a little dubious as our lieutenant, Sister Lampen, and "Auntie" (the matron) were over the brow of the hill searching for the missing pin! There seemed nothing else to be done, however, so in we all bundled. The officer was very sporting and wished us "good luck" as we sped off in his car.

Farther along, as we got nearer the front, all the sentries were English which seemed very strange to us. Passing through a village where a lot of our troops were billeted they gazed in wonder and amazement at the sight of English girls in that district.

One incident we thought specially funny—It may not seem particularly so now, but when you think that for months past we had only had dealings with French and Belgian soldiers, you will understand how it amused us. Outside an estaminet was a horse and cart partly across the road, and just sufficiently blocking it. The driver called out to a Tommy lounging outside the Inn to pull it over a little. He gave a truly British grunt, and went to the horse's head. Nothing happened for some seconds, and we waited impatiently. Presently he reappeared.

"Tied oop," he said laconically, in a broad north country accent, and washed his hands of the matter. How we laughed. Of course a Frenchman would have made the most elaborate apologies and explanations—a long conversation would have ensued, and finally salutes and bows exchanged, before we could have got on. "Tied oop" became quite a saying after that.

A F.A.N.Y. eventually coped with the matter, and on we went again. At last we espied some tents in the distance and struck off down a rutty lane in their direction. Here we said "goodbye" to our driver wondering if the other car did not turn up, just how we should get home. We plunged through mud that came well over the tops of our boots and, scrambling along some slippery duck boarding, arrived at the recreation tent. No sign of the other car, so we were obliged to draft out a fresh programme in the meantime.

We took off our heavy coats while two batmen used the back of their clasp knives to scrape off the first layers of mud (hardly the most attractive footlight wear) from our boots. We heard the M.C. announcing that the "Concert party" had arrived, and through holes in the canvas we could see the tent was full to overflowing. Cheers greeted the announcement, and we shivered with fright. There were hundreds there, and they had been patiently waiting for hours, singing choruses to pass the time.

As we crawled through the canvas at the back of the stage they cheered us to the echo. The platform was about the size of a dining table, which rather cramped our style. We always began our shows with a topical song, each taking a verse in turn, and then all singing the chorus. Towards the end of our first song the lieutenant and the others arrived. The guns boomed so loudly at times the words were quite drowned. The programme consisted of recitations, Songs at the piano, solo songs, choruses, violin, etc.; and to my horror I found they counted on me to do charcoal drawings, described out of courtesy as "Lightning sketches!" (an art only developed and cultivated at the insistence of Sergt. Wicks, who had once discovered me doing some in the wards to amuse the men).

There was nothing else for it, rolls of white paper were produced and pinned on a table placed on end, and off I started. I first drew them a typical Belgian officer with lots of medals which brought forth the remark that he "must have been through the South African Campaign!" When I got to his boots, which I did with a good high light down the centre, someone called out "Don't forget the Cherry Blossom boot polish, Miss." "What price, Kiwi?" etc. When he was finished they yelled "Souvenir, souvenir," so I handed it over amid great applause, and felt full of courage! The crown prince went down very well and I was grateful to him for having such a long nose. "We don't want him as no souvenir," they called—"Wish we drew our pay as fast as you draw little Willie, Miss." The *Kaiser* of course had his share, and in his first stages, to their great joy, evidently resembled one of their officers! (There's nothing Tommy enjoys quite so much as that.)

After the "Nut" before the war (complete in opera hat and monocle) and "now" in khaki, I could think of nothing more, and boldly, but with some trepidation, asked if any gentleman in the audience would care to be drawn. You can imagine the scene. A tent packed with Tommies, every available place taken up, and those who could not find seats sitting on the floor right up to the edge of the stage. Yells of delight greeted the invitation, and several made as if to come forward; finally, one unfortunate was heaved up from the struggling mass on to the stage. I always noticed after this that whenever I offered to draw anyone it was always a man with absolutely no particularly "salient" feature (I think that is the term) who presented himself. This individual could best be described as "sandy" in appearance, there was simply nothing about him to caricature, I thought in despair!

The remarks from the audience, which had been amusing before, now fairly bristled with wit, mostly of a personal nature. My subject became hotter and hotter as I seized the charcoal pencil and set off. "Wot would Liza say?" called out one in a horrified voice. "Don't smile, mate, yer might 'urt yer fice," called another. "Take 'is temperature, Miss," they called, as the perspiration began to roll off him in positive rivulets, and "Don't forget 'is auburn 'air," they implored. As the poor unfortunate had just been shorn like a lamb, preparatory to going into the trenches, this was particularly cutting. The remark, however, gave me an inspiration and the audience yelled delightedly while I put a few black dots, very wide apart, to indicate the shortage. When finished we shook hands to show there was no ill feeling, and quite cheerfully, with the expression of a hero, he bore his portrait off amid cheers from the men.

The show ended with a song, Sergeant Michael Cassidy, which was extremely popular at that time. For those who have not heard this classic, it might be as well to give one or two verses. We each had our own particular one, and then all sang the chorus.

> You've heard of Michael Cassidy, a strapping Irish bhoy.
> Who up and joined the Irish guards as Kitchener's pride and joy;
> When on the march you'll hear them shout, 'Who's going to win the war?'
> And this is what the khaki lads all answered with a roar:

Chorus
Cassidy, Sergeant Michael Cassidy,
He's of Irish nationality.
He's a lad of wonderful audacity,
Sergeant Michael Cassidy (bang), V.C.

Last Verse
Who was it met a dainty little Belgian refugee
And right behind the firing line, would take her on his knee?
Who was it, when she doubted him, got on his knees and swore
He'd love her for three years or the duration of the war?
Chorus, etc.

This was encored loudly, and someone called out for "Who's Your Lady Friend?" As there were not any within miles excepting ourselves, and certainly none in the audience, it was rather amusing.

We plunged through the mud again after it was all over and were taken to have coffee and sandwiches in the mess. We were just in time to see some of the men and wish them good luck, as they were being lined up preparatory to going into the trenches. Poor souls, I felt glad we had been able to do something to cheer them a little; and the guns, which we had heard distinctly throughout the concert, now boomed away louder than ever.

We had a fairly long walk back from the mess to where the Mors car had been left owing to the mud, and at last we set off along the dark and rutty road.

One facetious French sentry insisted on talking English and flashing his lantern into the back of the ambulance, saying, "But I will see the face of each Mees for fear of an *espion*." He did so, murmuring "*jolie—pas mal—chic*," etc.! He finally left us, saying: "I am an officer. Well, ladies, goodbye all!" We were convulsed, and off we slid once more into the darkness and rain, without any lights, reaching home about 12, after a very amusing evening.

Soon after this, we started our "Pleasant Sunday Evenings," as we called them, in the top room of the hospital, and there from 8 to 9.30 every Sunday gave coffee and held impromptu concerts. They were a tremendous success, and chiefly attended by the English. They were so popular we were often at a loss for seats. Of real furniture there was very little. It consisted mostly of packing cases covered with army blankets and enormous tumpties in the middle of the floor—these latter contained the reserve store of blankets for the hospital, and excellent "pouffs" they made.

Our reputation of being able to turn our hands to anything resulted in Mr. Sitters—rushing in during 10 o'clock tea one morning with the news that two English divisions were going south from Ypres in a few days' time, and the Y.M.C.A. had been asked by the army to erect a temporary canteen at a certain railhead during the six days they would take to pass through. There were no lady helpers in those days, and he was at his wits' end to know where to find the staff. Could any of us be spared? None of us could, as we were understaffed already, but Lieutenant Franklin put it to us and said if we were willing to undertake the canteen, as well as our hospital work, which would mean an average of only five hours sleep in the twenty-four—she had no objection. There was no time to get fresh Y.M.C.A. workers from England with the delay of passports, etc., and of course we decided to take it on, only too pleased to have the chance to do something for our own men.

A shed was soon erected, the front part being left open facing the railway lines, and counters were put up. The work, which went on night and day, was planned out in shifts, and we were driven up to the siding in Y.M.C.A. Fords or any of our own which could be spared. Trains came through every hour averaging about 900 men on board. There was just time in between the trains to wash the cups up and put out fresh buns and chocolates. When one was in, there was naturally no time to wash the cups up at all, and they were just used again as soon as they were empty. Canteen work with a vengeance! The whole of the Highland division passed through together with the 37th. They sat in cattle trucks mostly, the few carriages there were being reserved for the officers. It was amusing to notice that at first the men thought we were French, so unaccustomed were they then to seeing any English girls out there with the exception of army sisters and V.A.D.s.

"*Do chocolat, si voos play*," they would ask, and were speechless with surprise when we replied sweetly: "Certainly, which kind will you have?"

I asked one Scotchman during a pause, when the train was in for a longer interval than usual, how he managed to make himself understood up the line. "Och fine," he said, "it's not verra deefficult to *parley voo*. I gang into one o' them *estaminays* to ask for twa drinks, I say 'twa' and, would you believe it, they always hand out three—good natured I call that, but I hae to pay up all the same," he added!

Naturally the French people thought he said *trois*. This story sub-

73

sequently appeared in print, I believe.

One regiment had a goat, and Billy was let out for a walk and had wandered rather far afield, when the train started to move on again. Luckily those trains never went very fast, but it was a funny sight to see two Tommies almost throttling the goat in their efforts to drag it along, pursued by several F.A.N.Y.s (to make the pace), and give it a final shove up into a truck!

Towards the end of that week the entire staff became exceedingly short tempered. The loss of sleep combined with hospital work probably accounted for it; we even slept in the jolting cars on the way back. We were more than repaid though, by the smiles of the Tommies and the gratitude of the Y.M.C.A., who would have been unable to run the canteen at all but for our help.

It was at this period in our career we definitely became known as the "F.A.N.N.Y.s"—"F.A.N.Y.," spelt the passing Tommy—"FANNY," "I wonder what that stands for?"

"First anywhere," suggested one, which was not a bad effort, we thought!

The following is an extract from an account by Mr. Beach Thomas in a leading daily:

"Our Yeomanry nurses who, among other work, drive, clean, and manage their own ambulance cars, are dressed in khaki. Their skirts are short, their hats (some say their feet), are large! (this we thought hardly kind). They have done prodigies along the Belgian front. One of their latest activities has been to devise and work a peripatetic bath. By ingenious contrivances, tents, and ten collapsible baths, are packed into a motor car which circulates behind the lines. The water is heated by the engine in a cistern in the interior of the car and offers the luxury of a hot bath to several score men."

This was our famous motor bath called "James," and belonging to "Jimmy" Gamwell. She saw to the heating of the water and the putting up of the baths, with their canvas screens sloping from the roof of the ambulance and so forming at each side a bathroom annexe. A sergeant marshalled the soldiers in at one end and in about ten minutes' time they emerged clean, rosy, and smiling at the other!

The article continued:

These women have run a considerable hospital and its ambulances entirely by themselves. The work has been voluntary. By doing their own household work, by feeding themselves at their own expense (except for a few supplementary Belgian Army rations), by driving and cleaning their own cars, they have made such a success on the economical side that the money laboriously collected in England has all been spent on the direct service of the wounded, and not on establishment charges.

A Soup Kitchen brought out by Betty also belonged to our hospital equipment. It did excellent work down at the Gare Centrale, providing the wounded with hot soup on their arrival. Great was our excitement when it was commissioned by a battery up the line. Betty and Lewis set off in high spirits, and had the most thrilling escapes and adventures in the Ypres section that would alone fill a book. They were with the battery in the early summer when the first gas attack swept over, and caught them at "Hell fire Corner" on the Ypres-Menin road. It was they who improvised temporary masks for the men from wads of cotton wool and lint soaked in carbolic. Luckily they were not near enough to be seriously gassed, but for months after they both felt the after effects. Even where we were, we noticed the funny sulphurous smell in the air which seemed to catch one with a tight sensation in the throat, and the taste of sulphur was also perceptible on one's lips. We were to have taken turns with the kitchen, but owing to this episode the authorities considered the work too dangerous, and after being complimented on their behaviour they returned to Lamarck.

We had a lot of daylight Taube raids, Zeppelins for the moment confining all their efforts to England. It was fascinating to watch the little round white balls, like baby clouds, where the shrapnel burst in its efforts to bring the marauders down.

Very few casualties resulted from these raids and we rather enjoyed them. One that fell on the quay killed an old white horse; and a French sailor found the handle of the bomb among the shrapnel near by and presented it to me. It seemed odd to think that such a short while before it had been in the hands of a Boche.

Jan was a patient we had who had entirely lost his speech and memory. We could get nothing out of him but an expressive shrug of the shoulders and a smile. He was a good looking Belgian of about twenty-four; and it was my duty to take him out by the arm for a short walk each morning to try and reawaken his interest in life.

One day I saw the French governor of the town coming along on horseback followed by his ordnance (groom). How could I make Jan salute, I wondered? I knew the general was very particular about such things, and to all appearance Jan was a normal looking individual. *"Faut saluer le général, Jan,"* I said, while he was still some distance away, but Jan only shrugged his shoulders as much as to say, "I might do it, but on the other hand I might not!" What was I to do? As we drew nearer I again implored Jan to salute. He shrugged his shoulders, so in desperation, just as we came abreast I put my arm behind him and seizing his, brought it up to the salute! The general, whom I knew, seemed fearfully amused as he returned it, and the next time we met he asked me if I was in the habit of going for a walk arm in arm with Belgian soldiers, who had to be made to salute in such a fashion?

One day we saw an aeroplane falling. At first it was hard to believe it was not doing some patent stunt. Instead of coming down plumb as one would imagine, it fell first this way and then that, like a piece of paper fluttering down from a window. As it got nearer the earth though where the currents of air were not so powerful, it plunged straight downwards. Crowds witnessed the descent, and ran to the spot where it had fallen.

Greatly to their surprise the pilot was unhurt and the machine hardly damaged at all. It had fallen just into the sea, and its wings were keeping it afloat. The pilot was brought ashore in a boat, and when the tide went down a cordon of guards was placed round the machine till it was removed.

Bridget, our former housekeeper at the hospital, went home to England in the autumn for a rest and I was asked to take on her job. I moved to the hospital and slept in the top room, behind our sitting-room, together with the chauffeurs and Lieutenant Franklin.

I had to see that breakfast was all right, and at 7.30 lay the table in the big kitchen, get the jam out of our store cupboard, make the tea, etc. Breakfast over, I had the top room to sweep and dust, the beds to make, the linen to put out to air, and when that was done it was time to get "10 o'clocks" ready. After that I sallied forth armed with a big basket, a fat purse and a long list, and thoroughly enjoyed myself in the market.

In the afternoons there were always stacks of hospital mending to do, and then tea to get ready. Sometimes as many as twelve people—French, Belgian, or English—used to drop in, and it was no easy task to keep that teapot going; however it was always done somehow. Luckily we had a gas-ring, as it would have been an impossibility to run up and down the sixty-nine steps to the kitchen every time we wanted more hot water.

At six the housekeeper had to prepare the evening meal for 7.30, and the Flemish cooks looked on with great amusement at my concoctions—a lot of it was tinned stuff, so the cooking required was of the simplest. They always cooked the potatoes for me out of the kindness of their hearts. The reason they did not do the whole thing was that they were really off duty at six, but one of them usually stayed behind and helped.

Work at that time began to slacken off considerably.—A large hut hospital for typhoids was built and the casualties diminished, partly because most of the Belgians had already been killed or wounded, and partly because the remaining few had not much fighting to do except hold the line behind the inundations. A faint murmur reached us that a comb-out was going to take place among the British Red Cross Ambulance drivers, and we wondered who would replace them if they were sent up the line.

The anniversary of the opening of Lamarck hospital took place on the 31st October, 1915, and we had a tremendous gathering, French, English, and Belgians, described in the local rag as "*une réception intime, l'élite de tout ce que la ville renferme!*" The French governor-general of the town, accompanied by two *aides-de-camp*, came in state. All the guests visited the wards, and then adjourned for tea to the top room where the housekeeper had to perform miracles with the gas-ring. A speech of thanks was made to the corps, and "Scrubby" (the typhoid doctor) got up and in *quelques paroles émues* added his tribute as well. It was a most successful show and we thought the French governor would never depart, he seemed to enjoy himself so much!

Our next excitement was a big Allied concert given at the theatre. Several performances had taken place there since the one I described, but this was the first time Belgians, French, and English had collaborated.

Betty, who had been at Tree's School, was asked to recite, and I was asked to play the violin. She also got up a one-act farce with Lieutenant Raby. It is extremely hard to be a housekeeper for a hospital and work up for a concert at the same time. The only place I could practise in was the storeroom and there, surrounded by tins of McVitie's biscuits and Crosse & Blackwell's jam, I resorted when I could snatch a few minutes!

At last the day of the concert arrived and we rattled up to the theatre in "Flossie." A fairly big programme had been arranged, and the three Allies were well represented. There was an opera singer from

Paris resplendent in a long red velvet dress, who interested me very much, she behaved in such an extraordinary way behind the scenes. Before she was due to go on, she walked up and down literally snorting like a war-horse, occasionally bursting into a short scale, and then beating her breast and saying, "*Mon Dieu, que j'ai le trac,*" which, being interpreted, means, approximately, "My God, but I have got the wind up!" I sat in a corner with my violin and gazed at her in wonder. Everything went off very well, and we received many be-ribboned bouquets and baskets of flowers, which transformed the top room for days.

All lesser excitements were eclipsed when we heard further rumours that the English Red Cross might take us over to replace the men driving for them at that time.

MacDougal and Franklin, our two lieutenants, were constantly attending conferences on the subject.

At last an official requisition came through for sixteen ambulance drivers to replace the men by January 1, 1916. You can imagine our excitement at the prospect. The very first women to drive British wounded officially! It was an epoch in women's work in France and the forerunner of all the subsequent convoys.

Simultaneously an article appeared the 2nd December, 1915, headed "'Yeowomen,' a triumph of hospital organisation," which I may be pardoned for quoting:

A complete unit with sixteen to twenty motor ambulances, organised, worked, and driven by women, will next month be added to the British Army.

The women will drive their own cars and look after them in every way. One single male mechanic, and that is all, is to be attached to the whole unit. These ambulances may of course be summoned from their camp to hurry over any type of winter-worn road to the neighbourhood of the firing line.

What strength, endurance, and pluck such work demands from women can easily be understood by anyone who has ever tried to swing a car in cold weather or repair it by the roadside.

It is a very notable fact that for the first time under official recognition women have been allowed to share in what may be called a male department of warfare.

The Nursing Yeomanry have just extracted this recognition from the War Office and deserve every compliment that can be paid them; and the success is worth some emphasis as one of a series of victories for women workers and organisations, at the top of which is, of course, the Voluntary Aid Detachment.

The actual work of these Yeomen nurses, who rode horseback to the dressing stations when no other means of conveyance were available, has been in progress in France and Belgium almost since war was declared. Most of their work has been done in the face of every kind of discouragement, but they were never dismayed. Their khaki uniforms on more than one occasion in Ghent made German sentries jump. (Mrs. MacDougal arranging for F.A.N.Y. work with the Belgians in September, 1914).

This feat of the 'Yeowomen'—who have struggled against a certain amount of ridicule in England since they started a horse ambulance and camp some six or seven years ago—is worth emphasis because it is only one instance, striking but by no means unique, of the complete triumph of women workers during the past few months!

★★★★★★

The next question was to decide who would go to the new English convoy, and two or three left for England to become proficient in motor mechanics and driving.

I was naturally anxious after a year with the Allies, to work for the British, but as I could not be spared from housekeeping to go to England I was dubious as to whether I could pass the test or not. Though I had come out originally with the idea of being a chauffeur, I had only done odd work from time to time at Lamarck. "Uncle," however, was very hopeful and persuaded me to take the test in France before my leave was due. Accordingly, I went round to the English Mechanical Transport in the town for the exam., the same test as the men went through. I felt distinctly like the opera lady at the concert. It was a very greasy day and the road which we took was bordered on one side by a canal and on the other by a deep and muddy ditch. As we came to a cross road the A.S.C. lieutenant who was testing me, said, "There you see the marks where the last man I tested skidded with his car."

"Yes, rather, how jolly!" I replied in my agitation, wondering if my fate would be likewise. We passed the spot more by luck than good management, and then I reversed for some distance along that same road. At last I turned at the cross-roads, and after some traffic driving, luckily without any mishap, drove back to hospital. I was questioned about mechanics on the way, and at the end tactfully explained I was just going on leave and meant to spend every second in a garage! I got out at the hospital gates feeling quite sure I had failed, but to my intense relief and joy he told me I had passed, and he would send up the marks to hospital later on. I jumped at least a foot off the pavement!

I went in and told the joyful news to Lieutenant Franklin, who was to be boss of the new convoy, while Lieutenant MacDougal was to be head of the Belgian hospital, and of the unit down at the big convalescent *dépôt* in the S. of France, at Camp de Ruchard, where Lady Baird and Sister Lovell superintended the hospital, and Chris and Thompson did the driving.

It was sad to bid goodbye to Lamarck and the Belgians, but as the English Convoy was to be in the same town it was not as if we should never see them again.

"Camille," in Ward 1, whose back had been broken when the dugout collapsed on him during a bombardment, hung on to my hand while the tears filled his eyes. He had been my special case when he first arrived, and his gratitude for anything we could do for him was touching.

The Adjutant Heddebaud, who was the official Belgian head of the hospital, wrote out with many flourishes a panegyric of sorts thanking me for what I had done, which I duly pasted in my War Album; and so I said goodbye to Lamarck and the Belgians, and left for England, December, 1915.

CHAPTER 11

The English Convoy

My second leave was spent for the most part at a garage in the neighbouring town near the village where we lived. I positively dreamt of carburettors, magnetoes, and how to change tyres! The remaining three of my precious fourteen days were spent in London enjoying life and collecting kit and such like. We were to be entirely under canvas in our new camp, and as it was mid-winter you can imagine we made what preparations we could to avoid dying of pneumonia.

The presentation of a fox terrier, "Tuppence," by name, I hailed with delight. When all else froze, he would keep me warm, I thought!

It may be interesting to members of the corps to know the names of those who formed that pioneer Convoy. They are: Lieutenant Franklin, M. Thompson (Section Leader), B. Ellis, W. Mordaunt, C. Nicholson, D. Heasman, D. Reynolds, G. Quin, M. Gamwell, H. Gamwell, B. Hutchinson, N. F. Lowson, P. B. Waddell, M. Richardson, M. Laidley, O. Mudie-Cooke, P. Mudie-Cooke and M. Lean (the last three were new members). I met Lowson and Lean at Victoria on January 3, 1916, and between us we smuggled "Tuppence" into the boat train without anyone seeing him; likewise through the customs at Folkestone. Arrived there we found that mines were loose owing to the recent storms, and the boat was not sailing till the next day.

Then followed a hunt for rooms, which we duly found but in doing so lost "Tuppence." The rest of the time was spent looking for him; and when we finally arrived breathless at the police station, there was the intelligent dog sitting on the steps! I must here confess this was one of the few occasions he ever exhibited his talents in that direction, and as such it must be recorded. He was so well bred that sometimes he was positively stupid, however, he was beautiful to look at, and one can't have everything in this world.

The next morning the sea was still fairly rough; and I went in to the adjoining room to find that the gallant Lowson was already up and stirring, and had gone forth into the town in search of "Mother-sill." I looked out at the sea and hoped fervently she would find some.

We went on board at nine, after a good breakfast, and decided to stay on deck. A sailor went round with a megaphone, shouting, "All lifebelts on," and we were under way.

I confided "Tuppence" to the care of the ship's carpenter and begged him to find a spare lifebelt for him, so that if the worst came to the worst he could use it as a little raft!

We watched the two destroyers pitching black against the dashing spray as they sped along on either side convoying us across.

We arrived at Boulogne in time for lunch, and then set off for our convoy camp thirty kilometres away, in a British Red Cross touring car borrowed from the "Christol Hotel." We arrived there amid a deluge of rain, and the camp looked indeed a sorry spectacle with the tents all awry in the hurricane that was blowing.

Bell tents flanked one side of the large open space where the ambulances stood. A big store tent occupied another and the cook-house was in a shed at the extreme corner, with the mess tent placed about as far from it as possible! I fully appreciated this piece of staff work later. There were also a lot of bathing machines, which made me vaguely wonder if a Snark had once inhabited the place.

The fourth (viz. sign of a Snark) is its fondness for bathing machines
Which it constantly carries about,
And believes that they add to the beauty of scenes—
A sentiment open to doubt.

My surmises were brought to an abrupt end.

"Pat, dear old Pat. I say, old bird, you won't mind going into the cook-house for a bit, will you, till the real cook comes? You're so good-natured (?) I know you will, old thing."

Before I could reply, someone else said:

"That's settled then; it's perfectly ripping of you."

"Splendid," said someone else. Being the chief person concerned, I hadn't had a chance to utter word of protest one way or the other!

When I could gasp out something, I murmured feebly that I had thought I was going to drive a car, and had spent most of my leave sitting in a garage with that end in view.

"Oh, yes, of course you are, old thing, but the other cook hasn't turned up yet. Bridget (Laidlay) is worked off her feet, so we decided you'd be a splendid help to her in the meantime!"

There was nothing else for it.

I discovered I was to share a tent with Quin, and dragged my kit over to the one indicated. I found her wringing out some blankets and was greeted with the cheery "Hello, had a good leave? I say, old thing, your bed's a pool of water."

I looked into the tent and there it was sagging down in the middle with quite a decent sized pond filling the hollow! "What about keeping some goldfish?" I suggested, somewhat peevishly.

Whatever happened I decided I couldn't sleep there that night, and with Quin's help tipped it up and spread it on some boxes outside, as the sun had come out.

That night I spent at Lamarck on a stretcher—it at least had the virtue of being dry if somewhat hard.

When I appeared at the cook-house next morning with the words, "Please mum, I've come!" Bridget literally fell on my neck. She poured out the difficulties of trying to feed seventeen hungry people, when they all came in to meals at different hours, especially as the big stove wouldn't "draw." It had no draught or something (I didn't know very much about them then). In the meantime all the cooking was done on a huge Primus stove and the field kitchen outside. I took a dislike to that field kitchen the moment I saw it, and I think it was mutual. It never lost an opportunity of "going out on me" the minute my back was turned. We were rather at a loss to know how to cope with our army rations at first. We all worked voluntarily, but the army undertook to feed and house (or rather tent) us.

We could either draw money or rations, and at first we decided on the former. When, however, we realised the enormous price of the meat in the French shops we decided to try rations instead, and this latter plan we found was much the best. Unfortunately, as we had first drawn allowances it took some days before the change could be effected, and Bridget and I had the time of our lives trying to make both ends meet in the meantime. That first day she went out shopping it was my duty to peel the potatoes and put them on to boil, etc. Before she left she explained how I was to light the Primus stove. Now, if you've never lit a Primus before, and in between the time you were told how to do it you had peeled twenty or thirty potatoes, got two scratch breakfasts, swept the mess tent and kept that field kitchen from going out, it's quite possible your mind would be a little blurred.

Mine was.

When the time came, I put the methylated in the little cup at the top, lit it, and then pumped with a will. The result was a terrific roar and a sheet of flame reaching almost to the roof! Never having seen one in action before, I thought it was possible they always behaved like that at first and that the conflagration would subside in a few moments. I watched it doubtfully, arms *akimbo*. Bridget entered just then and, determined not to appear flustered, in as cool a voice as possible I said: "Is that all right, old thing?" She put down her parcels and, without a word, seized the stove by one of its legs and threw it on a sand heap outside! Of course the field kitchen had gone out—(I can't think who invented that rotten inadequate grating underneath, anyway), and I felt I was not the bright jewel I might have been.

Our mess was a huge Indian tent rather out of repair, and, though it had a bright yellow lining, dusk always reigned within. The mugs, tin plates, and the oddest knives and forks constituted the "service." It was windy and chilly to a degree, and one of the few advantages of being in the cook-house was that one had meals in comparative warmth.

My real troubles began at night when, armed with a heavy tray, I set off on the perilous journey across the camp to the mess tent to lay the table. There were no lights, and it was generally raining. The chief things to avoid were the tent ropes. As I left the cook-house I decided exactly in my own mind where the bell-tent ropes extended, *ditto* those of the store tent and the mess, but invariably, just as I thought I was clear, something caught my ankle as securely as any snake, and down I crashed on top of the tray, the plates, mugs, and knives scattering all around. Luckily it was months since the latter had been sharp, or a steel proof overall would have been my only hope. Distances and the supposititious length of tent ropes are inclined to be deceptive in the dark. Nothing will make me believe those ropes were inanimate— they literally lay in wait for me each night! When any loud crash was heard in camp it was always taken for granted it was "only Pat taking another toss."

The wind, too, seemed to take a special delight in doing his bit. Our camp was situated on the top of a small hill quite near the sea, and some of the only trees in the neighbourhood flourished there, protected by a deep thorn hedge. This, however, ended abruptly where the drive led down to the road. It was when I got opposite the opening where the wind swept straight up from the sea my real tussle began. As often as not the tin plates were blown off the tray high into the air! It was then I realised the value of a chin. Obviously it was meant to keep the lid on the soup tureen and in this acrobatic attitude, my feet dodging the tent ropes, I arrived breathless and panting at the door of the Mess tent. The oil lamp swinging on a bit of wire over the table was as welcome a sight as an oasis in the desert.

We had no telephone in those days, and orderlies came up from the Casino hospital and A.D.M.S. with buff slips when ambulances were wanted. At that time the cars, Argylls, Napiers, Siddeley-Deaseys, and a Crossley, inscribed "Frank Crossley, the Pet of Poperinghe," were just parked haphazard in the open square, some with their bonnets one way and some another—it just depended which of the two drives up to camp had been chosen. It will make some of the F.A.N.Y.s smile to hear this, when they think of the neat rows of cars precisely parked up to the dead straight, white-washed line that ultimately became the order of things!

The bathing machines had their uses, one near the cook-house acting as our larder, another as a store for spare parts, while several others were adopted by F.A.N.Y.s as their permanent abodes. One bore the inscription, "The Savoy—Every Modern Inconvenience!"

Some R.E.'s came to look at the big cook-house stove and decided it must be put on a raised asphalt sort of platform. Of course this took some time, and we had to do all the cooking on the Primus. The field kitchen (when it went) was only good for hot water. We were relieved to see tins of bully beef and large hunks of cheese arriving in one of the cars the first day we drew rations, "Thank heaven that at least required no cooking." It was our first taste of British bully, and we thought it "really quite decent," and so it was, but familiarity breeds contempt, and finally loathing. It was the monotony that did it. You would weary of the tenderest chicken if you had it every other day for months.

As luck would have it, Bridget was again out shopping when, the day following, a huge round of raw beef arrived. How to cope, that was the question? (The verb "to cope" was very much in use at that period.) Obviously it would not fit into the frying pan. But something had to be done, and done soon, as it was getting late. "They must just have chops," I said aloud, in desperation, and bravely seizing that round of beef I cut seventeen squares out of it (slices would have taken too long; besides, our knife wasn't sharp enough).

They fried beautifully, and no one in the mess was heard to murmur. When you've been out driving from 7.30 a.m. hunger covers a multitude of sins, and Bridget agreed I'd saved the situation.

The beef when I'd finished with it looked exactly as if it had been in a worry. No *wonder* cooks never eat what they've cooked, I thought.

To our great disappointment an order came up to the convoy that all cameras were to be sent back to England, and everyone rushed round frantically finishing off their rolls of films. Lowson appeared and took one of the cook-house "staff" armed with kettles and more or less covered with smuts. It was rightly entitled, "The abomination of desolation"—when it came to be gummed into my War Album!

Quin was a great nut with our tent ropes at night, and though she had not been in camp before the war, assured me she knew all about them. Needless to say, I was only too pleased to let her carry on.

When I rolled in at night after washing up in the cook-house she would say: "You must come out and tighten the tent ropes with this gale blowing, it won't be funny if the whole thing blows over in the night." But none of the horrors she depicted ever persuaded me to turn out once I was safely tucked up in my "flea bag" with "Tuppence" acting as a weight to keep the top blankets in place. In the morning when I awoke after a sound night's sleep, I would exclaim triumphantly: "There you are, 'Squig,' what price the tent blowing down? It's as safe as a rock and hasn't moved an inch!"

"No?" the long-suffering "Squig" would reply bitterly, "it may interest you to hear I've only been up twice in the night hammering in the pegs and fixing the ropes!"

The only time I didn't bless her manipulation of these things was when I rose at 6.30 a.m., by which time they had been frozen stiff and shrunk to boot. The ones lacing the flap leading out of the tent were as hard to undo as if they had been made of iron. On these occasions "Tuppence," who had hardly realised the seriousness of war, would wake up and want me instantly to go out, half dressed as I was, and throw stones for his benefit! That dog had no sense of the fitness of things. If I did not comply immediately he sat down, threw his head in the air, and "howled to the moon!" The rest of the camp did not appreciate this pastime; but if they had known my frenzied efforts with the stiffened ropes "Squig" had so securely fixed over-night, their sympathies would have been with, rather than against, me.

One night we had a fearful storm (at least "Squig" told me of it in the morning and I had no reason to doubt her word), and just as I was rolling out of bed we heard yells of anguish proceeding from one of the other tents.

That one had collapsed we felt no doubt, and, rushing out in pyjamas just as we were, in the wind and rain, we capered delightedly to the scene of the disaster. The Sisters Mudie-Cooke (of course it would be their tent that had gone) were now hidden from sight under the heavy mass of wet canvas on top of them. The F.A.N.Y.s, their hair flying in the wind, looking more like Red Indians on a scalping expedition than a salvage party, soon extricated them, and they were taken, with what clothes could be rescued, to another tent. Their fate, "Squig" assured me, would have assuredly been ours had it not been for her!

Madame came into existence about this time. She was a poor Frenchwoman whom we hired to come and wash the dishes for us. She had no teeth, wispy hair, and looked very underfed and starved. Her "man" had been killed in the early days of the war. Though she looked hardly strong enough to do anything, Bridget and I, who interviewed her jointly, had not the heart to turn her away, and she remained with us ever after and became so strong and well in time she looked a different woman.

The mess tent was at last moved nearer the cook-house (I had fallen over the ropes so often that, quite apart from any feelings I had left, it was a preventive measure to save what little crockery we possessed).

The cars were all left in a pretty rotten condition, and the petrol was none too good. How Kirkby, the one mechanic, coped at that time, always with a cheery smile, will never be known. As Winnie aptly remarked, "In these days there are only two kinds of beings in the convoy—a 'Bird' and a 'Blighter'!" Kirkby was decidedly in the "Bird" class.

"Be a bird, and do such and such a thing," was a common opening to a request. Of course if you refused you were a 'blighter' of the worst description.

As you will remember, I was only in the cook-house as a "temporary help," and great was my joy when Logan (fresh from the Serbian campaign) loomed up on the horizon as the *pukka* cook. I retired gracefully—my only regret being Bridget's companionship. Two beings could hardly have laughed as much as we had done when impossible situations had arisen, and when the verb "to cope" seemed ineffective and life just one "gentle" thing after the other.

I was given the little Mors lorry to drive. To say I adored that car would not be exaggerating my feelings about it at all. The seat was my chief joy, it was of the racing variety, some former sportsman having done away with the tool box that had served as one! "Tuppy" also appreciated that lorry, and when we set off to draw rations, lying almost flat, the tips of his ears could just be seen from the front on a line with the top of my cap.

One of my jobs was to take Sergeant McLaughlan to fetch the hospital washing from a laundry some distance out of the town. He was an old "pug," but had grown too heavy to enter the ring, and kept his hand in coaching the promising young boxers stationed in the vicinity. In consequence, what I did not know about all their different merits was not worth knowing, and after a match had taken place every round was described in full. I grew quite an enthusiast.

He could never bear to see another car in front without trying to pass it. "Let her rip, Miss," he would implore—"Don't be beat by them Frenchies." Needless to say I did not need much encouragement, and nothing ever passed us. (There are no speed limits in France.) There was a special hen at one place we always tried to catch, but it was a wily bird and knew a thing or two. McLaughlan was dying to take it home to the Sergeants' Mess, but we never got her.

One day, as we were rattling down the main street, one of the tyres went off like a "4.2." We drew to the side, and there it was, as flat as a pancake.

There are always a lot of people in the streets of a town who seem to have nothing particular to do, and very soon quite a decent-sized crowd had collected.

"We must do this in record time," I said to McLaughlan, who knew nothing about cars, and kept handing me the wrong spanners in his anxiety to help. "See," exclaimed one, "it makes her nothing to dirty her hands in such a manner."

"They work like men, these English young girls, is it not so?" said another. "*Sapristi, c'est merveilleux.*"

"One would truly say from the distance that they were men, but this one, when one sees her close, is not too bad!" said a third.

"Passing remarks about you, they are, I should say," said McLaughlan to me as I fixed the spare wheel in place.

"You wait," I panted, "I'll pay them out."

"See you her strong boots?" they continued. "Believe you that she can understand what we say?" asked one. "Never on your life," was the answer, and the wheel in place, they watched every movement as I wiped my hands on a rag and drew on my gloves. "Eight minutes exactly," whispered McLaughlan triumphantly, as he seated himself beside me on the lorry preparatory to starting.

The crowd still watched expectantly, and, leaning out a little, I said sweetly, in my best Parisian accent: "*Mesdames et Messieurs, la séance est terminée.*" And off we drove! Their expressions defied description; I never saw people look so astounded. McLaughlan was unfeignedly delighted. "Wot was that you 'anded out to them, Miss?" he asked. "Fair gave it 'em proper anyway, straight from the shoulder," and he chuckled with glee.

I frequently met an old A.S.C. driver at one of the hospitals where I had a long wait while the rations were unloaded. He was fat, rosy, and smiling, and we became great friends. He was at least sixty; and told me that when war broke out, and his son enlisted, he could not bear to feel he was out of it, and joined up to do his bit as well. He was a taxi owner-driver in peace times, and had three of them; the one he drove being fitted with "real silver vauses!" I heard all about the "missus," of whom he was very proud, and could imagine how anxiously she watched the posts for letters from her only son and her old man.

Some months later when I was driving an ambulance a message was brought to me that Stone was in hospital suffering from bronchitis. I went off to visit him.

"I'm for home this time," he said sadly, "but won't the old missus be pleased?" I looked at his smiling old face and thought indeed she would.

He asked particularly if I would drive him to the boat when he was sent to England. "Itll seem odd to be going off on a stretcher, Miss," he said sadly, "just like one of the boys, and not even so much as a scratch to boast of." I pointed out that there were many men in England half his age who had done nothing but secure cushy jobs for themselves.

"Well, Miss," he said, as I rose to leave, "it'll give me great pleasure to drive you about London for three days when the war's over, and in my best taxi, too, with the silver vauses!"

(*N.B.* I'm still looking for him.)

Life in the Convoy Camp was very different from Lamarck, and I missed the cheery companionship of the others most awfully. At meal times only half the drivers would be in, and for days at a time you hardly saw your friends.

There were no "10 o'clocks" either. Of course, if you happened to be in camp at that time you probably got a cup of tea in the cookhouse, but it's not much of a pastime with no one else to drink it with you. "Pleasant Sunday Evenings" were also out of the question for, with all the best intentions in the world, no one could have spent an evening in our mess tent (even to the accompaniment of soft music) and called it "pleasant!" They were still carried on at Lamarck, however, and whenever possible we went down in force.

A Black Day in the Life of a Convoy F.A.N.Y.
(From *Barrack Room Ballads of the F.A.N.Y. Corps.*)
Gentle reader, when you've seen this,
Do not think, please, that I mean this
As a common or garden convoy day,
For the Fany, as a habit
Is as jolly as a rabbit—
Or a jay.

But the're days in one's existence,
When the ominous persistence
Of bad luck goes thundering heavy on your track,
Though you shake him off with laughter,
He will leap the moment after—
On your back.

'Tis the day that when on waking,
You will find that you are taking,
Twenty minutes when you haven't two to spare,
And the bloomin' whistle's starting,
When you've hardly thought of parting—
Your front hair!

You acquire the cheerful knowledge,
Ere you rush to swallow porridge,
That "fatigue" has just been added to your bliss,
"If the weather's no objection,
There will be a car inspection—
Troop—dismiss!"

With profane ejaculation,
You will see "evacuation"
Has been altered to an earlier hour than nine,
So your 'bus you start on winding,
Till you hear the muscles grinding—
In your spine.

Let's pass over nasty places,

Where you jolt your stretcher cases
And do everything that's wrong upon the quay,
Then it's time to clean the boiler,
And the sweat drops from the toiler,
      Oh—dear me!

When you've finished rubbing eye-wash,
On your engine, comes a "Kibosch."
As the Section-leader never looks at it,
But a grease-cap gently twisting,
She remarks that it's consisting,—
      "Half of grit."

Then as seated on a trestle,
With the toughest beef you wrestle,
That in texture would out-rival stone or rock,
You are told you must proceed,
To Boulogne, with care and speed
      At two o'clock.

As you're whisking through Marquise
(While the patients sit at ease)
Comes the awful sinking sizzle of a tyre,
It is usual in such cases,
That your jack at all such places,
      Won't go higher.

A wet, cold rain starts soaking,
And the old car keeps on choking,
Your hands and face are frozen raw and red,
Three sparking-plugs are missing,
There's another tyre a-hissing,
      Well—! 'nuff said!

You reach camp as night's descending,
To the bath with haste you're wending,
A hot tub's the only thing to save a cough,
Cries the F.A.N.Y. who's still in it,
"Ah! poor soul, why just this minute,
      Water's off!"

N.B.—It was a popular pastime of the powers that be to turn the water off at intervals, without any warning, rhyme or reason—one of the tragedies of the war.

CHAPTER 12

The Passing of the Little Lorry, "Old Bill" and "'Erb" at Audricq

A mild sensation was caused one day by a collision on the Boulogne road when a French car skidded into one of ours (luckily empty at the time) and pushed it over into the gutter.

"Heasy" and Lowson were both requested to appear at the subsequent Court of Enquiry, and Sergeant Lawrence, R.A.M.C. (who had been on the ambulance at the time) was bursting with importance and joy at the anticipation of the proceedings. He was one of the chief witnesses, and apart from anything else it meant an extra day's pay for him, though why it should I could never quite fathom.

As they drove off, with Boss as chaperone, a perfect salvo of old shoes was thrown after them!

They returned with colours flying, for had not Lowson saved the situation by producing a tape measure three minutes after the accident, measuring the space the Frenchman swore was wide enough for his car to pass, and proving thereby it was a physical impossibility?

"How," asked the colonel, who was conducting the enquiry, "can you declare with so much certainty the space was 3 feet 8 inches?"

"I measured it," replied Lowson promptly.

"May I ask with what?" he rasped.

"A tape-measure I had in my pocket," replied she, smiling affably the while (sensation).

The Court of Enquiry went down like a pack of cards before that tape measure. Such a thing had never been heard of before; and from then onwards the reputation of the "lady drivers" being prepared for all "immersions" was established finally and irrevocably.

It was a marvel how fit we all kept throughout those cold months. It was no common thing to wake up in the mornings and find icicles on the top blanket of the "flea bag" where one's breath had frozen, and of course one's sponge was a solid block of ice. It was duly placed in a tin basin on the top of the stove and melted by degrees. Luckily we had those round oil stoves; and with flaps securely fastened at night we achieved what was known as a "perfectly glorious fug."

Engineers began to make frequent trips to camp to choose a suitable site for the huts we were to have to replace our tents.

My jobs on the little lorry were many and varied; getting the weekly beer for the Sergeants' Mess being one of the least important. I drew rations for several hospitals as well as bringing up the petrol and tyres for the convoy, rationing the Officers' Mess, etc.; and regularly at one o'clock just as we were sitting at mess, Sergeant Brown would appear (though we never saw more of him than his legs) at the aperture that served as our door, and would call out diffidently in his high squeaky voice: "Isolation, when you're ready, Miss," and as regularly the whole mess would go off into fits! This formula when translated meant that he was ready for me to take the rations to the Isolation hospital up the canal. Hastily grabbing some cheese I would crank up the little lorry and depart.

The little lorry did really score when an early evacuation took place, at any hour from 4 a.m. onwards, when the men had to be taken from the hospitals to the ships bound for England. How lovely to lie in bed and hear other people cranking up their cars!

Barges came regularly down the canals with cases too seriously wounded to stand the jolting in ambulance trains. One day we were all having tea, and some friends had dropped in, when a voice was heard calling "Barges, Barges." Without more ado the whole mess rose, a form was overturned, and off they scampered as fast as they could to get their cars and go off immediately. The men left sitting there gazed blankly at each other and finally turned to me for an explanation—(being a lorry, I was not required). "Barges," I said; "they all have to hurry off as quickly as possible to unload the cases." They thought it rather a humorous way of speeding the parting guest, but I assured them work always came before (or generally during) tea in our Convoy! Major S.P. never forgot that episode, and the next time he came, heralded his arrival by calling out at the top of his voice, "Barges, Barges!" with the result that half the convoy turned out *en masse*. He assured his friends it was the one method of getting a royal welcome.

I shall never forget with what fear and trepidation I drove my first lot of wounded. I was on evening duty when the message came up about seven that there were eight bad cases, too bad to stay on the barge till next morning, which were to be removed to hospital immediately. Renny and I set off, each driving a Napier ambulance. We backed into position on the sloping shingly ground near the side of the canal, and waited for the barge to come in.

Presently we espied it slipping silently along under the bridge. The cases were placed on lifts and slung gently up from the inside of the barge, which was beautifully fitted up like a hospital ward.

It is not an easy matter when you are on a slope to start off smoothly without jerking the patients within; and I held my breath as I declutched and took off the brake, accelerating gently the meanwhile. Thank heaven! We were moving slowly forward and there had been no jerk. They were all bad cases and an occasional groan would escape their lips in spite of themselves. I dreaded a certain dip in the road—a sort of open drain known in France as a *canivet*—but fortunately I had practised crossing it when out one day trying a Napier, and we manoeuvred it pretty fairly. My relief on getting to hospital was tremendous. My back was aching, so was my knee (from constant clutch-slipping over the bumps and cobbles), and my eyes felt as if they were popping out of my head. In fact I had a pretty complete "stretcher face!" I had often ragged the others about their "stretcher faces," which was a special sort of strained expression I had noticed as I skimmed past them in the little lorry, but now I knew just what it felt like.

The new huts were going apace, and were finished about the end of April, just as the weather was getting warmer. We were each to have one to ourselves, and they led off on each side of a long corridor running down the centre. These huts were built almost in a horse-shoe shape and—joy of joys! there were to be two bathrooms at the end! We also had a telephone fixed up—a great boon. The furniture in the huts consisted of a bed and two shelves, and that was all. There was an immediate slump in car cleaning. The rush on carpentering was tremendous. It was by no means safe for a workman to leave his tools and bag anywhere in the vicinity; his saw the next morning was a thing to weep over if he did. (It's jolly hard to saw properly, anyway, and it really looks such an easy pastime.)

The wooden cases that the petrol was sent over in from England, large enough to hold two tins, were in great demand. These we made into settees and stools, etc., and when stained and polished they looked quite imposing. The contractor kindly offered to paint the interiors of the huts for us as a present, but we were a little startled to see the brilliant green that appeared. Someone unkindly suggested that he could get rid of it in no other way.

When at last they were finished we received orders to take up our new quarters, but, funnily enough, we had become so attached to our tents by that time that we were very loath to do so. A fatigue party however arrived one day to take the tents down, so there was nothing for it. Many of the workmen were most obliging and did a lot of odd jobs for us. I rescued one of the Red Cross beds instead of the camp one I had had heretofore—the advantage was that it had springs—but there was only the mattress part, and so it had to be supported on two petrol cases for legs! The disadvantage of this was that as often as not one end slipped off in the night and you were propelled on to the floor, or else two opposite corners held and the other two see-sawed in mid-air. Both great aids to nightmares.

"Tuppence" did not take at all kindly to the new order of things; he missed chasing the mice that used to live under the tent boards and other minor attractions of the sort.

The draughtiness and civilization of the new huts compared with the "fug" of the tents all combined to give us chills! I had a specially bad one, and managed with great skill to wangle a fortnight's sick leave in Paris.

The journey had not increased much in speed since my last visit, but everything in Paris itself had assumed a much more normal aspect. The bridge over the Oise had long since been repaired, and hardly a shop remained closed. I went to see my old friend M. Jollivet at Neuilly, and had the same little English mare to ride in the Bois, and also visited many of the friends I had made during my first leave there.

I got some wonderful French grey Ripolin sort of stuff from a little shop in the "Boul' Mich" with which to tone down the violent green in my hut, that had almost driven me mad while I lay ill in bed.

The convoy was gradually being enlarged, and a great many new drivers came out from England just after I got back. McLaughlan gave me a great welcome when I went for the washing that afternoon. "It's good to see you back, Miss," he said, "the driver they put on the lorry was very slow and cautious—you know the 'en we always try to catch? Would you believe it we slowed down to walking pace so as to miss 'er!" and he sniffed disgustedly.

The news of the Battle of Jutland fell like a bombshell in the camp owing to the pessimistic reports first given of it in the papers. A witty

Frenchman once remarked that in all our campaigns we had only won one battle, but that was the last, and we felt that however black things appeared at the moment we would come out on top in the end. The news of Kitchener's death five days later plunged the whole of the B.E.F. into mourning, and the French showed their sympathy in many touching ways.

One day to my sorrow I heard that the little Mors lorry was to be done away with, owing to the shortage of petrol that began to be felt about this time, and that horses and G.S. wagons were to draw rations, etc., instead. It had just been newly painted and was the joy of my heart—however mine was not to reason why, and in due course Red Cross drivers appeared with two more ambulances from the Boulogne *dépôt*, and they made the journey back in the little Mors.

It was then that "Susan" came into being.

The two fresh ambulances were both Napiers, and I hastily consulted Brown (the second mechanic who had come to assist Kirkby as the work increased) which he thought was the best one. (It was generally felt I should have first choice to console me for the loss of the little Mors.)

I chose the speediest, naturally. She was a four cylinder Napier, given by a Mrs. Herbert Davies to the Red Cross at the beginning of the war (vide small brass plate affixed), and converted from her private car into an ambulance. She had been in the famous old Dunkirk Convoy in 1914, and was battle-scarred, as her canvas testified, where the bullets and shrapnel had pierced it. She had a fat comfortable look about her, and after I had had her for some time I felt "Susan" was the only name for her; and Susan she remained from that day onwards. She always came up to the scratch, that car, and saved my life more than once.

We snatched what minutes we could from work to do our "*cues*," as we called our small huts. It was a great pastime to voyage from hut to hut and see what particular line the "furnishing" was taking. Mine was closed to all intruders on the score that I had the "painters in." It was to be *art nouveau*. I found it no easy matter to get the stuff on evenly, especially as I had rather advanced ideas as to mural decoration! With great difficulty I stencilled long lean-looking panthers stalking round the top as a sort of fresco. I cut one pattern out in cardboard and fixing it with drawing pins painted the Ripolin over it, with the result that I had a row of green panthers prowling round against a background of French grey! I found them very restful, but of course opinions differ on these subjects. Curtains and cushions were of bright Reckitt's blue material, bought in the market, relieved by scrolls of dull pink wool embroidered (almost a stitch at a time) in between jobs. The dark stained "genuine antiques" or veritables imitations (as I once saw them described in a French shop) looked rather well against this background; and a tremendous house-warming took place to celebrate the occasion.

No. 30 Field hospital arrived one day straight from Sicily, where it had apparently been sitting ever since the war, awaiting casualties.

As there seemed no prospect of any being sent, they were ordered to France, and took up their quarters on a sandy waste near the French coastal forts. The orderlies had picked up quite a lot of Italian during their sojourn and were never tired of describing the wonderful sights they had seen.

While waiting for patients there one day, a corporal informed me that on the return journey they had "passed the volcano Etna, in rupture!"

A great many troops came to a rest camp near us, and I always feel that "Tuppence's" disappearance was due to them. He would be friendly with complete strangers, and several times had come in minus his collar (stolen by French urchins, I supposed). I had just bought his fourth, and rather lost heart when he turned up the same evening without it once more. Work was pouring in just then, and I would sometimes be out all day. When last I saw him he was playing happily with Nellie, another terrier belonging to a man at the Casino, and that night I missed him from my hut. I advertised in the local rag (he was well known to all the French people as he was about the only pure bred dog they'd ever seen), but to no avail. I also made visits to the Abattoir, the French slaughter house where strays were taken, but he was not there, and I could only hope he had been taken by some Tommies, in which case I knew he would be well looked after. I missed him terribly.

Work came in spasms, in accordance with the fighting of course, and when there was no special push on we had tremendous car inspections. Boss walked round trying to spot empty grease caps and otherwise making herself thoroughly objectionable in the way of gear boxes and universals. On these occasions "eye-wash" was extensively applied to the brass, the idea being to keep her attention fixed well to the front by the glare.

One day, when all manner of fatigues and other means of torture had been exhausted, Dicky and Freeth discovered they had a simultaneous birthday. Prospects of wounded arriving seemed nil, and permission was given for a fancy-dress tea party to celebrate the double event. It must be here understood that whether work came in or not we all had to remain on duty in camp till five every day, in case of the sudden arrival of ambulance trains, etc. After that hour, two of us were detailed to be on evening duty till nine, while all night duty was similarly taken in turns. Usually, after hanging about all day till five, a train or barges would be announced, and we were lucky if we got into bed this side of 12. Hardly what you might call a "six-hour day," and yet nobody went on strike.

The one in question was fine and cloudless, and birthday wishes in the shape of a Taube raid were expressed by the Boche, who apparently keeps himself informed on all topics.

The fancy dresses (considering what little scope we had and that no one even left camp to buy extras in the town) were many and varied. "Squig" and de Wend were excellent as bookies, in perfectly good toppers made out of stiff white paper with deep black ribbon bands and "THE OLD FIRM" painted in large type on cards. Jockeys, squaws, yokels, etc., all appeared mysteriously from nothing. I was principally draped in my Reckitts blue upholsterings and a brilliant Scherezade *kimono*, bought in a moment of extravagance in Paris.

The proceedings after tea, when the cooks excelled themselves making an enormous birthday cake, consisted of progressive games of sorts. You know the kind of thing, trying to pick up ten needles with a pin (or is it two?) and doing a Pelman memory stunt after seeing fifty objects on a tray, and other intellectual pursuits of that description. Another stunt was putting a name to different liquids which you smelt blindfold. This was the only class in which I got placed. I was the only one apparently who knew the difference between whisky and brandy! Funnily enough, would you believe it, it was the petrol that floored me. Considering we wallowed in it from morning till night it was rather strange. I was nearly spun altogether when it came to the game of Bridge in the telephone room. "I've never played it in my life," I said desperately. "Never mind," said someone jokingly, "just take a hand." I took the tip seriously and did so, looking at my cards as gravely as a judge—finally I selected one and threw it down. To my relief no one screamed or denounced me and I breathed again. (It requires some skill to play a game of Bridge when you know absolutely nothing about it.)

"Pity you lost that last trick," said my partner to me as we left the room; "it was absolutely in your hand."

"Was it?" I asked innocently.

We had a rush of work after this, and wounded again began to pour in from the Third Battle of Ypres.

Early evacuations came regularly with the tides. They would begin at 4 a.m. and get half an hour later each day. When we took "sitters" (i.e. sitting patients with "Blighty" wounds), one generally came in front and sat beside the driver, and on the way to the Hospital Ships we sometimes learnt a lot about them. I had a boy of sixteen one day, a bright cheery soul.

"How did you get in?" (meaning into the army), I asked.

"Oh, well, Miss, it was like this, I was afraid it would be over before I was old enough, so I said I was eighteen. The recruiting bloke winked and so did I, and I was through."

Another, when asked about his wound, said, "It's going on fine now, Sister (they always called us Sister), but I lost me conscience for two days up the line with it."

We had a bunch of Canadians to take one day. "D'you come from Sussex?" asked one, of me.

"No," I replied, "from Cumberland."

"That's funny," he said, "the V.A.D. who looked after me came from Sussex, and she had the same accent as you, I guess!"

Another man had not been home for five years, but had joined up in Canada and come straight over. A Scotsman had not been home for twenty, and he intended to see his "folks" and come out again as soon as he was passed fit by the doctors.

One fine morning at 5 a.m. we were awakened by a fearful din, much worse than the usual thing. The huts trembled and our beds shook beneath us, not to mention the very nails falling out of the walls! We wondered at first if it was a fleet of Zepps. dropping super-bombs, but decided it was too light for them to appear at that hour.

There it was again, as if the very earth was being cleft in two, and our windows rattled in their sockets. It is not a pleasant sensation to have steady old Mother Earth rocking like an "ashpan" leaf beneath your feet.

We dressed hurriedly, knowing that the cars might be called on to go out at any moment.

What the disaster was we could not fathom, but that it was some distance away we had no doubt.

At 7 a.m. the telephone rang furiously, and we all waited breathless for the news.

Ten cars were ordered immediately to Audricq, where a large ammunition dump had been set on fire by a Boche airman.

Heavy explosions continued at intervals all the morning as one shed after another became affected.

When our cars got there the whole dump was one seething mass of smoke and flames, and shells of every description were hurtling through the air at short intervals. Several of these narrowly missed the cars. It was a new experience to be under fire from our own shells. The roads were littered with live ones, and with great difficulty the wheels of the cars were steered clear of them!

Many shells were subsequently found at a distance of five miles, and one buried itself in a peaceful garden ten miles off!

A thousand 9.2's had gone off simultaneously and made a crater big enough to bury a village in. It was this explosion that had shaken our huts miles away. The neighbouring village fell flat like a pack of cards at the concussion, the inhabitants having luckily taken to the open fields at the first intimation that the dump was on fire.

The total casualties were only five in number, which was almost incredible in view of the many thousands of men employed. It was due to the presence of mind of the camp commandant that there were not more; for, once he realised the hopeless task of getting the fire under control, he gave orders to the men to clear as fast as they could. They needed no second bidding and made for the nearest estaminets with speed! The F.A.N.Y.s found that instead of carrying wounded, their task was to search the countryside (with sergeants on the box) and bring the men to a camp near ours. "Dead?" asked someone, eyeing the four motionless figures inside one of the ambulances.

"Yes," replied the F.A.N.Y. cheerfully—"drunk!"

The Boche had flown over at 3 a.m. but so low down the Archies were powerless to get him. As one of the men said to me, "If we'd had rifles, Miss, we could have potted him easy."

He flew from shed to shed dropping incendiary bombs on the roofs as he passed, and up they went like fireworks. The only satisfaction we had was to hear that he had been brought down on his way back over our lines, so the Boche never heard of the disaster he had caused.

Some splendid work was done after the place had caught fire. One officer, in spite of the great risk he ran from bursting shells, got the ammunition train off safely to the 4th army. Thanks to him, the men up the line were able to carry on as if nothing had happened, till further supplies could be sent from other dumps. It was estimated that four days' worth of shells from all the factories in England had been destroyed.

An M.T. officer got all the cars and lorries out of the sheds and instructed the drivers to take them as far from the danger zone as possible, while the captain in charge of the "Archie" Battery stuck to his guns; and he and his men remained in the middle of that inferno hidden in holes in their dug-out, from which it was impossible to rescue them for two days.

Five days after the explosion Gutsie and I were detailed to go to Audricq for some measles cases, and we reported first to the camp *commandant*, who was sitting in the remains of his office, a shell sticking up in the floor and half his roof blown away.

He gave us permission to see the famous crater, and instructed one of the subalterns to show us round. There were still fires burning and shells popping in some parts and the scenes of wreckage were almost indescribable.

The young officer was not particularly keen to take us at all and said warningly, "You come at your own risk—there are nothing but live shells lying about, liable to go off at any moment. Be careful," he said to me, "you're just stepping on one now." I hopped off with speed, but all the same we were not a whit discouraged, which seemed to disappoint him.

As Gutsie and I stumbled and rolled over 4.2's and hand grenades I quoted to her from the "Fuse-top collectors"—"You can generally 'ear 'em fizzin' a bit if they're going to go 'orf, 'Erb!" by way of encouragement. Trucks had been lifted bodily by the concussion, and could be seen in adjacent fields; many of the sheds had been half blown away, leaving rows of live shells lying snugly in neat piles, but as there was no knowing when they might explode it was decided to scrap the whole dump when the fires had subsided.

We walked up a small hill literally covered with shells and empty hand grenades of the round cricket ball type, two of which were given to us to make into match boxes. Every description of shell was there as far as the eye could see, and some were empty and others were not. We reached the summit, walking gingerly over 9.2's (which formed convenient steps) to find ourselves at the edge of the enormous crater already half filled with water. It was incredible to believe a place of that size had been formed in the short space of one second, and yet on the other hand, when I remembered how the earth had trembled, the wonder was it was not even larger.

It took weeks for that dump to be cleared up. Little by little the live shells were collected and taken out to sea in barges, and dropped in mid-ocean.

Not long after that the *Zulu*, a British destroyer, came into port half blown away by a mine. Luckily the engine was intact and still working, but the men, who had had marvellous escapes, lost all their kit and rations. We were not able to supply the former, unfortunately, but we remedied the latter with speed, and also took down cigarettes, which they welcomed more than anything.

We were shown all over the remains, and hearing that the *Nubia* had just had her engine room blown away, we suggested that the two ends should be joined together and called the *Nuzu*, but whether the Admiralty thought anything of the idea I have yet to learn!

Before the captain left he had napkin rings made for each of us out of the copper piping from the ship, in token of his appreciation of the help we had given.

The colonials were even more surprised to see girls driving in France than our own men had been.

One man, a dear old Australian, was being invalided out altogether and going home to his wife. He told me how during the time he had been away she had become totally blind owing to some special German stuff, that had been formerly injected to keep her sight, being now unprocurable. "Guess she's done her bit," he ended; "and I'm off home to take care of her. She'll be interested to hear how the lassies work over here," and we parted with a handshake.

Important conferences were always taking place at the Hôtel Maritime, and one day as I was down on the quay the French Premier and several other notabilities arrived. "There's Mr. Asquith," said an R.T.O. to me. "That!" said I, in an unintentionally loud voice, eyeing his long hair, "I thought he was a 'cellist belonging to a Lena Ashwell Concert party!" He looked round, and I faded into space.

Taking some patients to hospital that afternoon we passed some Australians marching along. "Fine chaps," said the one sitting on the box to me, "they're a good emetic of their country, aren't they?" (N.B. I fancy he meant to say emblem.)

Our concert party still flourished, though the conditions for practising were more difficult than ever. Our mess tent had been moved again on to a plot of grass behind the cook-house to leave more space for the cars to be parked, and though we had a piano there it was somehow not particularly inspiring, nor had we the time to practise. The Guards' Brigade were down resting at Beau Marais, and we were asked to give them a show. We now called ourselves the "FANTAS-TIKS," and wore a black *pierrette* kit with yellow bobbles.

The rehearsals were mostly conducted in the back of the ambulance on the way there, and the rest of the time was spent feverishly muttering one's lines to oneself and imploring other people not to muddle one. The show was held in a draughty tent, and when it was over the padre made a short prayer and they all sang a hymn. (Life is one continual paradox out in France.) I shall never forget the way those Guardsmen sang either. It was perfectly splendid. There they stood, rows of men, the best physique England could produce, and how they sang!

Betty drove us back to camp in the "Crystal Palace," so-called from its many windows—a six cylinder Delauney-Belville car used to take the army sisters to and from their billets. We narrowly missed nose-diving into a chalk pit on the way, the so-called road being nothing but a rutty track.

The Fontinettes ambulance train was a special one that was usually reported to arrive at 8 p.m., but never put in an appearance till 10, or, on some occasions, one o'clock. The battle of the Somme was now in progress; and, besides barges and day trains, three of these arrived each week. The whole convoy turned out for this; and one by one the twenty-five odd cars would set off, keeping an equal distance apart, forming an imposing looking column down from the camp, across the bridge and through the town to the railway siding. The odd makes had been weeded out and the whole lot were now Napiers. The French inhabitants would turn out *en masse* to see us pass, and were rather proud of us on the whole, I think. Arrived at the big railway siding, we all formed up into a straight line to await the train.

After many false alarms, and answering groans from the waiting F.A.N.Y.s, it would come slowly creaking along and draw up. The ambulances were then reversed right up to the doors, and the stretcher bearers soon filled them up with four lying cases. At the exit stood Boss and the E.M.O., directing each ambulance which hospital the cases were to go to. Those journeys back were perfect nightmares. Try as one would, it was impossible not to bump a certain amount over those appalling roads full of holes and cobbles. It was pathetic when a voice from the interior could be heard asking, "Is it much farther, Sister?" and knowing how far it was, my heart ached for them. After all they had been through, one felt they should be spared every extra bit of pain that was possible. When I in my turn was in an ambulance, I knew just what it felt like. Sometimes the cases were so bad we feared they would not even last the journey, and there we were all alone, and not able to hurry to hospital owing to the other three on board.

The journey which in the ordinary way, when empty, took fifteen minutes, under these circumstances lasted anything from three-quarters of an hour to an hour. "Susan" luckily was an extremely steady 'bus, and in 3rd. gear on a smooth road there was practically no movement at all. I remember once on getting to the Casino I called out, "I hope you weren't bumped too much in there?" and was very cheered when a voice replied, "It was splendid, Sister, you should have seen us up the line, jolting all over the place."

"Sister," another one called, "will you drive us when we leave for Blighty?" I said it was a matter of chance, but whoever did so would be just as careful. "No," said the voice decidedly, "there couldn't be two like you." (I think he must have been in an Irish Regiment.)

The relief after the strain of this journey was tremendous; and the joy of dashing back through the evening air made one feel as if weights had been taken off and one were flying. It was rather a temptation to test the speed of one's 'bus against another on these occasions; and "Susan" seemed positively to take a human interest in the impromptu race, all the more so as it was forbidden. The return journey was by a different route from that taken by the laden ambulances so that there was no danger of a collision.

We usually had about three journeys with wounded; twelve stretcher cases in all, so that, say the train came in at nine and giving an hour to each journey there and back, it meant (not counting loading and unloading) roughly 1 o'clock a.m. or later before we had finished. Then there were usually the sitting cases to be taken off and the stretcher bearers to be driven back to their camp. Half of one head light only was allowed to be shown; and the impression I always had when I came in was that my eyes had popped right out of my head and were on bits of elastic.

A most extraordinary sensation, due to the terrible strain of trying to see in the darkness just a little further than one really could. It was the irony of fate to learn, when we did come in, that an early evacuation had been telephoned through for 5 a.m. I often spent the whole night dreaming I was driving wounded and had given them the most awful bump. The horror of it woke me up, only to find that my bed had slipped off one of the petrol boxes and was see-sawing in mid-air!

The Red Cross Cars

They are bringing them back who went forth so bravely.
Grey, ghostlike cars down the long white road
Come gliding, each with its cross of scarlet
On canvas hood, and its heavy load
Of human sheaves from the crimson harvest
That greed and falsehood and hatred sowed.

Maimed and blinded and torn and shattered,
Yet with hardly a groan or a cry
From lips as white as the linen bandage;
Though a stifled prayer 'God let me die,'
Is wrung, maybe, from a soul in torment
As the car with the blood-red cross goes by.

Oh, Red Cross car! What a world of anguish
On noiseless wheels you bear night and day.
Each one that comes from the field of slaughter
Is a moving Calvary, painted grey.
And over the water, at home in England
'Let's play at soldiers,' the children say.

Anon.

CHAPTER 13

Convoy Life

The Prince of Wales was with the grenadiers at Beau Marais when they came in to rest for a time. One day, while having tea at the Sauvage, Mademoiselle Léonie, sister of the proprietor, came up to me in a perfect flutter of excitement to say that that very evening the prince had ordered the large room to be prepared for a dinner he was giving to his brother officers.

I was rather a favourite of hers, and she assured me if I wished to watch him arriving it would give her great pleasure to hide me in her paying-desk place where I could see everything clearly. She was quite hurt when I refused the invitation.

He was tremendously popular with the French people; and the next time I saw her she rushed up to me and said: "How your prince is beautiful, Mees; what spirit, what fire! Believe me, they broke every glass they used at that dinner, and then the prince demanded of me the bill and paid for everything." (Some lad!) "He also wrote his name in my autograph book," she added proudly. "Oh he is *chic*, that one there, I tell you!"

One warm summer day Gutsie and I were sitting on a grassy knoll, just beyond our camp overlooking the sea (well within earshot of the summoning whistle), watching a specially large merchant ship come in. Except for the distant booming of the guns (that had now become such a background to existence we never noticed it till it stopped), an atmosphere of peace and drowsiness reigned over everything. The ship was just nearing the jetty preparatory to entering the harbour when a dull reverberating roar broke the summer stillness, the banks we were on fairly shook, and there before our eyes, out of the sea, rose a dense black cloud of smoke 50 feet high that totally obscured the ship from sight for a moment. When the black fumes sank down, there, where a whole vessel had been a moment before, was only half a ship! We rubbed our eyes incredulously. It had all happened so suddenly it might have taken place on a cinema. She had, of course, struck a German mine, and quick as lightning two long, lithe, grey bodies (French destroyers) shot out from the port and took off what survivors were left. Contrary to expectation she did not sink, but settled down, and remained afloat till she was towed in later in the day.

A "Y.M.C.A." article on "Women's work in France," that appeared in a magazine at home, was sent out to one of the girls. The paragraph relating to us ran:—

Then there are the 'F.A.N.N.I.E.S.,' the dear mud-besplashing F.A.N.Y.s. (to judge from the language of the sometime bespattered, the adjective was not always 'dear'), with them cheeriness is almost a cult; at 6 a.m. in the morning you may always be sure of a smile, even when their sleep for the week has only averaged five hours per night.

There were not many parties at Filbert during that summer. Off-time was such an uncertain quantity. We managed to put in several though, likewise some gallops on the glorious sands stretching for miles along the coast. (It was hardly safe to call at the convoy on your favourite charger. When you came out from tea it was more than probable you found him in a most unaccountable lather!) Bathing during the daytime was also a rare event, so we went down in an ambulance after dark, macs covering our bathing dresses, and scampered over the sands in the moonlight to the warm waves shining and glistening with phosphorus.

Zeppelin raids seemed to go out of fashion, but Gothas replaced them with pretty considerable success. As we had a French Archie battery near us it was no uncommon thing, when a raid was in progress, for our souvenirs and plates, etc., to rattle off the walls and bomb us (more or less gently) awake!

There was a stretch of asphalt just at the bottom of our camp that had been begun by an enterprising burgher as a tennis club before the war, though others *did* say it was really intended as a secret German gun emplacement. It did not matter much to us for which purpose it had been made, for, as it was near, we could play tennis and still be within call. There was just room for two courts, and many a good game we enjoyed there, especially after an early evacuation, in the long empty pause till "brekker" at eight o'clock.

"Wuzzy," or to give him his proper name, "Gerald," came into existence about this time. He arrived from Peuplinghe a fat fluffy puppy covered with silky grey curls. He was of nondescript breed, with a distinct leaning towards an old English sheep dog. He had enormous fawn-coloured silky paws, and was so soft and floppy he seemed as if he had hardly a bone in his body. We used to pick him up and drop him gently in the grass to watch him go out flat like a tortoise. He belonged to Lean, and grew up a rather irresponsible creature with long legs and a lovable disposition. He adored coming down to the ambulance trains or sitting importantly on a car, jeering and barking at his low French friends in the road, on the "I'm the king of the castle" principle.

Another of his favourite tricks was to rush after a car (usually selecting Lean's), and keep with it the whole time, never swerving to another, which was rather clever considering they were so much alike. On the way back to camp he had a special game he played on the French children playing in the Petit Courgain. He would rush up as if he were going to fly at them. They would scream and fall over in terror while he positively laughed at them over his shoulder as he cantered off to try it on somewhere else. The camp was divided in its opinion of Wuzzy, or rather I should say quartered—*viz.*—one quarter saw his points and the other three-quarters decidedly did not!

A priceless article appeared in one of the leading dailies entitled, "*Women Motor Drivers.—Is it a suitable occupation?*" and was cut out by anxious parents and forwarded with speed to the convoy.

The headlines ran: "The lure of the Wheel." "Is it necessary?" "The after effects." We lapped it up with joy. Phrases such as "Women's outlook on life will be distorted by the adoption of such a profession, her finer instincts crushed," pleased us specially. It continued "All the delicate things that mean, must mean, life to the feminine mind, will lose their significance"—(cries of "What about the frillies you bought in Paris, Pat?") "The uncongenial atmosphere"—I continued, reading further— "of the garage, yard, and workshops, the alien companionship of mechanics and chauffeurs will isolate her mental standing" (shrieks of joy), "the ceaseless days and dull monotony of labour will not only rob her of much feminine charm but will instil into her mind bitterness that will eat from her heart all capacity for joy, steal away her youth, and deprive her of the colour and sunlight of life" (loud sobs from the listening F.A.N.Y.s, who still, strangely enough, seemed to be suffering from no loss of *joie de vivre!*) When the noise had subsided I continued: "There is of course the possibility that she will become conscious of her condition and change of mind, and realise her level in time to counteract the ultimate effects(!). The realisation however may come too late. The aptitude for happiness will have gone by for the transitory joys of driving, the questionable intricacies of the magneto—" but further details were suspended owing to small bales of cotton waste hurtling through the air, and in self defence I had to leave the "intricacies of the magneto" and pursue the offenders round the camp! The only reply Boss could get as a reason for the tumult was that the F.A.N.Y.s were endeavouring to "realise the level of their minds."

"Humph," was Boss's comment, "First I've heard that some of them even had any," and retired into her hut.

We often had to take wounded German prisoners to No. 14 hospital, about 30 kilometres away. On these occasions we always had three armed guards to prevent them from escaping. The prisoners looked like convicts with their shorn heads and shoddy grey uniforms, and I always found it very difficult to imagine these men capable of fighting at all. They seemed pretty content with their lot and often tried to smile ingratiatingly at the drivers. One day going along the sea road one of them poked me in the back through the canvas against which we leant when driving and said, "*Ni—eece Englessh Mees!*" I was furious and used the most forcible German I could think of at a moment's notice. "Cheek!" I said to the guard sitting beside me on the box, "I'd run them over the cliff for tuppence."

He got the wind up entirely: "Oh, Miss," he said, in an anxious voice, "for Gawd's sake don't. Remember we're on board as well."

The Rifle brigade came in to rest after the Guards had gone, and before they left again for the line, gave a big race meeting on the sands. Luckily for us there was no push on just then, and work was in consequence very slack. A ladies' race was included in the Programme for our benefit. It was one of the last events, and until it came off we amused ourselves riding available mules, much to the delight of the Tommies, who cheered and yelled and did their best to get them to "take off!" They were hard and bony and had mouths like old sea boots, but it was better than toiling in the deep sand.

There were about fourteen entries for our race, several of them from Lamarck, and we all drew for polo ponies lent from the brigade. Their owners were full of instructions as to the best method to get them along. We cantered up to the starting post, and there was some delay while Renny got her stirrups right. This was unfortunate, as our ponies got a bit "cold." At last the flag fell, and we were off! It was ripping; and the excitement of that race beat anything I've ever known. As we thundered over the sands I began to experience the joys of seeing the horses in front "coming back" to me, as our old jockey stable-boy used to describe. Heasy came in first, MacDougal second, and Winnie and I tied third. It was a great race entirely, and all too short by a long way.

One day I was detailed to drive the matron and our section leader to a *fête* of sorts for Belgian refugee orphans. On the way back, crossing the swing bridge, we met Betty driving the sisters to their billets. I thought matron wanted to speak to them and luckily, as it turned out, I slowed down. She changed her mind, however, and I was just picking up again as we came abreast, when from behind Betty's car sprang a woman right in front of mine (after her hat it appeared later, which the wind had just blown across the road). The apparition was so utterly unforeseen and unexpected that she was bowled over like a rabbit in two shakes. I jammed on the brakes and we sprang out, and saw she was under the car in between the wheel and the chassis. Luckily she was a small thin woman, and as Gaspard has so eloquently expressed it on another occasion, *platte comme une punaise* (flat as a drawing-pin). I was horrified, the whole thing had happened so suddenly.

A crowd of French and Belgian soldiers collected, and I rapidly directed them to lift the front of the car up by the springs, as it seemed the only way of getting her out without further injury. I turned away, not daring to look, and as I did so my eye caught sight of some hair near one of the back wheels! That finished me up! I did not stop to reason that of course the back wheels had not touched her, and thought, "My God, I've scalped her!" and I leant over the railings feeling exceedingly sick.

A friendly M.P. who had seen the whole thing, patted me on the arm and said, "Now, then, Miss, don't you take on, that's only her false 'air," as indeed it proved to be! The woman was yelling and groaning, "*Mon Dieu, je suis tuée,*" but according to the "red hat" she was as "right as rain, nothing but 'ysteria." I blessed that M.P. and hoped we would meet again. We helped her on to the front seat, where Thompson supported her, while I drove to hospital to see if any damage had been done. Singularly enough, she was only suffering from bruises and a torn skirt, and of course the loss of her "false 'air" (which I had refused to touch, it had given me such a turn). I can only hope her husband, who was with her at the time, picked it up. He followed to hospital and gave her a most frightful scolding, adding that of course the "Mees" could not do otherwise than knock her down if she so foolishly sprang in front of cars without warning; and she might think herself lucky that the "Mees" would not run her in for being in the way! It has always struck me as being so humorous that in England if you knock a pedestrian over they can have you up, while in France the law is just the reverse. She sobbed violently, and I had to tell him that what she wanted was sympathy and not scolding.

It took me a day or two to get over that scalping expedition (of course the story was all round the camp within the hour!) and for some time after I slowed down crossing the bridge. This was the one and only time anything of the sort ever happened to me, thank goodness!

Our camp began to look very smart, and the seeds we had sown in the spring came up and covered the huts with creepers. We had as many flowers inside our huts as we could possibly get into the shell cases and other souvenirs which perforce were turned into flower vases—a change they must have thought rather singular. The steady boom of the guns used to annoy me intensely, for it shook the petals off the roses long before they would otherwise have fallen, and I used to call out, crossly, "Do stop that row, you're simply ruining my flowers." But that made no difference to the distant gunners, who carried on night and day causing considerably more damage than the falling petals from my roses!

We began to classify the new girls as they came out, jokingly calling them "Kitchener's" Army, "Derby's Scheme," and finally, "Conscripts." The old "regulars" of course put on most fearful side. It was amusing when an air-raid warning (a siren known as "mournful Mary") went at Mess and the shrapnel began to fly, to see the new girls all rush out to watch the little white balls bursting in the sky, and the old hands not turning a hair but going on steadily with the bully beef or Maconochie, whichever it happened to be. Then one by one the new ones would slink back rather ashamed of their enthusiasm and take their seats, and in time they in turn would smile indulgently as the still newer ones dashed out to watch.

We had no dugout to go to, even if we had wanted to. Our new mess tent was built in the summer; and we said goodbye for ever to the murky gloom of the old Indian flapper.

One day I had gone out to tea with Logan and Chris to an "Ar-

111

chie" station at Pont le Beurre. During a pause I heard the following conversation take place.

Host to Logan: "I suppose, being in a Convoy Camp, you hear nothing but motor shop the whole time, and get to know quite a lot about them?"

"Rather," replied Logan, who between you and me hardly knew one end of a car from the other, "I'm becoming quite conversant with the different parts. One hears people exclaiming constantly: 'I've mislaid my big end and can't think where I've put the carburettor!'" The host, who appeared to know as much as she did, nodded sympathetically.

Chris and I happened to catch the captain's eye, and we laughed for about five minutes. That big-end story went the round of the camp too, you may be quite sure.

Besides the regular work of barges, evacuation, and trains we had to do all the ambulance work for the outlying camps, and cars were regularly detailed for special *dépôts* the whole day long. Barges arrived mostly in the mornings, and I think the patients in them were more surprised than anyone to see girls driving out there, and were often not a little fearful as to how we would cope! It was comforting to overhear them say to each other on the journey: "This is fine, mate, ain't it?"

When we drove the cases to the hospital ships the long quay along which we took them barely allowed two cars to pass abreast. Turning when the car was empty was therefore a ticklish business, and there was only one place where it could be done. If you made a slip, there was nothing between you and the sea 50 feet below. There was a dip in the platform at one point, and by backing carefully on to this, it was just possible to turn, but to do so necessitated running forward in the direction of the quay, where there was barely the space of a foot left between the front wheel and the edge. I know, sitting in the car, I never could see any edge at all. If by any chance you misjudged this dip and backed against the edge of the platform by mistake the car, unable to mount it, rebounded and slid forward!

It was always rather a breathless performance at first; and beginners, rather than risk it, backed the whole length of the quay. I did so myself the first time, but it was such a neck-twisting performance I felt I'd rather risk a ducking. With practice we were able to judge to a fraction just how near the edge we could risk going, and the men on the hospital ships would hold their breath at the (I hope pardonable) swank of some of the more daring spirits who went just as near as they could and then looked up and laughed as they drove down the quay. After I was in hospital in England, I heard that a new hand lost her head completely, and in Eva's newly painted 'bus executed a spinning nose-dive right over the quay.

A sight I wouldn't have missed for worlds. As she "touched water," however, the F.A.N.Y. spirit predominated. She was washed through the back of the ambulance (luckily the front canvas was up), and as it sank she gallantly kicked off from the roof of the fast disappearing car. She was an excellent swimmer, but two R.A.M.C. men sprang overboard to her rescue, and I believe almost succeeded in drowning her in their efforts! This serves to show what an extremely touchy job it was, and one we had to perform in fogs or the early hours of a winter's morning when it was almost too dark to see anything. Some Red Cross men drivers from Havre watched us once, and declared their quay down there was wider by several feet, but no one ever turned on it. It seemed odd at home to see two girls on army ambulances. We went distances of sixty miles or more alone, only taking an orderly when the cases were of a very serious nature and likely to require attention en route.

Once I remember I was returning from taking a new medical officer (a cheerful individual, whose only remark during the whole of that fifteen-mile run was, "I'm perished!") to an outlying camp. I wondered at first if that was his name and he was introducing himself, but one glance was sufficient to prove otherwise! On the way back alone, I paused to ask the way, as I had to return by another route. The man I had stopped (whom at first I had taken to be a Frenchman) was a German prisoner, so I started on again; but wherever I looked there were nothing but Germans, busily working at these quarries. No guards were in sight, as far as I could see, and I wondered idly if they would take it into their heads to hold up the car, brain me, and escape. It was only a momentary idea though, for looking at these men, they seemed to be quite incapable of thinking of anything so original.

Coming back from B. one day I started a huge hare, and with the utmost difficulty prevented the good Susan from turning off the road, lepping the ditch, and pursuing 'puss' across the flat pastures. Some sporting 'bus, I tell you!

The tanks made their first appearance in September, and weird and wonderful were the descriptions given by the different men I asked whom I carried on my ambulance. They appeared to be anything in size from a hippopotamus to Buckingham Palace. It was one of the best kept secrets of the war. When anyone asked what was being made in the large foundries employed they received the non-committal reply "Tanks," and so the name stuck.

My last leave came off in the autumn, and while I was at home Lamarck Hospital closed on its second anniversary—October 31, 1916. The Belgians now had a big hut hospital at the Porte de Gravelines, and wished to concentrate what sick and wounded they had there, instead of having so many small hospitals. A great celebration took place, and there was much bouquet handing and speechifying, etc.

Our work for the Belgians did not cease with the closing of Lamarck, and a convoy was formed with the Gare Centrale as its headquarters, and so released the men drivers for the line. The hospital staff and equipment moved to Epernay, where a hospital was opened for the French in an old Monastery and also a convoy of F.A.N.Y. ambulances and cars was attached, so that now we had units working for the British, French, and Belgians. Another unit was the one down at Camp de Ruchard, where Crockett so ably ran a canteen for 700 convalescent Belgian soldiers, while Lady Baird, with a trained nurse, looked after the consumptives, of whom there were several hundreds. It will thus be seen that the F.A.N.Y. was essentially an "active service" Corps with no units in England at all.

I had a splendid leave, which passed all too quickly, and oddly enough before I left home I had a sort of premonition that something was going to happen; so much so that I even left an envelope with instructions of what I wanted done with such worldly goods as I possessed. I felt that in making such arrangements I might possibly avert any impending catastrophe!

Heasy was on leave as well, and the day we were due to go back was a Sunday. The train was to leave Charing Cross at four, which meant that we would not embark till seven or thereabouts. It was wet and blustery, and I did not relish the idea of crossing in the dark at all, and could not help laughing at myself for being so funky. I had somehow quite made up my mind we were going to be torpedoed. The people I was staying with ragged me hard about it. It was the 5th of November, too! As I stepped out of the taxi at Charing Cross and handed my kit to the porter, he asked: "Boat train, Miss?" I nodded. "Been cancelled owin' to storm," he said cheerfully. I leapt out, and I think I shook him by the hand in my joy. France is all right when you get there; but the day you return is like going back to school.

The next minute I saw Heasy's beaming face, and we were all over each other at the prospect of an extra day. My old godfather, who had come to see me off, was the funniest of all—a peppery Indian edition. "Not going?" he exclaimed, "I never heard of such a thing! In my day there was not all this chopping and changing." I pointed out that he might at least express his joy that I was to be at home another day, and fuming and spluttering we returned to the D's. It's rather an anti-climax, after saying goodbye and receiving everyone's blessing, to turn up suddenly once more!

Heasy and I duly met at Charing Cross next morning, to hear that once more the leave boat had been cancelled owing to loosened mines floating about. Again I returned to my friends who by this time seemed to think I had "come to stay." On the Wednesday (we were now getting to know all the porters quite well by sight) we really did get off; but when we arrived at Folkestone it was to find the platform crammed with returning leave-men and officers, and to hear the same tale—the boat had again been cancelled. None of the officers were being allowed to return to town, but by dint of good luck and a little palm oil, we dashed into a cab and reached the other station just in time to catch the up-going train. "We stay at an hotel tonight," I said to Heasy, "I positively won't turn up at the D's again." We got to town in time for lunch, and then went to see the Happy Day, at Daly's (very well named we thought), where Heasy's brother was entertaining a party. He had seen us off, "positively for the last time," at 7.30 that morning. We saw him in the distance, and in the interval we instructed the programme girl to take round a slip of paper on which we printed:—

If you will come round to Stalls 21 and 22 you will hear of something to your advantage.

George Heasman came round utterly mystified, and when he saw us once more, words quite failed him!

On the Thursday down we went again, and this time we actually did get on board, though they kept us hanging about on the Folkestone platform for hours before they decided, and the rain dripped down our necks from that inadequate wooden roofing that had obviously been put up by some war profiteer on the cheap. The congestion was something frightful, and there were twelve hundred on board instead of the usual seven or eight. "We can't blow over at any rate," I said cheerfully to Heasy, in a momentary lull in the gale. There were so many people on board that there was just standing room and that was all. We hastily swallowed some more Mother-sill and hoped for the best (we had consumed almost a whole boxful owing to our many false starts). We were in the highest spirits. The only other woman on board was an army sister, who came and stood near us. Lifebelts were ordered to be put on, and as I tied Heasy's the aforementioned sister turned to me and said: "You ought to tie that tighter; it will come undone very easily in the waves!"

Heasy and I were convulsed, and so were all the people within earshot. "You mustn't be so cheerful," I said, as soon as I could speak.

It was the roughest crossing I've ever experienced, and there was no time to indulge in "*that periscope feeling*," so aptly described by Bairnsfather; we were too busy exercising Christian Science on our "innards" and trying not to think of all the indigestible things we'd eaten the night before! We rose on mountains of waves one moment and then descended into positive valleys the next. I swear I would have been perfectly all right if I had not heard an officer say "I hope it will not be too rough to get into Boulogne harbour. The last time I crossed we had to return to Folkestone!"......

Luckily his fears were incorrect, and at last we arrived in the harbour, and I never was so glad to see France in all my life! The F.A.N.Y.s had almost given us up for good, and were all very envious when they heard of our adventures.

Towards the end of that month the *Britannic*, a hospital ship, was torpedoed. As a preventive measure against future outrages of the kind (not that it would have made the Germans hesitate for a moment) twenty prisoners were detailed to accompany each hospital ship on the voyage to England. These men, under one of their own sergeant-majors, sat on the edge of the platform until all the wounded were on board, and then were marched on into a little wooden shelter specially erected. As they sat on the edge, their feet rested on the narrow quay along which we drove, and I loved to go as near as possible and pretend I was going over them, just for the fun of watching the Boches roll on their backs in terror with their feet high in the air. A new method of saying *Kamerad!* Those prisoners did not care for me very much, I don't think, and I always hope I shan't meet any of them après la guerre. Unfortunately this pastime was stopped by the vigilant E.M.O.

My hut was closed for "winter decorations," and the *crème de menthe* coloured panthers were covered up by a hunting *frieze*. It was a priceless show, one of the field appearing in a chic pair of red gloves! I suppose they had some extra paint over from the pink coats. Scene 1. was the meet, with the fox lurking well within sight behind a small gorse bush, but funnily enough not a hound got wind of him. Scene 3. was a good water-jump where one of the field had taken a toss right into the middle of a stream. Considering the sandy spot he had chosen as a take-off, he had no one to thank but himself. A lady further up on a grey, obviously suffering from spavin, was sailing over like a two-year old. The last scene was of course a kill, the gentleman in the pink gloves on the black horse being well to the fore. Altogether it was most pleasing. Silk hunting "hankies" in yellow and other vivid colours, *ditto* with full field, took the place of the now chilly looking Reckitt's blue, and a Turkey rug on the floor completed the transformation.

When an early evacuation was not in progress, breakfast was at eight o'clock, and at 10 minutes to, the whistles went for parade, which was held in the square just in front of the cars. Those who were late were put on fatigues without more ado, but in the ordinary way if there were no delinquents we took it in turns, two every day.

Often when that first whistle went, it found a good many of us still "complete in flea-bag," and that scramble to get into things and appear "fully dressed" was an art in itself. An overcoat, muffler, and a pair of field boots went a long way to complete this illusion. Once however, Boss, to everyone's pained surprise, said, "Will the troopers kindly take off their overcoats!" With great reluctance this was done amid shouts of laughter as three of us stood divested of coats in gaudy pyjamas.

Fatigue consisted of two things: One—"Tidying up the Camp," which was a comprehensive term and meant folding up everyone's bonnet covers and putting them in neat piles near the mess hut, collecting cotton waste and grease tins, etc., and weeding the garden (a rotten job). The second was called "Doing the stoke-hole," i.e. cleaning out the ashes from the huge boiler that heated the bath water, chopping sticks, laying the fire, and brushing the "hole" up generally.

Opinions were divided as to the merits of those two jobs. Neither was popular of course, but we could choose. The latter certainly had its points, because once done it was done for the day, while the former might be tidy at nine, and yet by 10 o'clock lumps of cotton waste might be blowing all over the place, tins and bonnet covers once more in untidy heaps. I often "did the boiler," but I simply hated chopping

117

the sticks. One day the axe was firmly fixed in a piece of hard wood and I was vainly hitting it against the block, with eyes tight shut, when I heard a chuckle from the top of the steps. I looked up and there was a Tommy looking down into the hole, watching the proceedings. Where he'd come from I don't know. "Call those 'ands?" he asked. "'Ere, give it to me"—indicating the axe. "I guess y'aint chopped many sticks, 'ave yer?"

"No," I said; "and I'm terrified of the thing!" I sat on the steps and watched him deftly slicing the wood into thin slips. "This is a fatigue," I said, by way of an explanation.

That tickled him! He stopped and chuckled, "You do fatigues just the same as we do?" he asked. "I never heard anything to beat that. Well I never, wot's the crime, I wonder? Look 'ere," he added, "I'll chop you enough to last fatigues for a month, and you put 'em somewhere in the meantime," and in ten minutes, mark you, there was a pile that rejoiced my heart. He was a "Bird," that man, and no mistake.

After brekker was over the first thing that had to be done before anything else was to get one's 'bus running and in order for the day. Once that was done we could do our huts, provided no jobs had come in; and when that was done the engine had to be thoroughly cleaned, and then the car. I might add that this is an ideal account of the proceedings for, as often as not, we went out the minute the cars were started. Three days elapsed sometimes before the hut could have a "turn out." On these occasions one just rolled into one's bed at night unmade and unturned, too tired to care one way or the other.

Some of the girls got a Frenchwoman, "Alice" by name, to do their "cues" for them. She used to bring her small baby with her and dump him down anywhere in the corridor, sometimes in a waste paper basket, till she was done. One morning he howled bitterly for about an hour, and at last I went out to see what could be the matter. "Oh, Mees, it is that he has burnt himself against the stove, the careless one" (he couldn't walk, so it must have been her own fault). "I took him to a *pharmacie* but he has done nothing but cry ever since."

Now I had fixed up a small *pharmacie* in one of the empty "cues," complete with sterilised dressings and rows of bottles, and bandaged up whatever cuts and hurts there were, in fact my only sorrow was there were not more "cases." Considering the many men we had had at Lamarck burnt practically all over from fire-bombs, I suggested that she should bring the baby into the *pharmacie* and see if I could do anything for it. She was quite willing, and carried it in, when I undid

118

the little arm (only about six inches long) burnt from the elbow to the wrist! The chemist had simply planked on some zinc ointment and lint. I got some warm *boracic* and soaked it off gently, though the little thing redoubled its yells, and a small crowd of F.A.N.Y.s dashed down the passage to see what was up. "It's only Pat killing a baby" was one of the cheerful explanations I heard. So encouraging for me. I dressed it with Carron oil and to my relief the wails ceased. She brought it every morning after that, and I referred proudly to my "out-patient" who made great progress. Within ten days the arm had healed up, and Alice was my devoted follower from that time on.

We had a lot of work that autumn, and barges came down regularly as clockwork. Many of these cases were taken to the Duchess of Sutherland's Hospital. She had given up the Bourbourg Belgian one some time before and now had one for the British, where the famous Carroll-Dakin treatment was given. One night, taking some cases to the Casino hospital, there was a boy on board with his eyes bandaged. He had evidently endeared himself to the sister on the train, for she came along with the stretcher bearers and saw him safely into my car. "Goodbye, Sister," I heard him say, in a cheery voice, "thank you a thousand times for your kindness—you wait till my old eyes are better and I'll come back and see you. I know you must look nice," he continued, with a laugh, "you've got such a kind voice."

Tears were in her eyes as she came round to speak to me and whisper that it was a hopeless case; he had been so severely injured he would never see again.

I raged inwardly against the powers that cared not a jot who suffered so long as their own selfish ends were achieved.

That journey was one of the worst I've ever done. If the boy had not been so cheerful it would have been easier, but there he lay chatting breezily to me through the canvas, wanting to know all about our work and asking hundreds of questions. "You wait till I get home," he said, "I'll have the best eye chap there is, you bet your life. By Jove, it will be splendid to get these bandages off, and see again."

Was the war worth even one boy's eyesight? No, I thought not.

CHAPTER 14

Christmas, 1916

Taking some wounded Germans to No. 14 hospital one afternoon we were stopped on the way by a road patrol, a new invention to prevent joy-riding. Two Tommies rushed out from the hedges, like highwaymen of old, waving little red flags (one of the lighter efforts of the War Office). Perforce we had to draw up while one of them went into the estaminet (I noticed they always chose their quarters well) to bring out the officer. His job was to examine papers and passes, and sort the sheep from the goats, allowing the former to proceed and turning the latter away!

The man in question was evidently new to the work and was exceedingly fussy and officious. He scanned my pink pass for some time and then asked, "Where are you going?"

"Wimereux," I replied promptly.

He looked at the pass again—"It's got 'Wimeroo,' here, and not what you said," he answered suspiciously.

"Some people pronounce it 'Vimerer,' nevertheless," I could not refrain from replying, rather tartly.

Again he turned to the pass, and as it started to snow in stinging gusts (and I was so obviously one of the "sheep"), I began to chafe at the delay.

As if anyone would joy-ride in such weather without a wind screen, I thought disgustedly. (None of the cars had them.)

"Whom have you got in behind?" was the next query.

I leant forward as if imparting a secret of great importance, and said, in a stage whisper: "Germans!"

He jumped visibly, and the two flag-wagging Tommies grinned delightedly. After going to the back to find out if this was so, he at last very reluctantly returned my pass.

"Thinks we're all bloomin' spies," said one of the guards, as at last we set off to face the blinding snow, that literally was blinding, it was so hard to see. The only method was to shut first one eye and then the other, so that they could rest in turns!

On the way back we passed a motor hearse stuck on the Wimereux hill with four coffins in behind, stretcher-wise.

The guard gave a grunt. "Humph," said he, "They makes yer form fours right up to the ruddy grave, they do!"

We were not so far from civilization in our convoy as one might have supposed, for among the men in the M.T. yard was a hairdresser from the Savoy Hotel!

He made a diffident call on Boss one day and said it would give him great pleasure to shampoo and do up the "young ladies' hair" for them in his spare time "to keep his hand in." He was afraid if the war lasted much longer he might forget the gentle art!

We rose to the occasion and were only too delighted, and from then onwards he became a regular institution up at the convoy.

News was brought to us of the torpedoing of the *Sussex*, and the terrible suffering the crew and passengers endured. It was thought after she was struck she would surely sink, and many deaths by drowning occurred owing to overcrowding the lifeboats. Like the *Zulu*, however, when day dawned it was found she was able to come into Boulogne under her own steam. After driving some cases over there, I went to see the remains in dry dock. It was a ghastly sight, made all the more poignant as one could see trunks and clothes lying about in many of the cabins, which were open to the day as if a transverse section had been made.

The only humorous incident that occurred was that King Albert was arrested while taking a photo of it! I don't think for a moment they recognized who he was, for, with glasses, and a slight stoop, he does not look exactly like the photos one sees, and they probably imagined he was bluffing. He was marched off looking intensely amused! One of the French guards, when I expressed my disappointment at not being able to get a photo, gave me the address of a friend of his who had taken some official ones for France, so I hurried off, and was lucky to get them.

The weather became atrocious as the winter advanced and our none too water-tight huts showed distinct signs of warping. We only had one thickness of matchboarding in between us and the elements, and, without looking out of the windows, I could generally ascertain through the slits what was going on in the way of weather. I had chosen my "*cue*" looking sea-ward because of the view and the sunsets, but then that was in far away Spring. Eva's was next door, and even more exposed than mine. When we happened to mention this state of affairs to Colonel C., he promised us some asbestos to line the outer wall if we could find someone to put it up.

Another obliging friend lent us his carpenter to do the job—a burly Scot. The fact that we cleaned our own cars and went about the camp in riding breeches and overalls, not unlike land-girls' kit, left him almost speechless.

The first day all he could say was, "Weel, weel, I never did"—at intervals.

The second day he had recovered himself sufficiently to look round and take a little notice.

"Ye're one o' them artists, I'm thinkin'," he said, eyeing my panthers disparagingly. (The hunting *frieze* had been taken down temporarily till the asbestos was fixed.) "No, you mustn't think that," I said apologetically.

"Ha ye no men to do yon dirty worrk for ye?" and he nodded in direction of the cars. "Scandalizing, and no less," was his comment when he heard there were not. In two days' time he reported to his C.O. that the job was finished, and the latter overheard him saying to a pal, "Aye mon, but A've had ma outlook on life broadened these last two days." B. 'phoned up hastily to the convoy to know what exactly we had done with his carpenter.

Work was slack in the Autumn owing to the fearful floods of rain, and several of the F.A.N.Y.s took up fencing and went once a week at eight o'clock to a big "*Salle d'Escrime*" off the Rue Royale. A famous Belgian fencer, I forget his name, and a Frenchman, both stationed in the vicinity, instructed, and "Squig" kindly let me take her lessons when she was on leave. Fencing is one of the best tests I know for teaching you to keep your temper. When my foil had been hit up into the air about three times in succession to the triumphant Riposte! of the little Frenchman, I would determine to keep "Quite cool."

In spite of all, however, when I lunged forward it was with rather a savage stamp, which he would copy delightedly and exclaim triumphantly—"*Mademoiselle se fâche!*" I could have killed that Frenchman cheerfully! His quick orders "*Paré, paré—quatre, paré—contre—Riposté!*" etc. left me completely bewildered at first. Hope was a great nut with the foils and she and the Frenchman had veritable battles, during which the little man, on his mettle and very excited, would squeal exactly like a rabbit. The big Belgian was more phlegmatic and not so easily moved.

One night I espied a pair of boxing gloves and pulled them on while waiting for my turn. "*Mademoiselle* knows *la boxe?*" he asked interestedly.

"A little, a very little, *Monsieur*," I replied. "Only what my brother showed me long ago."

"*Montrez*," said he, drawing on a pair as well, and much to the amusement of the others we began preliminary sparring. "*Mademoiselle* knows *ze-k-nock-oot?*" he hazarded.

I did not reply, for at that moment he lifted his left arm, leaving his heart exposed. Quick as lightning I got in a topper that completely winded him and sent him reeling against the wall. When he got his breath back he laughed till the tears rolled down his cheeks, and whenever I met him in the street he flew up a side alley in mock terror. I was always designated after that as *Mademoiselle qui sait la boxe—oh, la la!*

In spite of repeated efforts on the part of R.E.s. there was a spot in the roof through which the rain persistently dripped on to my face in the night. They never could find it, so the only solution was to sleep the other way up! *C'est la guerre*, and that's all there was to it.

One cold blustery day I had left "Susan" at the works in Boulogne and was walking along by the fish market when I saw a young fair-haired staff officer coming along the pavement toward me. "His face is very familiar," I thought to myself, and then, quick as a flash—"Why, it's the Prince of Wales, of course!" He seemed to be quite alone, and except for ourselves the street was deserted. How to cope? To bob or not to bob, that was the question? Then I suddenly realised that in a stiff pair of Cording's boots and a man's sheepskin-lined mackintosh, sticking out to goodness knows where, it would be a sheer impossibility. I hastily reviewed the situation. If I salute, I thought, he may think I'm taking a liberty! I decided miserably to do neither and hoped he would think I had not recognised him at all.

As we came abreast I looked straight ahead, getting rather pink the while. Once past and calling myself all manner of fools, I thought "I'm going to turn round, and stare. One doesn't meet a prince every day, and in any case a cat may look at a king!" I did so—the prince was turning round too! He smiled delightfully, giving me a wonderful salute, which I returned and went on my way joyfully, feeling that it had been left to him to save the situation, and very proud to think I had had a salute all to myself.

Christmas came round before we knew where we were, and Boss gave the order it was to be celebrated in our own mess. Work was slack just then and Mrs. Williams gave a tea and dance in the afternoon at her canteen up at Fontinettes. It was a picturesque-looking place with red brick floor, artistic-looking tables with rough logs for legs and a large open fireplace, typically English, which must have rejoiced the hearts of men so far from Blighty.

It was a very jolly show, in spite of my partner bumping his head against the beam every time we went round, and people came from far and near. It was over about five, and we hastened back to prepare for our Christmas dinner in mess.

Fancy dress had been decided on, and as it was to be only among ourselves we were given *carte blanche* as to ideas. They were of course all kept secret until the last moment. Baby went as a Magpie and looked very striking, the black and white effect being obtained by draping a white towel straight down one side over the black nether garments belonging to our concert party kit.

I decided to go as a *Vie Parisienne* cover. A study in black and daffodil—a ravishing confection—and also used part of our "FAN-TASTIK" kit, but made the bodice out of crinkly yellow paper. A chrysanthemum of the same shade in my hair, which was skinned back in the latest door-knob fashion, completed the get-up.

Baby and I met on our way across the camp and drifted into mess together, and as we slowly divested ourselves of our grey wolf-coats we were hailed with yells of delight.

Dicky went as Charlie's Aunt, and Winnie as the irresistible nephew. Eva was an art student from the Quartier Latin, and Bridget a charming two-year old. The others came in many and various disguises.

We all helped to clear away in order to dance afterwards, and as I ran into the cook-house with some plates I met the mechanic laden with the tray from his hut.

The momentary glimpse of the *Vie Parisienne* was almost too much for the good Brown. I heard a startled "Gor blimee! Miss" and saw his eyes popping out of his head as he just prevented the tray from eluding his grasp!

Soon after Christmas a grain-ship, while entering Boulogne harbour in a storm, got blown across and firmly fixed between the two jetties, which are not very wide apart. To make matters worse its back broke and so formed an effectual barrier to the harbour and took from a fortnight to three weeks to clear away.

Traffic was diverted to the other ports, and for the time being Boulogne became almost like a city of the dead.

One port had been used solely for hospital ships up till then, and the scenes of bustle and confusion that replaced the comparative calm were almost indescribable. We saw many friends returning from Christmas leave, who for the most part had not the faintest idea where they had arrived. There were not enough military cars to transport the men to Fontinettes, so besides our barge and hospital work we were temporarily commissioned by the Local Transport Office.

I was detailed to take two officers inspecting the Archic stations north of St. Omer one wet snowy afternoon, and many were the adventures we had. It was a great thing to get up right behind our lines to places where we had never been before, and Susan ploughed through the mud like a two-year old, and never even so much as punctured. We were on our way back at a little place called Pont l'Abbesse, about 6.30, when the snow came down in blinding gusts. With only two side lamps, and a pitch dark night, the prospect of ever finding our way home seemed nil, and every road we took was bordered by a deep canal, with nothing in the way of a fence as protection. It was bitterly cold, and once we got completely lost; three-quarters of an hour later finding ourselves at the same cottage where we had previously asked the way!

At last we found a staff car that promised to give us a lead, and in time we reached the main St. Omer road, finally getting back to Pont-le-Beurre about 10 p.m. I 'phoned up to the convoy to tell them I was still in the land of the living, and after a bowl of hot soup sped back to camp.

My hands were so cold I had to sit on them in turns, and as for feet, I didn't seem to have any. Still it was "some run," and the next day I spent a long time hosing off the thick clay which almost completely hid the good Susan from sight.

Another temporary job we had was to drive an army sister (a sort of female Military Landing officer) to the boat every day, where she met the sisters coming back from leave and directed them to the different units and hospitals.

One of the results of the closing of Boulogne harbour was that instead of the patients being evacuated straight to England we had to drive them into Boulogne, where they were entrained for Havre!

A terrible journey, poor things. Twenty to twenty-four ambulances would set off to do the thirty kilometres in convoy, led at a steady pace by the Section Leader. These journeys took place three times a week, and often the men would get bitterly cold inside the cars. If there was one puncture in the convoy we all had to stop till a spare wheel was put on. We eagerly took the opportunity to get down and do stamping exercises and "cabby" arms to try and get warm. To my utmost surprise, on one of these occasions my four stretcher patients got up and danced in the road with me. Why they were "liers" instead of "sitters" I can't think, as there was not much wrong with them.

À propos I remember asking one night when an ambulance train came in in the dark, "Are you liers or sitters in here?" and one humorist scratched his head and replied, "I don't rightly know, Sister, I've told a few in my time!" To return to our long convoy journeys: once we had deposited our patients it was not unnaturally the desire of this "dismounted cavalry" unit to try the speed of its respective 'buses one against the other on the return journey; to our immense disappointment this idea was completely nipped in the bud, for Boss rode on the first car.

Permission however was given to pass on hills, as it was considered a pity to overheat a car going down to second gear when it could easily have done the hill on third! That Boulogne road is one of the hilliest in France, and Susan was a nailer on hills. I remember arriving in camp second one day. "How have you got here?" asked Boss in surprise, "I purposely put you nineteenth!" Heasy, Betty, and I in celebration of two years' active service had permission to give a small dance in the mess at the beginning of the new year. We trembled lest at the last moment an ambulance train might arrive, but there was nothing worse than an early evacuation next morning and all went off excellently. I was entrusted to make the "cup," and bought the ingredients in the town (some cup), and gravely assured everyone there was absolutely "nothing in it." The *boracic* powder was lifted in my absence from the *pharmacie* to try and get the first glimmerings of a slide on that sticky creosoted floor. The ambulances, fitted with paper Chinese lanterns, were temporarily converted into sitting out places. It was a great show.

There was one job in the convoy we all loathed like poison; it was known as "corpses." There was no chance of dodging unpopular jobs, for they worked out on an absolutely fair system. For instance, the first time the telephone bell went after 8 a.m. (anything before that was counted night duty) it was taken by a girl whose name came first in alphabetical order. She rushed out to her car, but before going "warned" B. that when the bell next went it would be her job, and so on throughout the day. If you were "warned," it was an understood thing that you did not begin any long job on the car but stayed more or less in readiness. If the jobs got half through the alphabet by nightfall the last girl warned knew she was first for it the next morning.

To return to the corpses. What happened was that men were frequently falling into the canals and docks and were not discovered till perhaps three weeks later. An ambulance was then rung up, and the corpse, or what remained of it, was taken to the mortuary.

One day Bobs was called on to give evidence at a Court of Enquiry with regard to a corpse she had driven, as there was some mystification with regard to the day and hour at which it was found. As she stepped smartly up to the table the colonel asked her how, when it occurred some ten days ago, she could be sure it was 4.30 when she arrived on the scene.

"It was like this," said she. "When I heard it was a corpse, I thought I'd have my tea first!" (This was almost as bad as the tape measure episode and was of course conclusive. I might add, corpses were the only jobs that were not allowed to interfere with meals.)

"Foreign bodies," in the shape of former Belgian patients, often drifted up to camp in search of the particular "Mees" who had tended them at Lamarck, as often as not bringing souvenirs made at great pains in the trenches as tokens of their gratitude. It touched us very much to know that they had not forgotten.

One night when my evening duty was nearing its close and I was just preparing to go to my hut the telephone bell rang, and I was told to go down to the hospital ship we had just loaded that afternoon for a man reported to be in a dying condition, and not likely to stand the journey across to England—I never could understand why those cases should have been evacuated at all if there was any possibility of them becoming suddenly worse; but I suppose a certain number of beds had to be cleared for new arrivals, and individuals could not be considered. It seemed very hard.

I drove down to the quay in the inky blackness, it was a specially dark night, turned successfully, and reported I had come for the case.

An orderly, I am thankful to say, came with him in the car and sat behind holding his hand.

The boy called incessantly for his mother and seemed hardly to realise where he was. I sat forward, straining my eyes in the darkness along that narrow quay, on the look-out for the many holes I knew were only too surely there.

The journey seemed to take hours, and I answered a query of the orderly as to the distance.

The boy heard my voice and mistook me for one of the Sisters, and then followed one of the most trying half-hours I have ever been through.

He seemed to regain consciousness to a certain extent and asked me from time to time,

"Sister, am I dying?"

"Will I see me old mother again, Sister?"

"Why have you taken me off the Blighty ship, Sister?"

Then there would be silence for a space, broken only by groans and an occasional "Christ, but me back 'urts crool," and all the comfort I could give was that we would be there soon, and the doctor would do something to ease the pain.

Thank God, at last we arrived at the Casino. One of the most trying things about ambulance driving is that while you long to get the patient to hospital as quickly as possible you are forced to drive slowly. I jumped out and cautioned the orderlies to lift him as gently as they could, and he clung on to my hand as I walked beside the stretcher into the ward.

"You're telling me the truth, Sister? I don't want to die, I tell you that straight," he said. "Goodbye and God bless you; I'll come and see you in the morning," I said, and left him to the nurses' tender care. I went down early next day but he had died at 3 a.m. Somebody's son and only nineteen. That sort of job takes the heart out of you for some days, though Heaven knows we ought to have got used to anything by that time.

To make up for the wet autumn a hard frost set in early in the year.

The M.T. provided us with anti-freezing mixture for the radiators, but the anti-freezing cheerfully froze! We tried emptying them at night, turning off the petrol and running the engine till the carburettor was dry (for even the petrol was not above freezing), and wrapping up the engines as carefully as if they were babies, but even that failed.

Starting the cars up in the morning (a detail I see I have not mentioned so far), even in ordinary times quite a hard job, now became doubly so.

It was no uncommon sight to see F.A.N.Y.s lying supine across the bonnets of their cars, completely winded by their efforts. The morning air was full of sobbing breaths and groans as they swung in vain! This process was known as "getting her loose"—(I'm referring to the car not the F.A.N.Y., though, from personal experience, it's quite applicable to both.)

Brown or Johnson (the latter had replaced Kirkby) was secured to come if possible and give the final fillip that set the engine going. It's a well-known thing that you may turn at a car for ten minutes and not get her going, and a fresh hand will come and do so the first time.

This swinging left one feeling like nothing on earth, and sometimes was a day's work in itself.

In spite of all the precautions we took, whatever water was left in the water pipes and drainings at the bottom of the radiators froze solidly, and sure enough, when we had got them going, clouds of steam rose into the air. The frost had come to stay and moreover it was a black one.

Something had to be done to solve the problem for it was imperative for every car to be ready for the road first thing in the morning.

Camp fires were suggested, but were impracticable, and then it was that "Night Guards" were instituted.

Four girls sat up all night, and once every hour turned out to crank up the cars, run them with bonnet covers on till they were thoroughly warm, and then tuck them up again till the next time. We had from four to five cars each, and it will give some idea of the extreme cold to say that when we came to crank them again, in roughly three-quarters of an hour's time, they were almost cold. The noise must have been heard for some distance when the whole convoy was roaring and racing at once like a small inferno. But in spite of this, I know that when it was not our turn to sit up we others never woke.

As soon as the cars were tucked up and silent again we raced back to the cook-house, where we threw ourselves into deck chairs, played the gramophone, made coffee to keep us awake, or read frightening books—I remember I read *Bella Donna* on one of these occasions and wouldn't have gone across the camp alone if you'd paid me. A grand midnight supper also took up a certain amount of time.

That three-quarters of an hour positively flew, and seemed more like ten minutes, but punctually at the second we had to turn out again, willy-nilly—into that biting cold with the moon shining frostily over everything apparently turning it into steel.

The trouble was that as the frost continued water became scarce—baths had stopped long ago—and it began to be a question of getting even a basinful to wash in. Face creams were extensively applied as the only means of saving what little complexions we had left! The streets of the town were in a terrible condition owing principally to the hygienic customs of the inhabitants who would throw everything out of their front doors or windows. The consequence was that, without exaggeration, the ice in some places was two feet thick, and every day fresh layers were formed as the French housewives threw out more water. No one remained standing in a perpendicular position for long, and the difficulty was, once down, how to get up again.

Finally water became so scarce we had to bring huge cans in a lorry from the M.T., one of the few places not frozen out, and there was usually ice on them when they arrived in camp. Then the water even began to freeze as we filled up our radiators; and, finally, we were reduced to chopping up the ice in our tank and melting it for breakfast! One morning, however, Bridget came to me in great distress. "What on earth shall I do," said she, "I've finished all the ice, and there's not a bit left to make the tea for breakfast? I know you'll think of something," she added hopefully.

I had been on night guard and the idea of no hot tea was a positive calamity.

I thought for some minutes. "Here, give me the jug," I said, and out I went. After looking carefully round to see that I was not observed, I quietly tapped one of the radiators.

"I'll tell you after breakfast where it came from," I said, as I returned with the full jug. Bridget seized it joyfully and must have been a bit suspicious as it was still warm, but she was much too wise to ask any questions.

We had a cheery breakfast, and when it was over I called out, "I hope you all feel very much better and otherwise radiating? You ought to at all events!"

"Why?" they asked curiously. "Well, you've just drunk tea made out of 'radium,'" I replied. "Absolutely priceless stuff, known to a few of the first families by its original name of 'radiator water,'" and I escaped with speed to the fastnesses of my hut.

The Story of a Perfect Day
(From *Barrack Room Ballads of the F.A.N.Y. Corps,*)
We were smoking and absently humming
To anyone there who could play—
We'd finished our tea in the Mess hut

Awaiting an ambulance train—)
Roasting chestnuts some were, while the rest,
Cut up toffee or sang a refrain.
Outside was a bitter wind shrieking—
(Thank God for a fug in the Mess!)
Never mind if the old stove is reeking
If only the cold's a bit less—
But one of them starts and then shivers
(A goose walking over her tomb)
Gazes out at the rain running rivers
And says to the group in the room:
"Just supposing the 'God of Surprises'
Appeared in the glow of a coal,
With a promise before he demises
To take us away from this hole
And do just whatever we long to do.
Tell me your perfect day."
Said one, "Why, to fly to an island
Far away in a deep blue lagoon;
One would never be tired in my land
Nor ever get up too soon."
"Every time," cried the girl darning stockings,
"We'd surf-ride and bathe in the sea,
We'd wear nothing but little blue smockings
And eat mangoes and crabs for our tea."
"Oh no!" said a third, "that's a rotten
Idea of a perfect day;
I long to see mountains forgotten,
Once more hear the bells of a sleigh.
I'd give all I have in hard money
For one day of ski-ing again,
And to see those white mountains all sunny
Would pretty well drive me insane."
Then a girl, as she flicked cigarette ash
Most carelessly on to the floor,
Had a feeling just then that her pet "pash"
Would be a nice car at the door,
To motor all day without fagging—
Not to drive nor to start up the thing.
Oh! the joy to see someone else dragging

A tow-rope or greasing a spring!
Then a fifth murmured, "What about fishing?
Fern and heather right up to your knees
And a big salmon rushing and swishing
'Mid the smell of the red rowan trees."
So the train of opinions drifted
And thicker the atmosphere grew,
Till piercing the voices uplifted
Rang a sound I was sure I once knew.
A sound that set all my nerves singing
And ran down the length of my spine,
A great pack of hounds as they're flinging
Themselves on a new red-hot line!
A bit of God's country is stretching
As far as the hawk's eye can see,
The bushes are leafless, like etching,
As all good dream fences should be.
There isn't a bitter wind blowing
But a soft little southerly breeze,
And instead of the grey channel flowing
A covert of scrub and young trees.
The field of course is just dozens
Of people I want to meet so—
Old friends, to say nothing of cousins
Who've been killed in the war months ago.
Three F.A.N.Y.s are riding like fairies
Having drifted right into my dreams,
And they're riding their favourite "hairies"
That have been dead for years, so it seems.
A ditch that I've funked with precision
For seasons, and passed by in fear,
I now leap with a perfect decision
That never has marked my career.
For a dream-horse has never yet stumbled;
Far away hounds don't know how to flag.
A dream-fence would melt ere it crumbled,
And the dream-scent's as strong as a drag.
Of course the whole field I have pounded
Lepping high five-barred gates by the score,
And I don't seem the least bit astounded,

Though I never have done it before!
At last a glad chorus of yelling,
Proclaims my dream-fox has been viewed—
But somewhere some stove smoke is smelling
Which accounts for my feeling half stewed—
And somewhere the F.A.N.Y.s are talking
And somebody shouts through the din:
"What a horrible habit of snoring—
Hit her hard—wake her up—the train's in."

CHAPTER 15

Convoy Pets, Commandeering, and the "Fantastiks"

We took turns to go out on "all-night duty"; a different thing from night guards, and meant taking any calls that came through after 9 p.m. and before 8 a.m. next morning.

They were usually from outlying camps for men who had been taken ill or else for stranded army sisters arriving at the *gare* about 3 a.m. waiting to be taken to their billets.

It was comparatively cheery to be on this job when night guards were in progress, as there were four hefty F.A.N.Y.s sitting up in the cook-house, your car warm and easy to crank, and, joy of joys, a hot drink for you when you came back!

In the ordinary way as one scrambled into warm sweaters and top coats the dominant thought was, would the car start all right out there, with not a hand to give a final fillip once the "getting loose" process was accomplished?

Luckily my turns came round twice during night guards, and the last time I had to go for a pneumonia case to Beau Marais. It was a bright moonlight night, almost as light as day, with everything glittering in the frozen snow. Susan fairly hopped it! After having found the case, which took some doing, and deposited him in No. 30 hospital, I sped back to camp.

As I crossed the Place d'Armes and drove up the narrow Rue de la Mer, Susan seemed to take a sudden header and almost threw a somersault! I had gone into an invisible hole in the ice, two feet deep, extending half across the street. For some reason it had melted (due probably to an underground bakery in the vicinity). I reversed anxiously and then hopped out to feel Susan's springs as one might a horse's knees. Thank goodness they had not snapped, so backing all the way down the street again, relying on the moon for light, I proceeded cautiously by another route and got back without further mishap.

Our menagerie was gradually increasing. There were now three dogs and two cats in camp, not to mention a magpie and two canaries, more of which *anon*. There was Wuzzy, of course, and Archie (a naughty looking little Sealyham belonging to Heasy) and a mongrel known as G.K.W. (God knows what) that ran in front of a visiting Red Cross touring car one day and found itself in the position of the young lady of Norway, who sat herself down in the doorway! I did not witness the untimely end, but I believe it was all over in a minute.

One cat belonged to Eva, a plain-looking animal, black with a half-white face, christened "Miss Dip" (an inspiration on my part suggested by the donor's name, on the "Happy Family" principle). She was the apple of her eye, nevertheless, and nightly Eva could be heard calling "Dip, Dip, Dip," all over the camp to fetch her to bed. Incidentally it became quite an Angelus for us.

Considering the way she hunted all the meat shops for tit bits, that cat ought to have been a show animal—but it wasn't. One day as our fairy Lowson was lightly jumping from a windowsill she inadvertently "came in contact" with Dip's tail, the extreme tip of which was severed in consequence! In wrathful indignation Eva rushed Dip down to the Casino in an ambulance, where one of the foremost surgeons of the day operated with skill and speed and made a neat job of it, to the entire satisfaction of all concerned. If her tail still remains square at the end she can tell her children she was *blessée dans la guerre*. The other cat was a tortoiseshell and appropriately called "Melisande in the Wood," justified by the extraordinary circumstances in which she was discovered.

One day at No. 35 hut hospital I saw three of the men hunting in a bank opposite, covered with undergrowth and small shrubs. They told me that for the past three days a kitten had been heard mewing, but in spite of all their efforts to find it, they had failed to do so. I listened, and sure enough heard a plaintive mew. The place was a network of clinging roots, but presently I crawled in and found it was just possible to get along on hands and knees. It was most mysterious—the kitten could be heard quite loud one minute, and when we got to the exact spot it would be some distance away again. (It reminded me of the Dutch ventriloquist's trick in Lamarck). It was such a plaintive mew I was determined to find that kitten if I stayed there all night. At last it dawned on me, it must be in a rabbit hole; and sure enough after pushing and pulling my way along to the top of the bank, I found one over which a fall of earth had successfully pushed some wire netting from the fence above.

I waited patiently, and in due time caught sight of a little black, yellow, and white kitten; but the minute I made a grab for it, it bolted. I pulled the netting away, but the hole was much too deep for so small a creature to get out by itself, and it was much too frightened to let me catch it. With great difficulty I extricated myself and ran to the cook-house, where I soon enlisted Bridget's aid. We got some small pieces of soft raw meat and crawled to the top of the bank again. After long and tedious coaxing I at last grabbed the little thing spitting furiously while Bridget gave it some food, and in return for my trouble it bit and scratched like a young devil! It was terribly hungry and bolted all we had brought. When we got her to the cook-house she ran round the place like a mad thing, and turned out to be rather a fast cat altogether when she grew up. We tossed for her, Bridget won, and she was duly christened with a drop of tinned milk on her forehead, "Melisande in the Wood."

The magpie belonged to Russell, and came from Peuplinghe. Magpies are supposed to be unlucky birds. This one certainly brought no luck to its different owners. Shortly after its arrival Russell was obliged to return to England for good. Before going, however, she presented Jacques to Captain White at Val de Lièvre. Sure enough after some time he was posted to the Boche prisoner camp at Marquise—a job he did not relish at all. I don't know if he took Jacques with him, but the place was bombed shortly after and the Huns killed many of their own men, and presumably Jacques as well. So he did his bit for France.

The canaries belonged to Renny—at least at first she had only one. It happened in this wise. The man at the disinfector (where we took our cars and blankets to be syringed after an infectious case), had had a canary given him by his "best girl" (French). He did not want a canary and had nowhere to keep it, but, as he explained, he did not know enough of the language to say so, and thought the easiest way out of the difficulty was to accept it. "Give me the bird, proper, she 'as," he added.

The trouble was he did not reckon on her asking after it, which she most surely did. He could hardly confess to her that he had passed the present on so instead he conveyed the news to her, somehow, that the "pore little bird had gone and died on 'im." She expressed her horror and forthwith produced a second!

"Soon 'ave a bloomin' aviary at this rate," he remarked as he handed the second one over! No more appeared, however, and the two little birds, both presumably dead, twittered and sang merrily the length of the "cues."

As the better weather arrived so our work increased again, and in March the Germans began a retreat in the west along a front of 100 miles. We worked early and late and reached the point of being able to drive almost asleep. An extraordinary sensation—you avoid holes, you slip the clutch over bumps, you stop when necessary, and go on *ditto*, and at the same time you can be having dreams! More a state of coma than actual sleep, perhaps. I think what happened was one probably slept for a minute and then woke up again to go off once more.

I became "Wuzzy's" adopted mother about now and, whenever I had time, combed and brushed his silver curls till they stood out like fluff. He could spot Susan miles away, and though it was against rules I sometimes took him on board. As we neared camp I told him he must get down, but he would put on an obstinate expression and deliberately push himself behind my back, in between me and the canvas, so that I was almost on the steering wheel. At other times he would listen to me for awhile, take it all in, and then put his head on my shoulder with such an appealing gesture that I used to risk being spotted, and let him remain. He simply adored coming out if I was going riding, but I disliked having him intensely, for he ran about under the horses, nibbling at them and making himself a general nuisance. He would watch me through half shut eyes the minute I began polishing my riding boots; and try as I would to evade him he nearly always came in the end.

He got so crafty in time he would wait for me at the bottom of the drive and dash out from among the shrubs just as I was vanishing. One day we had trotted some distance along the Sangatte road, and I was just congratulating myself I had given him the slip, when looking up, there he was sitting on a grassy knoll just ahead, positively laughing and licking his chops with self-satisfied glee. I gave it up after that, I felt I couldn't cope with him, and yet there were those who called him stupid! I grant you he had his bad days when he was referred to as my "idiot son," but even then he was only just "peculiar"—a world of difference.

One job we had was termed "lodgers" and consisted of meeting the "sitting" cases from an ambulance train, taking them to the different hospitals for the night, and then back to the quay early next morning in time to catch the hospital ship to England. The stretcher cases had been put on board the night before, but there was no sleeping accommodation for so many "sitters." An ordinary evacuation often took place as well, so that before breakfast we had sometimes carried as many as thirty-five sitting cases, and done journeys with twelve stretchers. One day at No. 30 hospital I saw several of the girls beside a stretcher, and there was the "Bovril king" lying swathed in blankets, chatting affably! He was the cook at No. 30, a genial soul, who always rushed out in the early hours of the morning when one was feeling emptiest, with a cup of hot soup. He called it doing his bit, and always referred to himself proudly as the "Bovril king." Alas, he was now being invalided home with bronchitis!

Hope came back from leave and told me she had been pursued half way down Regent Street by a fat old taxi driver who asked after me. It was dear old Stone, of course, now returned to civil life and his smart taxi with the silver "vauses!" I have hunted the stands in vain for his smiling rosy face, but hope to spot him some day and have my three days' joy ride.

One precious whole afternoon off, a very rare event, I went out for a ride with Captain D. He rode "Baby," a little bay mare, and I rode a grey, a darling, with perfect manners and the "sweetest" mouth in the world. He was devoted to "Baby," and wherever she went he went too, as surely as Mary's little lamb.

We struck off the road on to some grass and after cantering along for some distance found we were in a network of small canals—the ground was very spongy and the canal ahead of us fortunately not as wide as the rest. We got over safely, landing in deep mud on the other side, and decided our best plan was to make for the road again. We espied a house at the end of the strip we were in with a road beyond, and agreed that there must be a bridge or something leading to it. Captain D. went off at a canter and I saw Baby break into a startled gallop as a train steamed up on the line beyond the road. They disappeared behind the house and I followed on at a canter. I turned the corner just in time to see them almost wholly immersed in a wide canal and the gallant captain crawling over Baby's head on to the bank! It was one of those deceptive spots where half the water was overgrown with thick weeds and cress, making the place appear as narrow again.

The grey was of course hot on Baby's track. Seeing her plight I naturally pulled up, but he resented this strongly and rose straight on his hind legs. Fearing he would over-balance, I quickly slacked the reins and leant forward on his neck. But it was too late; that slippery mud was no place to try and regain a foothold, and over he came. I just had time to slip off sideways, promptly lost my foothold and collapsed as well. How I laughed! There was Captain D. on one side of the canal vainly trying to capture his "wee red tourie" floating down stream, and Baby standing by with the mud dripping from her once glossy flanks; and on the other was I, sitting laughing helplessly in the mud, and the grey (now almost brown) softly nosing my cap and eyeing his beloved on the further bank with pained surprise!

To crown all, the train, which had come to a standstill, was by the irony of fate full of Scottish soldiers on their way up the line. Such a bit of luck in the shape of a free cinema show had rarely come their way and they were bent on enjoying it to the fullest extent. The fact that the officer now standing ruefully on the bank was in Tartan riding "troos" of course added to the piquancy of the situation.

The woman had come out of her cottage by this time and kept exclaiming at intervals, "Oh, la-la, Oh, la-la," probably imagining that this mudbath was only a new pastime of the mad English. She at last was kind enough to open the gate; and thither I led the grey and then across a plank bridge beyond, previously hidden from sight.

We scraped the mud off the saddles under a running fire of witty comments from the train. I knew the whole thing had given them so much enjoyment that I bore them no illwill. I could see their point of view so well, it must have been such fun to watch! "Hoots, mon," they called to the now thoroughly embarrassed D., as we mounted, "are ye no going to lift the lassie oop?" I was glad we were "oop" and away before the train started again, and as we trotted along the road, cries of "Guid luck to ye!" "May ye have a happy death!" (which is a regular north-country wish, and a very nice one when you come to think of it), followed us. The batman eyed us suspiciously as we reached Fontinettes where he was waiting for the horses, and remarked that they seemed to have had a "bit roll." My topcoat I'm glad to say covered all traces of the "bit roll" I had indulged in on my own. It was a great ride entirely.

One night for some reason I was unable to sleep—a rare occurrence—and bethought me of an exciting spy book, called the German Submarine Base, I had begun weeks before but had had no time to finish. All was dead quiet with the exception of the distant steady boom of the guns, which one of course hardly noticed. I had just got to the most thrilling part and was holding my breath from sheer excitement when *whiz! sob! bang!* and a shell went spinning over the huts. For a moment I thought I must be dreaming or that the book was bewitched. Next minute I was out of bed like a rabbit, and turning off the light, dashed outside just as the second went over. I naturally looked skyward, but there was not a sign of anything and, stranger still, not even the throb of an engine.

A third went over with a loud screech, and my hair was blown into the air by the rushing wind it caused. I saw a flash from the sea and Thompson said she was wakened by my voice calling, "I say, come out and see this new stunt." Soon everyone was up and the shells came on steadily, blowing our hair about, and making the very pebbles rush rattling along the ground, hitting against our feet with such force we thought at first it must be spent shrapnel. Some of those shells screeched and some miauled like huge cats hurtling through the air to spring on their prey. These latter made a cold shiver run down my spine; the noise they made was so blood-curdling. One could cope with the ordinary ones, but frankly, these were beastly.

Luckily they only went over about every tenth. It was something quite new getting shells of this calibre from such a short range, and "side-ways," too, as someone expressed it; quite a different sensation from on top. The noise was deafening; and then one struck the bank our camp was built on. We had no dugout and seemingly were just waiting to be potted at. We got the cars ready in case we were called up, and the shells whizzed over all the time. There was another explosion—one had landed in our incinerator! Good business! Another hit the bank again! Once more the fact of being so near the danger proved our safety, for with these three exceptions, they all passed over into the town beyond. The smell of powder in the air was so strong it made us sneeze. It was estimated roughly that 300 shells were lobbed into the town, and all passing over us on the way.

It was a German destroyer that had somehow got down the coast unchallenged, and was—we heard afterwards—only at a distance of 100 yards! What a chance for good shooting on our part; but it was a pitch black night and somehow she got away in the velvet darkness. Sounds of firing at sea—easily distinguishable from those on land because of the "*plop*" after them—continued throughout the night and we thought a naval battle was in progress somewhere; however, it proved to be one of the bombardments of England, according to the papers next day. To our great disappointment, our little "drop in the bucket" of 300 odd shells was not even mentioned.

There was much eager scratching in the bank for bits of shells the next day. One big piece was made into a paperweight by the old Scotch carpenter, and another was put on the "narrow escape" shelf among the other bits that had "nearly, but not quite!"

Wild rumours had got round the camps and town that the "lady drivers had got it proper," been "completely wiped out," in fact not one left alive to tell the lurid tale. So that wherever we drove the next morning we were greeted with cheery nods and smiles by everyone. The damage to the town was considerable, but the loss of life singularly small. The Detail Issue Stores had gone so far as to exchange bets as to whether we would appear to draw rations that morning, and as I drove up with Bridget on the box we were greeted right royally. One often found large oranges in one's tool box, or a bag of nuts, or something of the kind, popped in by a kindly Tommy who would pass the car and merely say: "Don't forget to look in your tool-box when you get to camp, Miss," and be gone before you could even thank him! All the choicest "cuts" were also reserved for us by the butcher and we were altogether spoilt pretty generally.

Tommy is certainly a nailer at what he terms "commandeering." I was down at the M.T. yard one day and as I left, was told casually to look in the box when I got to camp. I did so, and to my horror saw a wonderful foot pump—the pneumatic sort. I had visions of being hauled up before a Court of Enquiry to produce the said pump, which was a brand new one and painted bright red. On my next job I made a point of going round by the M.T. yard to return the "present." I found my obliging friend, who was pained in the extreme at the mere mention of a pump. "Never 'eard of one," he affirmed stoutly. "Leastways," he said reminiscently, looking at me out of the corner of his eye, "I do seem to remember something about a stawf car bein' in 'ere this morning when yours was"—and he smiled disarmingly. "Look 'ere," he continued, "you forget all about it, Miss. I 'ates to see yer puffing at the tyres with them old-fashioned ones, and anyway," with a grin, "that car's in Abbeville now!"

Another little example of similar "commandeering" was when my friend of the chopped sticks turned up one day with a small Primus stove: "I 'eard you was askin' for one, and 'ere it is," and with that he put it down and fled. After the pump episode I was full of suspicions about little things that "turned up" from nowhere, but for a long time

I had no opportunity of asking him exactly where the gift had come from. One night, however, one of the doctors from the adjacent hut hospital was up in camp, and Primus stoves suddenly cropped up in the conversation. "Most extraordinary thing," said he, "my batman is as honest as the day, and can't account for the disappearance of my stove at all. No one went into my hut, he declares, and yet the stove is gone, and not so much as a sign of it. One thing is I'd know it if I saw it again."

I started guiltily at this, and got rather pink—"Look here," I said, "come into my hut a moment."

He did so. "By Jove! that's my stove right enough," he cried, "I know the scratches on it. How on earth did you get it?"

"That I can't tell you," I replied, "but you can have it back" (graciously), "and look here, it wasn't your batman, so rest easy."

He was too wise to ask unnecessary questions (one didn't in France), and only too thankful to get his Primus, which he joyfully carried back in state. It was a pity about it, because they were impossible to get at that time, and our huts had already been raided for electric kettles.

Gothas came frequently to visit us at night and terrible scenes took place, during which we were ordered out amid the dropping bombs to carry the injured to hospital, but more often than not to collect the dead, or what was left of them.

One morning I was in great distress, for I lost my purse through the lining of my wolf-coat. It was not the loss of the purse that worried me, but the fact that I always kept the little medal of the Virgin and Child in there, given me by the old Scotch nun in Paris "for protection." "Eva," I called, "I've lost my luck—that little charm I had given me in 1915—I do wish I hadn't. I'm not superstitious in the ordinary way, but I kind of believe in that thing;" she only laughed however. But I took the trouble to advertise for it in the local paper—unfortunately with no result. I was very distressed.

Our concert party got really quite a slap-up show going about this time. We also had a drop scene behind—a huge white linen sheet on which we appliquéd big black butterflies fluttering down to a large sunflower in the corner, the petals of which were the same yellow as the bobbles on our dresses. We came to the conclusion that something of the sort was necessary, for as often as not we had to perform in front of puce-coloured curtains that hardly showed us up to the best advantage.

One of the best shows we ever gave I think was for the M.T. *dépôt*. They did so much for us one way and another repairing cars (not to mention details like the foot pump episode), that we were only too glad to do something for them in return. The *pièce de résistance* (at least, Dicky and I thought so) was a skit we got up on one of "Lena's" concert party stars[1]—a ventriloquist stunt. We thought of it quite suddenly and only had time for one rehearsal before the actual performance. I paid a visit to Corporal Coy of the mortuary (one of the local low comedians, who, like the coffin-cart man at Lamarck, "had a merry eye!" and was a recognised past-master in the art of make-up), and borrowed his little bowler hat for the occasion. He listened solemnly to the scheme, and insisted on making me a fascinating little Charlie Chaplin moustache (the requisites for which he kept somewhere in the mortuary with the rest of his disguises!) and he then taught me to waggle it with great skill!

Dicky was the "doll" with round shiny patches of red on her cheeks and a Tommy's cap and hospital blue coat. She supplied the glassy stare herself most successfully. For these character stunts we simply put on caps and coats over our "Fantastik" kit and left the rest to the imagination of the audience who was quick (none quicker) to grasp the implied suggestion. I was "Mr. Lenard Ashwell" in aforementioned bowler, moustache, and coat. We made up the dialogue partly on the basis of the original performance, and added a lot of local colour. I asked the questions, and was of course supposed to ventriloquize the answers, and, thanks to the glassy stare of my doll, her replies almost convinced the audience I was doing so.

They had all seen the real thing a fortnight before, so that we were greeted with shouts of laughter as the curtain went up.

The trouble was, as we had only written the book of words that day it was rather hard for me to remember them, so I had taken the precaution of safety-pinning them on my doll's back. It was all right for her as she got the cue from me. It was not difficult, half supporting her as I appeared to be, to squint behind occasionally for the next jest! On one of these occasions my incorrigible doll horrified me by winking at the audience and exclaiming, to their delight, "The bloke's got all the words on my back!" She then revolved out of my grasp, and spun slowly round on her stool. This unrehearsed effect quite brought

<hr />

1. *Entertaining the Boys 'Over There'* by Leonaur contains three books-*Modern Troubadours* by Lena Ashwell along with two others, Entertaining the American Army by James W Evans & Gardner L. Harding and *Trouping for the Troops* by Margaret Mayo.

the house down, and not to be outdone, I raised my small bowler repeatedly in acknowledgment!

I was a little taken aback the next morning when the man at the petrol stores said, "My, but you wos a fair treat as Charlie Chaplin last night, Miss." (It must have been Corporal Coy's moustache that did it, not to mention lifting my bowler from the rear!)

The more local colour you get in a show of that sort the better the men like it, and we parodied all the latest songs as fast as they came out. Winnie and "Squig" in Unity More's "*Clock strikes Thirteen*" were extremely popular, especially when they sang with reference to cranking up in the mornings:

Wind, wind. Oh what a grind!
I could weep, I could swear, I could scream,
Both my arms ache, and my back seems to break
But she'll go when the clock strikes thirteen.

Oh, oh (with joy), at last she will go!
There's a spark from the bloomin' machine,
She's going like fire, when bang goes a tyre
And we'll start when the clock strikes thirteen!

The whole programme was as follows:—

1. The FANTASTIKS announce their shortcomings in chorus of original words to the opening music of the Bing Boys— " We're the FANTASTIKS, and we rise at six and don't get much time to rehearse, so if songs don't go, and the show is slow, well, we hope you'll say it might have been worse," etc., etc.
2. *Violin* . . 1. " Andantino " (Kreisler) } P. B. WADDELL
           2. " Capriccioso " (Drdla) }
3. *Recitation* . . Humorous . N. F. LOWSON
4. *Chorus Song* . " Piccadilly " . FANTASTIKS (in monocles)
5. *Stories* . . . . . M. RICHARDSON
6. *China Town* . . . . . FANTASTIKS
    (Sung in the dark with lighted Chinese lanterns, quite professional in effect—at least we hoped so !)
7. *Recitation* . . Serious . . B. HUTCHINSON
8. Mr. Lenard Ashwell and his } . { M. RICHARDSON
    Ventriloquist Doll } . { P. B. WADDELL
9. *Duet* " When the Clock strikes Thirteen " G. QUIN AND W. MORDAUNT
10. *Violin Solo* " Zigeunerweisen " (Sarasate) P. B. WADDELL
11. *Song* . . " Au Revoir " . W. MORDAUNT
12. *The Kangaroo Hop* . . . . . FANTASTIKS

The chorus wore their goat-coats for this last item, and with animal masks fixed by elastic, bears, wolves, elephants, etc., it was distinctly realistic.

When "God save the King" had been sung, and the usual thanks and cheers given, and received, the sergeant-major from the canteen (with the beautiful waxed moustache) rushed forward to say that light refreshments had been provided. The "grizzly bears" were only too thankful, as they had had no time to snatch even a bun before they left camp.

CHAPTER 16

The Last Ride

The hardest job in the convoy was admittedly that of the big lorry, for, early and late, it was first and last on the field.

It took all the stretchers and blankets to the different hospitals, cleared up the quay after an early evacuation, brought stretchers and blankets up to the convoy, took the officers' kits to hospital and boats, and rationed the ambulance trains and barges. "Jimmy" took to the Vulcan instinctively when the convoy was first started and jealously kept to the job, but after a time she was forcibly removed therefrom in order to take a rest. I could sympathize—I knew how I had felt about the little lorry.

The job was to be taken in fortnightly turns, and while the old Vulcan lorry was being overhauled a Wyllis-Overland was sent in its place.

The disadvantage of the lorry was that you never saw any of your friends, for you were always on duty when they were off, and vice versa; also you hardly ever had meals when they did. Eva's fortnight was almost up, and I was hoping to see something of her before I went on leave when one night in she came with the news that I was the next one for it—hardly a welcome surprise; and down at barges that evening—it was a Sunday—Gamwell, the sergeant, told me officially I was to take on the job next morning at 5 a.m.

When I got back to camp I went for a preliminary run on it, as I had never driven that make before. The tyres were solid, all vestige of springs had long since departed from the seat and the roof was covered with tin that bent and rattled like stage thunder. The gears were in the middle and very worn, and the lever never lost an opportunity of slipping into first as you got out, and consequently the lorry tried to run over you when you cranked up! Altogether a charming car. You drove along like a travelling thunder-clap, and coming up the slope into camp the earth fairly shook beneath you. I used to feel like the whole of Valhalla arriving in a Wagner Opera! It was also quite impossible to hear what anyone said sitting on the seat beside you.

The third day, as I got out, I felt all my bones over carefully. "When I come off this job," I called to Johnson, "I shall certainly swallow a bottle of gum as a wise precaution." He grinned appreciatively.

Lowson, who had had her turn before Eva, appropriately christened it "Little Willie," and I can affirm that that car had a Hun soul.

You were up and dressed at 5 a.m. and waited about camp till the telephone bell rang to say the train had arrived. Schofield, the incinerator man who was usually in the camp at that hour, never failed to make a cup of tea—a most welcome thing, for one never got back to camp to have breakfast till 11 or 11.30 a.m. I used to spend the interval, after "Little Willie" was all prepared for the road, combing out Wuzzy's silver curls. He always accompanied the lorry and was allowed to sit, or rather jolt, on the seat beside me, unrebuked. After breakfast there was the quay to clear up and all the many other details to attend to, getting back to camp about 3 to go off in an hour's time to barges. When a Fontinettes ambulance train came down, the lorry driver was lucky if she got to bed this side of 2 a.m.

All social engagements in the way of rides, etc., had to be cancelled in consequence, but the Monday before I went into hospital the grey and Baby appeared up in camp about 5.30. I was hanging about waiting for the telephone to say the barge had arrived, but as there was a high wind blowing it was considered very unlikely it would come down the canal that evening. I 'phoned to a station several miles up to enquire if it was in sight, and the reply came back "Not a sign," and I accordingly got permission to go out for half an hour. I was so afraid Captain D. might not consider it worth while and could have almost wept, but fortunately he agreed half an hour was better than nothing, and off we went up the sands, leaving the bob-tailed Wuzzy well in the rear.

What a glorious gallop that was—my last ride! The sands appeared almost golden in the sun and the wind was whipping the deep blue waves into little crests of foam against the paler turquoise of the sky. Already the flowers on the dunes had burst into leaf, for it was the "*merrie month of May*," and there, away on the horizon, the white cliffs of England could just be discerned. Altogether it was good to be alive. "Hurrah," I cried, as we slowed down to a walk, "five more days and then on leave to England!" and I rubbed the grey's neck with joy. Alas! that half hour flew like ten minutes and we turned all too soon and raced back, thudding along over the glorious sands as we went.

I got to the convoy to find there was no news of the barge, but I had to dismount all the same—duty is duty—and I kissed the grey's nose, little thinking I should never see him again. The barge did not come down till 9 o'clock the next morning. *C'est la guerre*—and a very trying one to boot!

The weather was ideal just then: warm and sunny and not a cloud in the sky except for those little round white puffs where the Archie shells burst round the visiting Huns.

One afternoon about 5 o'clock, when breakfast had been at lunch time and consequently that latter meal had been n'apoo'd altogether, I went into the E.M.O.'s for the chits before leaving for camp. (These initials stood for "Embarkation Medical Officer" and always designated the office and shed where the blankets and stretchers were kept; also, incidentally, the place where the corporal and two men slept.) As I entered a most appetising odour greeted my nostrils and I suddenly realised how very hungry I was. I sniffed the air and wondered what it could be.

"Just goin' to have a cockle tea," explained the corporal. "I suppose, Miss, you wouldn't care to join us?" I knew the brew at the convoy would be long since cold, and accepted the invitation joyfully.

Their "dining-room" was but the shed where the stretchers were piled up, many of them brown and discoloured by blood, and bundles of fusty army blankets, used as coverings for the wounded, reached almost to the ceiling. They were like the stretchers in some cases, and always sticky to the touch. I could not repress a shudder as I turned away to the much more welcome sight of tea. A newspaper was spread on the rough table in my honour and Wheatley was despatched "at the double" to find the only saucer! (Those who knew the good Wheatley will perhaps fail to imagine he could attain such a speed—dear Wheatley, with his long spindle legs and quaint *serio-comic* face. He was a man of few words and a heart of gold.)

I look back on that "cockle tea" as one of my happiest memories. It was so jolly and we were all so gay and full of hope, for things were going well up the line.

I had never tasted cockles before and thought they were priceless. We discussed all manner of things during tea and I learnt a lot about their aspirations for *après la guerre*. It was singular to think that within a short month, of that happy party Headley the corporal alone remained sound and whole. One was killed by a shell falling on the E.M.O. One was in hospital crippled for life, and the third was brought in while I was there and died shortly after from septic pneumonia. Little did we think what was in store as we drank tea so merrily!

Wheatley insisted on putting a bass bag full of cockles into the lorry before I left, and when I got to camp I ran to the cook-house thinking how they would welcome a variation for supper.

"Cockles?" asked Bridget. "Humph, I suppose you know they grow on sewers and people who eat them die of ptomaine poisoning?" "No," I said, not at all crestfallen, "do they really, well I've just eaten a whole bag full! If they give me a military funeral I do hope you'll come," and I departed, feeling rather hurt, to issue further invitations.

I was drawing petrol at the stores the next day and as I was signing for it the man there (my Charlie Chaplin friend) kindly began to crank up.

As he did so I saw Little Willie move gently forward, and ran out to slip the gear back into "neutral."

"It's a Hun and called 'Little Willie,'" I explained as I did so.

"Crikey, wot a car," he observed, "no wonder you calls it that. Don't you let him put it acrosst you, Miss."

"He's only four more days to do it in," I thought joyfully, as I rattled off to the Quay, and yet somehow a premonition of some evil thing about to happen hung over me, and again I wished I hadn't lost my charm.

The next day was Wednesday, and I had been up since 5 and was taking a lorry-full of stretchers and blankets past a French battery to the E.M.O.'s. It was about midday and there was not a cloud in the sky. Then suddenly my heart stood still. Somehow, instinctively, I knew I was "for it" at last. Whole eternities seemed to elapse before the crash. There was no escape. Could I urge Little Willie on? I knew it was hopeless; even as I did so he bucketed and failed to respond. He would! How I longed for Susan, who could always be relied upon to sprint forward. At last the crash came. I felt myself being hurled from the car into the air, to fall and be swept along for some distance, my face being literally rubbed in the ground.

I remember my rage at this, and even in that extreme moment managed to seize my nose in the hope that it at least might not be broken! Presently I was left lying in a crumpled heap on the ground.

149

My first thought, oddly enough, was for the car, which I saw stand-ing sulkily and somewhat battered not far off. "There will be a row," I thought. The stretcher bearer in behind had been killed instantane-ously, but fortunately I did not know of this till some time later, nor did I even know he had jumped in behind. The car rattled to such an extent I had not heard the answer to my query, if anyone was coming with me to unload the stretchers.

I tried to move and found it impossible. "What a mess I'm in," was my next thought, "and how my legs ache!" I tried to move them too, but it was no good. "They must both be broken," I concluded. I put my hand to my head and brought it away all sticky. "That's funny," I thought, "where can it have come from?" and then I caught sight of my hand. It was all covered with blood. I began to have a panic that my back might be injured and I would not be able to ride again. That was all that really worried me. I had always dreaded anything happen-ing to my back, somehow.

The French soldiers were down from their battery in a trice, all great friends of mine to whom I had often thrown ration cigarettes.

Gaspard (that was not his name, I never knew it, but always called him that in my own mind after Raymond's hero) gave a cry and was on the ground beside me, calling me his "little cabbage," his "poor lit-tle pigeon," and presently he half lifted me in his arms and cradled me as he might a baby. I remained quite conscious the whole time. "Will I be able to ride again?" kept hammering through my brain. The pain was becoming rapidly worse and I began to wonder just where my legs were broken. As I could move neither I could not discover at all, and presently I gave a gasp as I felt something tighten and hurt terribly. It was a boot lace they were fixing to stop the haemorrhage (bootlaces are used for everything in France).

The men stood round, and I watched them furtively wiping the tears away that rolled down their furrowed cheeks. One even put his arm over his eyes as a child does. I wondered vaguely why they were crying; it never dawned on me it had anything to do with me. "Com-plètement coupée," I heard one say, and quick as a shot, I asked, "Où est-ce que c'est qu'est coupé?" and those tactful souls, just rough soldiers, replied without hesitation, "La jaquette, Mademoiselle."

"Je m'en fiche de la jaquette," I answered, completely reassured.

I wished the ambulance would come soon. "I am in a beastly mess," I thought again. "Fancy broken legs hurting like this. What must the men go through!"

It was singular I was so certain they were broken. But a month before I had received a wire from the War Office stating one of my brothers had crashed 1,000 feet and had two legs fractured, and without more ado I took it for granted I was in a similar plight. "I won't sit up and look," I decided, "or I shall think I'm worse than I am. There's sure to be some blood about," and the sun beat down fiercely, drying what there was on my face into hard cakes. My lower lip had also been cut inside somehow. One man took off his coat and held it high up to form a shade. I saw everything that happened with a terrible distinctness. They had already bound up my head, which was cut and bleeding profusely.

The pain was becoming almost intolerable and I wondered if in time I would cry, but luckily one does not cry on those occasions; it becomes an impossibility somehow. I even began to wish I could. I asked to have my legs lifted a little and the pain seemed to ease somewhat. I shall never forget those Frenchmen. They were perfect. How often I had smiled at them as I passed, and laughed to see them standing in a ring like naughty schoolboys, peeling potatoes, their sergeant walking round to see that it was done properly!

The little French doctor from the battery, who had once helped me change a tyre, came running up and I covered the scratched side of my face lest he should get too much of a shock. "*Je suis joliment dans la soupe*," I said, and saw him go as white as a sheet. "These Frenchmen are very sympathetic," I thought, for it had dawned on me what they were crying about by that time.

Just then an ambulance train came down the line and the two English doctors were fetched. A tourniquet which seemed like a knife, and hurt terribly, was applied as well as the bootlace. I was also given some morphia. "This will hurt a little," he said as he pushed in the needle, which I thought distinctly humorous. As if a prick from a hypodermic could be anything in comparison with what was going on "down there" where I hadn't courage to look! His remark had one good effect though, because I thought: "If he thinks that will hurt there can't be much to fuss over down there."

Would the ambulance never arrive? I wondered if we were always so long—which F.A.N.Y. would come? "She's cranked up by now and on the way, probably as far as the bridge," I thought. I drove all the way down in my own mind and yet she did not arrive, but they had 'phoned to the French hospital in the town and not the convoy. I did not know this till I saw the French car arrive.

It seemed an age. Gaspard never moved once from his cramped position and kept saying soothingly from time to time: "*Allons, p'tit chou, mon pauvre petit pigeon, ça viendra tout à l'heure, hé la petite.*"

At last the ambulance came. I dreaded being lifted, but those soldiers raised me so tenderly the wrench was not half as bad as I had anticipated. I had been there just over forty minutes. Then began the journey in the ambulance. The men gave me a fine salute as I was taken off and I waved goodbye. One of the sisters from the train came in the car with me and also the little French doctor whose hand I hung on to most of the way, and which incidentally must have been like pulp when we arrived.

As luck would have it the driver was a new man, and neither the doctor nor the sister knew the way, so I had to give the directions. The doctor was all for taking me to the French military hospital, but I asked to be taken to the Casino.

"So this is what the men go through every day," I thought, as we were into a hole and out again with a bump and the pain became almost too much to bear. The doctor swore at the driver, and I took another grip of his hand. "*Bien difficile de ne pas faire ça,*" I murmured, for I knew he had really manoeuvred it well. The constant give of the springs jiggling endlessly up and down, up and down, was as trying as anything. The trouble was I knew every hole in that road and soon we had to cross railway lines! The sister, who was a stranger too, began to worry how she would find her way back to the train, but I assured her once arrived at the Casino, she only had to walk up to our camp to get a F.A.N.Y. car. "I hope there won't be many people there when I'm pulled out," I thought, "I hate being stared at in such a beastly mess," above all I hated a fuss.

Now we had come to the railway lines. "What would it have been like without morphia?" I wondered. Of course the drawbridge was up and that meant at least ten minutes wait till the ships went through. My luck seemed dead out. At last I heard the familiar clang as it rattled into place, and we were over.

I dared not close my eyes, as I had a sort of feeling I'd never be able to open them again. "Only up the slope and then I'm there. If I can't keep them open till then, I'm done." The pain was getting worse again, and from what the sister said I gathered something down there had begun to haemorrhage once more. Still no thought of the truth ever dawned on me.

At last we arrived and slowly backed into place. I could not help seeing the grim humour of the situation; I had driven so many wounded men there myself. The colonel, who must have heard, for he was waiting, looked very white and worried, and Leather, one of the Duchess' drivers, started visibly as I was pulled out. I was told after that my complexion, or what could be seen of it, was ashen grey in colour and if my eyes had not been open they would have thought the worst. I was carried into the big hall and there my beloved Wuzzy found me. I heard a little whine and felt a warm tongue licking my face—luckily he had not been with me that morning.

"Take that —— dog away, someone," cried the colonel, who was peevish in the extreme.

"He's not a —— dog," I protested, and then up came a *padre* who asked gravely, "What are you, my child?"

Thinking I was now fairly unrecognisable by this time with the Frenchman's hanky round my head, etc., I replied, "A F.A.N.Y., of course!" This completely scandalized the good *padre*. When he had recovered, he said, "No, you mistake me, what religion I mean?"

"He wants to know what to bury me under," I thought, "what a thoroughly cheerful soul!"

"C. of E.," I replied as per identity disc.

He then took my home address, which seemed an unnecessary fuss, and I was left in peace. Captain C. was there as well and came over to the stretcher.

"I've broken both legs," I announced, "will I be able to ride again?"

"Of course you will," he said.

"Sure?" I asked.

"Rather," he replied, and I felt comforted.

I was then carried straight through Ward 1 into the operating theatre. The men in bed looked rather startled, and Barratt, a man I had driven and been visiting since, was near the door. What he said is hardly repeatable. When the British Tommy is much moved he usually becomes thoroughly profane! I waved to him as I disappeared through the door into the theatre.

I was speedily undressed. Dicky appeared mysteriously from somewhere and was a brick. The room seemed to be full of nurses and orderlies and then I went slipping off into oblivion as the chloroform took effect (my first dose and at that time very welcome) and at last I was in a land where pain becomes obliterated in one vast empty space.

★★★★★★

I woke that afternoon and of course wondered where I was. Everything seemed to be aching and throbbing at once. I tried to move, but I felt as if I was clamped to the bed. "This is terrible," I thought, "I must be having a nightmare." Then I saw the cradle covering my legs. "What could it be?" I wondered, and then in a flash the scenes of that morning (or was it a week ago?) came back to me. I wondered if my back was all right and felt carefully down the side. No, there was no bandage, and I sighed with relief, though it ached like fury. I could feel the top of the wooden splints on the one leg but nothing but bandages on the other.

My head had been sewn up, also my lip, and a nice tight bandage replaced the hanky.

It was thumping wildly and presently an unseen figure gave me something very cool to sip out of a feeding mug. Things straightened out a bit after that, and I saw there were quantities of flowers in the room, jugfuls in fact, which had been sent to cheer me along. Then something in my leg, the one that was hurting most, gave a fearful tug and a jump and I drew in my breath with a sobbing gasp. What could it be? It felt just as if someone had tugged it on purpose, and it took ages to settle down again. I looked mutely at my nurse for an explanation, and she put a cool hand on mine.

It was the severed nerve, and I learnt to dread those involuntary jumps that came so suddenly from nowhere and seized one like a deadly cramp.

Everything, including my back, was one vast ache punctuated by those appalling nerve jumps that set every other one in my body tingling.

How I longed to turn on my side, but that was a luxury denied me for weeks.

My friend Eva had heard the cheerful news when she returned from Boulogne, where she had been all day, and she and Lowson were allowed to come and see me for a few minutes.

"I've broken both legs," I stated. "Isn't it the limit? They don't half hurt." They nodded sympathetically, not daring to give me a hint of the real state of affairs.

"Captain C. says I'll be able to ride again though," I added, and once more they nodded.

"I told you what would happen when I lost that charm," I said to Eva.

I asked after "Little Willie," and heard his remains had been towed to camp, though being a Hun he would of course manage to escape somehow!

I had an adorable V.A.D. to look after me. The best I ever want to have. She seemed to know exactly what I wanted without being told. I felt almost too tired to speak, and in any case it's not easy with stitches in your mouth.

The *padre*, not my friend of the entrance hall I was glad to note, came to see me and I had a Communion Service all to myself, as they thought I might possibly die in the night.

I dreaded the nights as I'd dreaded nothing before in my life; with darkness everything seemed to become intensified. Whenever I did manage to snatch a few moments' sleep the dreadful demon that seemed to lurk somewhere just out of sight would pop up and jerk my leg again. I would think to myself "Now I will really catch him next time," and I would lie waiting in readiness, but just as I thought I was safe, jerk! and my leg would jump worse than ever. I clenched my fists in rage, and the V.A.D. came from behind the screen to smooth the pillows for me. I used to lie and think of all the thousands of men in hospital and perhaps even lying untended in No-man's-land going through twice as much as I, and wondered if the world would really be any the better for all this suffering or if it would be forgotten as soon as the war was over. It seemed to be rather a waste if it was to be so.

When morning came there were the dressings to be done. At 10 o'clock I used to try and imagine it was really 11, and all over, but the rattle of the trolley and terribly cheerful voice of Sister left room for no illusions on that score. My hands were useful on these occasions, and at the end of the half hour were excellent examples of the shape of my teeth! They were practically the only parts completely uninjured, and I knew that whatever happened I could still play the violin again.

I could not understand why one leg had jumping nerves and the other apparently had none and argued that the one must be half-broken to account for it. The B.E.F. specialist also paid frequent visits.

Then one evening, the third or fourth I think, Captain C. came in and sat down in the shadow, looking very grave.

I think it must have been one of the worst half-hours he ever spent. It is not a job any man would relish to tell someone who is particularly fond of life that they have lost one leg and the other has only

155

just been saved! I was speechless for some minutes; in fact I refused to believe it. It took a long time for the full horror of the situation to dawn on me. It will seem odd that I did not feel I had lost my leg, but one never has that sensation even when on crutches; the nerves are unfortunately too much alive.

Captain C. stayed a long time and the evening drew on but still he sat there and talked to me quietly in the darkness. I wondered why I couldn't cry, but somehow it seemed to have nothing to do with me at all. I was not the girl who had lost a leg. It was merely someone else I was hearing about. "Jolly bad luck on them," I thought, "rotten not to be able to run about any more."

Then my leg jumped and it began to dawn on me that I was the girl to whom those things had happened. Still, I could not cry. Useless to urge how lucky it was my knee had just been saved. What use was a knee, I thought bitterly, if I could never fly round again! When was the very soonest I could get about with one of these artificial legs, I asked, and he swore to me that if all went well, in a year's time. A year! I had fancied the autumn at latest. Little did I know it would be even longer. That night was the worst I'd had. It is a useless occupation to kick against the pricks anyway, and the hours dragged slowly on till morning came at last.

When it was light enough I looked round, as well as I could at least, lying flat on my back, for something to distract my thoughts. Seeing a *Pearson's Magazine* with George Robey on the cover, I drew it towards me and saw there was an article by him inside. Quite sure that "George" would cheer me up if anyone could I turned the pages and found it. It not only cheered me but gave me the first real ray of hope. There in print was all Captain C. had told me the night before, and somehow, to see a thing in print is doubly convincing. It was on disabled soldiers and the pluck with which they bore their misfortunes.

There was one story of two of his friends who walked into his dressing-room one day. After dancing about the place they told him they were out of the army.

"I don't see much wrong with you," said G., eyeing them up and down. They then whacked their legs soundly and never flinched once, for they each had an artificial one! I blessed George from the bottom of my heart. Someone told him this, and he promptly sat down and wrote to me, enclosing several signed postcards and a drawing of himself at the end of the letter—his own impression of what he looked like in the pre-historic scene in Zigzag—and a promise of a box for the show as soon as I got to Blighty. Some jolly good fellow!

The countless flowers I received were one of the chief joys. I simply adored lying and looking at them.

Every single person I knew seemed to have remembered me, and boxes of chocolates filled my shelf as well.

The *Parc d'Automobiles* Belges sent such a huge gerbe that two men had to carry it, and, emblazoned on a broad ribbon of the Belgian colours, spanning the whole thing, was my name and an inscription in letters of gold! Captain Saxon Davies, from the Christol in Boulogne, had fruit sent over in the boat from Covent Garden delivered at the hospital every morning by motorcycle. I felt quite overwhelmed; everyone seemed determined to spoil me.

One day the *padre* had come in to see me and was just concluding a prayer when there was a tap, and the door opened on the instant. A large bottle, the size of a magnum, was pushed in by an orderly, who, seeing the *padre*, departed in haste. (I was squinting up through my eyelashes and saw it all and just pulled myself together in time to say "Amen.")

I knew who had sent it and hastened to explain: "It's not champagne, *padre*, it's *Eau de Cologne!*"

That surprising sportsman replied: "Isn't it? Bad luck. Have you a scent spray? No? Well, I'll get you one!" (Some *padre!*)

On the Sunday one of my people came over, thanks to the cheery telegrams the War Office had been dispatching. It seemed an unnecessary fuss—the colonel, too, showed distinct signs of "needle"—but it was a dear little aunt who is never flustered by anything and who greeted me as if we had parted only yesterday. The word "leg" was not included in her dictionary at all. One is apt to be a bit touchy at first about these little things, and though I had seen the most terrible wounds in our hospital, amputations had always rattled me thoroughly.

The little aunt subsequently entertained the austere A.P.M., while her papers were being put in order, with most interesting details of my childhood and how she had brought me up from a baby! The whole interview was described to me as "utterly priceless," by the F.A.N.Y. who had taken her there.

The French battery sent daily to enquire and presently I was allowed visitors. I began to realise after a while that in losing a leg you find out exactly who your real friends are. There are those whom I shall never forget who came day after day to read or talk to me—friends who paid no attention when the leg gave one of its violent jerks, but went on talking as if nothing had happened, a fact that helped me to bear it more than all the expressed sympathy in the world. The type who says "Whatever was that? How dreadful!" fortunately never came. It was only due to those real friends that I was saved from slipping into a slough of despond from which I might never have hoped to rise. Eva gave up rides and tennis in order to come down every day, and considering the little time there was to devote to these pastimes I appreciated it all the more.

To say I was the best posted person in the place is no exaggeration. I positively heard both sides of every question (top and bottom as well sometimes) and did my best to make as little scandal as possible!

I was in a room off the "Grand Circle" of the one-time Casino, an officers' ward. One night the sister had left me for a moment and I could have sworn I saw three Germans enter. I thought they said to me that they had come to hide and if I gave them away they would hit my leg. The mere suggestion left me dumb and I distinctly seemed to see them getting under the two other empty beds in the room.

After a few minutes it dawned on me what a traitor I was, and bit by bit I eased myself up on my elbows. "I must go and tell someone these Germans are here," I thought, and turned back the clothes. After throwing the small sand bags on the floor that kept my bad leg in position, I next seized the cradle and pitched that overboard. I then carefully lifted first one leg round and then the other and sat swaying on the side of the bed. The splints naturally jutted out some distance from the end of my one leg and this struck me as being very funny. I wondered just how I could walk on them. Then I looked down at the other and the proposition seemed funnier still; though I could feel as if the leg was there, when I looked there was nothing. It was really extremely odd! I sat there for some time cogitating these matters and was just about to try how I could walk when very luckily in came an orderly.

"Germans!" I gasped, pointing to the two beds. I must have looked a little odd sitting swaying there in a very inadequate "helpless" shirt belonging to the hospital! With a muttered exclamation he rushed forward just catching me in his arms, and I was back in bed in a twinkling. The whole thing was so clear to me; even now I can fancy I really saw those Germans, and the adorable V.A.D., after searching under the beds at my request, sat with me for the rest of the night. My "good" leg was tied securely down after that episode.

I was dead and buried (by report) several times that first week in hospital and Sergeant Richardson from the Detail Issue Stores, who saw we always had the best rations, came up to see me one afternoon. He was so spick and span I hardly recognised him, and in his hand was a large basket of strawberries. The very first basket that had appeared in the fruiterers' that year. He sat down and told me how anxious "the boys" were to hear how I really was. All sorts of exaggerated rumours had been flying about.

He related how he had first heard the news on that fatal Wednesday and how "a bloke" told him I had been killed outright. "I knocked 'im down," said the sergeant with pride, "and when he comes to me the next morning to tell to me you wos still alive, why, I was so pleased I knocked 'im down again!"

Bad luck on the "bloke," what? I was convulsed, only the trouble was it hurt me even to laugh, which was trying.

He had been out in Canada before the war as a cowboy and had always promised to show me some day how to pick things off the ground when galloping, a pastime we agreed I should now have to forgo. I assured him if I couldn't do that, however, I had every intention of riding again. Had I not heard that morning of someone who even hunted! I began to appreciate the fact that I had my knee.

CHAPTER 17

Hospitals: France and England

An old Frenchman came to the hospital every day with the English papers, and looked in to leave me the *Mirror,* for which he would never accept any payment. He had very few teeth and talked in an indistinct sort of *patois* and insisted on holding long conversations in consequence! He told me he would be *enchanté* to bring me some novels *bien choisis par ma femme* (well chosen by my wife) one day, and in due course they arrived—the 1 *franc* 25 edition.

The names in most cases were enough, and the pictures in some a little more! If they were his wife's idea of suitable books for *jeunes filles* I wondered vaguely with what exactly the grown-ups diverted themselves! I had not the heart to tell him I never read them.

All the French people were extraordinarily kind and often came in to see me. They never failed to bring a present of some sort either. Mademoiselle Marguerite, the dear fat old lady who kept the flower shop in the Rue, always brought some of her flowers, and looking round would declare that I was trying to run an opposition to her! *Madame* from the *pharmacie* came with a large bottle of scent, the little dressmaker brought some lace. *Monsieur* and *Madame* from the "Omelette Shop" (a popular resort of the F.A.N.Y.s) arrived very hot and smart one Sunday afternoon. *Monsieur,* who was fat, with large rolls at the back of his neck, was rather ill at ease and a little panting from the walk upstairs.

He had the air of a man trying to appear as if he were somewhere else. He tiptoed carefully to the window and had a look at the *plage.* "The *bonhomme* wished to come and assure himself which of the *demoiselles anglaises* it was, to whom had arrived so terrible a thing," said *Madame,* "but me, I knew. Is it not so, Henri?" she cried to her husband. "I said it was this one there," and she pointed triumphantly to me. As they were going he produced a large bottle of Burgundy from a voluminous pocket in his coat tails. "*Ha! le bonhomme!*" cried the incorrigible wife, "he would first see which *demoiselle* it was before he presented the bottle!" Hubby appeared to be slightly discomfited at this and beat a hasty retreat.

And one day "Alice," whose baby I had doctored, arrived, and even she, difficult as she found it to make both ends meet, had not come without something. As she left she produced a little packet of lace wrapped in newspaper, which she deposited on my bed with tears in her eyes.

I used to lie awake at nights and wonder about those artificial legs, just what they were like, and how much one would be able to cope with them. It was a great pastime! Now that I really know what they are like it seems particularly humorous that I thought one would even sleep in them. My great idea was to have the whole thing clamped on and keep it there, and not tell anyone about it! Little did I know then what a relief it is to get them off. One can only comfort oneself on these occasions with the ancient jest that it is "the first seven years that are the worst!"

It is surprising how the illusions about artificial legs get knocked on the head one by one. I discussed it with someone at Roehampton later. I thought at least I should have jointed toes! An enterprising French firm sent me a booklet about them one day. That really did bring things home to me and I cried for the first time.

My visitors varied in the social scale from French guttersnipes (Jean-Marie, who had been wont to have my old boots, etc.), to brigadier-generals. One afternoon Corporal Coy dropped in to enquire how I was. As he remarked cheerfully, "It would have fair turned me up if you'd come round to the mortuary, miss!"

He then settled himself comfortably in the armchair and proceeded to entertain me. I only wished it didn't hurt so much to laugh. I asked him if he had any new songs, and he accordingly gave me a selection *sotto voce*. He would stop occasionally and say, "Noa, I can't sing you that verse, it's too bad, aye, but it's a pity!" and shaking his head mournfully he would proceed with the next!

He was just in the middle of another when the door opened suddenly and Sir A—— S—— (Inspector-General of Medical Services) was ushered in by the colonel. (The little corporal positively faded out of existence!) I might add he was nearly if not quite as entertaining.

"Nobby" Clark, a scion of the Labour Battalion, was another visitor who called one afternoon, and I got permission for him to come up. He was one of the local comedians and quite as good as any professional. I would have gone miles to hear him. His famous monologue with his imaginary friend "Linchpin" invariably brought the house down. He was broad Lancashire and I had had a great idea of taking him off at one of the FANTASTIK Concerts some time, but unfortunately, it was not to be. He came tiptoeing in. "I thought I might take the liberty of coming to enquire after you," he said, twisting his cap at the bottom of my bed (I had learnt by this time to keep both hands hidden from sight as a hearty shake is a jarring event). I asked him to sit down. "Bein' as you might say fellow *artistes*; 'aving appeared so often on the same platform, I had to come," he said affably! "I promised 'the boys' (old labour men of about fifty and sixty years) I'd try and get a glimpse of you," he continued, and he sat there and told me all the funny things he could think of, or rather, they merely bubbled forth naturally.

The weather—it was June then—got fearfully hot, and I found life irksome to a degree, lying flat on my back unable to move, gazing at the wonderful glass candelabra hanging from the middle of the ceiling. How I wished each little crystal could tell me a story of what had happened in this room where fortunes had been lost and won! It would have passed the time at least.

A friend had a periscope made for me, a most ingenious affair, through which I was able to see people walking on the sands, and above all horses being taken out for exercise in the mornings.

The first W.A.A.C.s came out to France about this time, and I watched them with interest through my periscope. I heard that a sandbagged dugout had also been made for us in camp, and tin hats handed out; a wise precaution in view of the bricks and shrapnel that rattled about when we went out during air raids. I never saw the dugout of course. We had a mild air-raid one night, but no damage was done.

My faithful friends kept me well posted with all the news, and I often wonder on looking back if it had not been for them how ever I could have borne life. The leg still jumped when I least expected it, and of course I was never out of actual pain for a minute.

One day, it was June then, the dressings were done at least an hour earlier than usual, and the colonel came in full of importance and ordered the other two beds to be taken out of the ward. The sister could get nothing out of him for a long time. All he would say was that the French governor-general was going to give me the freedom of the city! She knew he was only ragging and got slightly exasperated. At last, as a great secret, he whispered to me that I was going to be decorated with the French *Croix de Guerre* and silver star. I was dumbfounded for some minutes, and then concluded it was another joke and paid no more attention. But the room was being rapidly cleared and I was more and more puzzled. He arranged the vases of flowers where he thought they showed to the best advantage, and seemed altogether in extremely good form.

At last he became serious and assured us that what he had said was perfectly true. The mere thought of such an event happening made me feel quite sick and faint, it was so overwhelming.

The colonel offered to bet me a box of chocolates the general would embrace me, as is the custom in France on these occasions, and the suggestion only added to my fright!

About 11 o'clock as he had said, General Ditte, the governor of the town, was announced, and in he marched, followed by his two *aides-de-camp* in full regalia, the English Base *commandant* and staff captain, the colonel of the hospital, the Belgian general and his two *aides-de-camp*, as well as some French naval officers and *attachés*. Boss, Eva, and the sister were the only women present. The little room seemed full to overflowing, and I wondered if at the supreme moment I would faint or weep or be sick, or do something similarly foolish. The general himself was so moved, however, while he read the "citation," and so were all the rest, that that fact alone seemed to lend me courage. He turned half way through to one of the *aides-de-camp*, who fumbled about (like the best man at a wedding for the ring!) and finally, from his last pocket, produced the little green case containing the *Croix de Guerre*.

The supreme moment had arrived. The general's fingers trembled as he lifted the medal from its case and walked forward to pin it on me. Instead of wearing the usual "helpless" shirt, I had been put into some of the afore-mentioned Paris frillies for the great occasion, and suddenly I saw two long skewer-like prongs, like foreign medals always have, bearing slowly down upon me! "Heavens," I thought, "I shall be harpooned for a certainty!" Obviously the rest of the room thought so too, and they all waited expectantly. It was a tense moment—something had to be done and done quickly. An inspiration came to me. Just in the nick of time I seized an unembroidered bit firmly between the finger and thumb of both hands and held it a safe distance from me for the medal to be fixed; the situation was saved. A sigh of relief (or was it disappointment?) went up as the general returned to finish the citation, and contrary to expectation he had not kissed me! He confided to someone later I looked so white he was afraid I might faint. (It was a pity about that box of chocolates, I felt!)

Two large tears rolled down his cheeks as he finished, and then came forward to shake hands; after that they all followed suit and I held on to the bed with the other, for in the fullness of their hearts they gave a jolly good shake!

I was tremendously proud of my medal—a plain cross of bronze, with crossed swords behind, made from captured enemy guns, with the silver star glittering on the green and red ribbon above. It all seemed like a dream, I could not imagine it really belonged to me.

I was at the Casino nearly two months before I was sent to England in a hospital ship. It was a very sad day for me when I had to say goodbye to my many friends. Johnson and Marshall, the two mechanics, came up the day before to bid goodbye, the former bringing a wonderful paper knife that he had been engaged in making for weeks past. A F.A.N.Y button was at the end of the handle, and the blade and rivets were composed of English, French, and Boche shells, and last, but by no means least, he had "sweated" on a ring from one of Susan's plugs! That pleased me more than anything else could have done, and I treasure that paper knife among my choicest souvenirs. Nearly all the F.A.N.Y.s came down the night before I left, and I felt I'd have given all I possessed to stay with them, in spite of the hard work and discomfort, so aptly described in a parody of one of Rudyard Kipling's poems:

The F.A.N.Y.

I wish my mother could see me now with a grease-gun under my car,
Filling my differential, ere I start for the camp afar,
Atop of a sheet of frozen iron, in cold that'd make you cry.
"Why do we do it?" you ask. "Why? We're the F.A.N.Y."
I used to be in Society—once;
Danced, hunted, and flirted—once;
Had white hands and complexion—once:
Now I'm an F.A.N.Y.

That is what we are known as, that is what you must call,
If you want "Officers' Luggage," "Sisters," "Patients" an' all,
"Details for Burial Duty," "Hospital Stores" or "Supply,"
Ring up the ambulance convoy,

"Turn out the F.A.N.Y."They used to say we were idling—once; Joy-
riding round the battle-field—once; Wasting petrol and carbide—once:
Now we're the F.A.N.Y.

That is what we are known as; we are the children to blame,
For begging the loan of a spare wheel, and fitting a car to the same;
We don't even look at a workshop, but the Sergeant comes up with a
sigh:
"It's no use denyin' 'em nothin'!
Give it the F.A.N.Y."
We used to fancy an air raid—once;
Called it a bit of excitement—once;
Prided ourselves on our tin-hats once:
Now we're the F.A.N.Y.

That is what we are known as; we are the girls who have been
Over three years at the business; felt it, smelt it and seen.
Remarkably quick to the dugout now, when the Archies rake the sky;
Till they want to collect the wounded, then it's
"Out with the F.A.N.Y."
"Crank! crank! you Fannies;
Stand to your 'buses again;
Snatch up the stretchers and blankets,
Down to the barge through the rain."
Up go the 'planes in the dawning;
'Phone up the cars to "Stand by."
There's many a job with the wounded:
"Forward, the F.A.N.Y."

I dreaded the journey over, and, though the sea for some time past
had been as smooth as glass, quite a storm got up that evening. All the
orderlies who had waited on me came in early next morning to bid
goodbye, and Captain C. carried me out of my room and downstairs
to the hall. I insisted on wearing my F.A.N.Y. cap and tunic to look as
if nothing was the matter, and once more I was on a stretcher. A bouquet of red roses arrived from the French doctor just before I was carried out of the hall, so that I left in style! It was an early start, for I was
to be on board at 7 a.m., before the ship was loaded up from the train.
Eva drove me down in her ambulance and absolutely crawled along,
so anxious was she to avoid all bumps. One of the sisters came with
me and was to cross to Dover as well (since the Boche had not even
respected hospital ships, sisters only went over with special cases).

It struck me as odd that all the trees were out; they were only in bud when I last saw them.

Many of the French people we passed waved *adieu*, and I saw them explaining to their friends in pantomime just what had happened. On the way to the ship I lost my leg at least four times over!

The French battery had been told I was leaving, and was out in full force, and I stopped to say goodbye and thank them for all they had done and once again wave farewell—so different from the last time! They were deeply moved, and followed with the doctor to the quay where they stood in a row wiping their eyes. I almost felt as if I was at my own funeral!

The old stretcher-bearers were so anxious not to bump me that they were clumsier in their nervousness than I had ever seen them! As I was pulled out I saw that many of my friends, English, French, and Belgian, had come down to give me a send off. They stood in absolute silence, and again I felt as if I was at my own funeral. As I was borne down the gangway into the ship I could bear it no longer, and pulled off my cap and waved it in farewell. It seemed to break the spell, and they all called out "Goodbye, good luck!" as I was borne round the corner out of sight to the little cabin allotted me.

Several of them came on board after, which cheered me tremendously. I was very keen to have Eva with me as far as Dover, but, unfortunately, official permission had been refused. The captain of the ship, however, was a tremendous sportsman and said: "Of course, if my ship starts and you are carried off by mistake, Miss Money, you can't expect me to put back into port again, and I shan't have seen you," he added with a twinkle in his eye as he left us. You may be sure Eva was just too late to land! He came along when we were under way and feigned intense surprise. As a matter of fact he was tremendously bucked and said since his ship had been painted grey instead of white and he had been given a gun he was no longer a "hospital," but a "wounded transport," and therefore was within the letter of the law to take a passenger if he wanted to.

The cabin was on deck and had been decorated with flowers in every available space. The crossing, as luck would have it, was fairly rough, and one by one the vases were pitched out of their stands on to the floor. It was a tremendous comfort to me to have old Eva there. Of course it leaked out as these things will, and there was even the question of quite a serious row over it, but as the captain and everyone else responsible had "positively not seen her," there was no one to swear she had not overstayed her time and been carried off by mistake! At Dover I had to say goodbye to her, the sister, and the kindly captain, and very lonely I felt as my stretcher was placed on a trolley arrangement and I was pushed up to the platform along an asphalt gangway. The orderlies kept calling me "Sir," which was amusing. "Your kit is in the front van, sir," and catching sight of my face, "I mean—er—Miss, Gor'blimee! well, that's the limit!" and words failed them.

I was put into a ward on the train all by myself. I didn't care for that train much, it stopped and started with such jolts, otherwise it was quite comfy, and all the orderlies came in and out on fictitious errands to have a look and try and get me anything I wanted. The consequence was I had no less than three teas, two lots of strawberries, and a pile of books and periodicals I could never hope to read! I had had lunch on board when we arrived at one o'clock, before I was taken off. The reason the journey took so long was that the loading and unloading of stretchers from ship to train is a lengthy job and cannot be hustled. We got to London about five.

The E.M.O. was a cheery soul and came and shook hands with me, and then, joy of joys, got four stretcher-bearers to take me to an ambulance. With four to carry you there is not the slightest movement, but with two there is the inevitable up and down jog; only those who have been through it will know what I mean. I had got Eva to wire to some friends, also to Thompson, the section leader who was on leave, and by dint of Sherlock Holmes stunts they had discovered at what station I was arriving. It was cheering to see some familiar faces, but the ambulance only stopped for a moment, and there was no time to say anything.

As I was driven out of the station—it was Charing Cross—the old flower women were loud in their exclamations. "Why, it's a dear little girl!" cried one, and she bombarded Thompson with questions. (I felt the complete fool!) "Bin drivin' the boys, 'as she? Bless 'er," and they ran after the car, throwing in whole bunches of roses galore! I could have hugged them for it, dear fat old things! They did their bit as much as any of them, and never failed to throw their choicest roses to "the boys" in the ambulances as they were driven slowly past.

My troubles, I am sorry to say, began from then onwards. England seemed quite unprepared for anything so unorthodox, and the general impression borne in on me was that I was a complete nuisance. There was no recognized hospital for "the likes of us" to go to, and I was taken to a civilian one where war-work seemed entirely at a discount. I was carried to a lift and jerked up to the top floor by a housemaid, when I was put on a trolley and taken into a ward full of people. A sister came forward, but there was no smile on her face and not one word of welcome, and I began to feel rather chilled. "Put the case there," she said, indicating an empty bed, and the "case," feeling utterly miserable and dejected, was deposited! The rattle and noise of that ward was such a contrast to my quiet little room in France (rather humorous this) that I woke with a jump whenever I closed my eyes.

Presently the matron made her rounds, and very luckily found there was a vacant room, and I was taken into it forthwith. There was a notice painted on the wall opposite to the effect that the bed was "given in remembrance" of the late so-and-so of so-and-so—with date and year of death, etc. I can see it now. If only it had been on the door outside for the benefit of the visitors! It had the result of driving "the case" almost to the verge of insanity. I could say the whole thing backwards when I'd been in the room half an hour, not to mention the number of letters and the different words one could make out of it! There was no other picture in the room, as the walls were of some concrete stuff, so, try as one would, it was impossible not to look at it. "Did he die in this bed?" I asked interestedly of the sister, nodding in the direction of the "In Memoriam."

"I'm sure I don't know," said she, eyeing me suspiciously. "We have enough to do without bothering about things like that," and she left the room. I began to feel terribly lonely; how I missed all my friends and the cheerful, jolly orderlies in France! The frowsy housemaid who brought up my meals was anything but inspiring. My dear little "helpless" shirt was taken away and when I was given a good stuff nightdress in its place, I felt my last link with France had gone!

The weather—it was July then—got terribly hot, and I lay and sweltered. It was some relief to have all bandages removed from my right leg.

There were mews somewhere in the vicinity, and I could smell the horses and even hear them champing in their stalls! I loved that, and would lie with my eyes shut, drinking it in, imagining I was back in the stables in far away Cumberland, sitting on the old corn bin listening to Jimmy Jardine's wonderful tales of how the horses "came back" to him in the long ago days of his youth. When they cleaned out the stables I had my window pulled right up! "Fair sick it makes me," called my neighbour from the next room, but I was quite happy. Obviously everyone can't be satisfied in this world!

The doctor was of the "bluff and hearty" species and, on entering the first morning, had exclaimed, in a hail-fellow-well-met tone, "So you're the young lady who's had her leg chopped off, are you? ha, ha!" Hardly what one might call tactful, what? I withdrew my hand and put it behind my back. In time though we became fairly good friends, but how I longed to be back in France again!

Being a civilian hospital they were short-staffed. "Everyone seems mad on war work," said one sister to me peevishly, "they seem to forget there are civilians to nurse," and she flounced out of the room.

A splendid diversion was caused one day when the Huns came over in full force (thirty to forty Gothas) in a daylight raid. I was delighted! This was something I really did understand. It was topping to hear the guns blazing away once more. Everyone in the place seemed to be ringing their electric bells, and, afraid I might miss something, I put my finger on mine and held it there. Presently the matron appeared: "You can't be taken to the cellar," she said, "it's no good being nervous, you're as safe here as anywhere!"

"It wasn't that," I said, "I wondered if I might have a wheelchair and go along the corridor to see them."

"Rubbish," said she, "I never heard of such a thing," and she hurried on to quiet the patient in the next room. But by dint of screwing myself half on to a chair near the window I did just get a glimpse of the sky and saw about five of the Huns manoeuvring. Good business!

One of the things I suffered from most, was visitors whom I had never seen in my life before. There would be a tap at the door; enter lady, beautifully dressed and a large smile. The opening sentence was invariably the same. "You won't know who I am, but I'm Lady L——, Miss so-and-so's third cousin. She told me all about you, and I thought I really must come and have a peep." Enters and subsides into chair near bed smiling sweetly, and in nine cases out of ten jiggles toes against it, which jars one excessively. "You must have suffered terribly! I hear your leg was absolutely crushed! And now tell me all about it! Makes you rather sick to talk of it? Fancy that! Conscious all the time, dear me! What you must have gone through! (Leg gives one of its jumps.) Whatever was that? Only keeping your knee from getting stiff, how funny! Lovely having the *Croix de Guerre*. Quite makes up for it. What? Rather have your leg. Dear me, how odd! Wonderful what they do with those artificial limbs nowadays. Know a man and really you can't tell which is which. (Naturally not, any fool could make a leg the shape of the other!) Well, I really must be going. I shall be able to tell all my friends I've seen you now and been able to cheer you up a little. Poor girl! So unfortunate! Terribly cheerful, aren't you? Don't seem to mind a bit. Would you kindly ring for the lift? I find these stairs so trying. I've enjoyed myself so much. Goodbye." Exit (goodby-ee).

In its way it was amusing at first, but one day I sent for the small porter, Tommy, aged twelve (I had begun to sympathise with the animals in the Zoo). "Tommy," I said, "if you dare to let anyone come up and see me unless they're personal friends, you won't get that shell head I promised you. Don't be put off, make them describe me. You'll be sorry if you don't."

Tremendous excitement one day when I went out for my first drive in a car sent from the Transport Department of the Red Cross. Two of the nurses came with me, and I was lifted in by the stalwart driver. "A quiet drive round the park, I suppose, Miss?" he asked.

"No," I said firmly, "down Bond Street and then round and round Piccadilly Circus first, and then the Row to watch the people riding" (an extremely entertaining pastime). He had been in the Argentine and "knew a horse if he saw one," and no mistake.

The next day a huge gilded basket of blue hydrangeas arrived from the "bird" flower shop in Bond Street, standing at least three feet high, the sole inscription on the card being, "From the Red Cross driver." It was lovely and I was extremely touched; my room for the time being was transformed.

I was promised a drive once a week, but they were unfortunately suspended as I had an operation on July 31st for the jumping sciatic nerve and once more was reduced to lying flat on my back. There was a man over the mews who beat his wife regularly twice per week, or else she beat him. I could never discover which, and used to lie staring into the darkness listening to the "sounds of revelry by night," not to mention the choicest flow of language floating up into the air. I was measured for a pair of crutches some time later by a lugubrious individual in a long black frock coat looking like an undertaker. I objected to the way he treated me, as if I were already a "stiff," ignoring me completely, saying to the nurse: "Kindly put the case absolutely flat and full length," whereupon he solemnly produced a tape measure!

I was moved to a nursing home for the month of August, as the hospital closed for cleaning, and there, quite forgetting to instruct the people about strangers, I was beset by another one afternoon. A cousin who has been gassed and shell-shocked had come in to read to me. There was a tap on the door. "Mrs. Fierce," announced the porter, and in sailed a lady whom I had never seen in my life before. (I want the readers of these "glimpses" to know that the following conversation is absolutely as it took place and has not been exaggerated or added to in the very least.)

She began with the old formula. "You won't know me, etc., but I'm so-and-so." She did not pause for breath, but went straight ahead. "It's the second time I've been to call on you," she said, in an aggrieved voice. "I came three weeks ago when you were at —— Hospital. You had just had an operation and were coming round, and would you believe it, though I had come all the way from West Kensington, they wouldn't let me come up and see you—positively rude the boy was at the door." (I uttered a wordless prayer for Tommy!)

"It was very kind of you," I murmured, "but I hardly think you would have liked to see me just then; I wasn't looking my best. Chloroform has become one of my *bêtes noires.*"

"Oh, I shouldn't have minded," said the lady; "I thought it was so inconsiderate of them not to let me up. So sad for you, you lost your foot," she chattered on, eyeing the cradle with interest. I winked at my cousin, a low habit but excusable on occasions. We did not enlighten her it was more than the foot. Then I was put through the usual inquisition, except that it was if possible a little more realistic than usual. "Did it bleed?" she asked with gusto. I began to enjoy myself (one gets hardened in time).

"Fountains," I replied, "the ground is still discoloured, and though they have dug it over several times it's no good—it's like Rizzio's blood at Holyrood, the stain simply won't go away!" My cousin hastily sneezed.

"How very curious," said the lady, "so interesting to hear all these details first hand! Young man," and she fixed Eric with her lorgnettes, "have you been wounded—I see no stripe on your arm?" and she eyed him severely.

Now E. has always had a bit of a stammer, but at times it becomes markedly worse. We were both enjoying ourselves tremendously: "N-n-n-no," he replied, "s-s-s-shell s-s-s-shock!"

"Dear me, however did that happen?" she asked.

"I w-w-was b-b-b-blown i-i-i-into t-t-t-the air," he replied, smiling sweetly.

"How high?" asked the lady, determined to get to the bottom of it, and not at all sure in her own mind he wasn't a conscientious objector masquerading in uniform.

"As all t-t-the other m-m-men were k-k-killed b-b-b-by t-t-t-the same s-s-shell, t-t-there was n-n-no one t-t-there t-t-t-to c-c-c-count," he replied modestly. (I knew the whole story of how he had been left for two whole days in No-man's-land, with Boche shells dropping round the place where he was lying, and could have killed her cheerfully if the whole thing had not been so funny.)

Having gleaned more lurid details with which we all too willingly supplied her, she finally departed.

"Fierce by name and fierce by nature," I said, as the door closed. "I wonder sometimes if those women spend all their time rushing from bed to bed asking the men to describe all they've been through—I feel like writing to John Bull about it," I added, "but I don't believe the average person would believe it. Tact seems to be a word unknown in some vocabularies." The cream of the whole thing was that, not content with the information she had gleaned, when she got downstairs, she asked to see my nurse. The poor thing was having tea at the time, but went running down in case it was something important.

"Will you tell me," said Mrs. F. confidentially, "if that young man is engaged to Miss B.?" (The "young man," I might add, has a very charming *fiancée* of his own), and how we all laughed when she came up with the news!

The faithful "Wuzzy" had been confided to the care of a friend at the Remount Camp, and I was delighted to get some snaps of him taken by a Frenchman at Neuve-Chapelle—I felt my "idiot son" was certainly seeing life! "In reply to your question" (said my friend in a letter), "as to whether I have discovered Wuzzy's particular 'trait' yet, the answer as far as I can make out appears to be 'chickens'!"

In time I began to get about on crutches, and the question next arose where I was to go and convalesce, and the then strange, but now all too familiar phrase was first heard. "If you were only a man, of course it would be so easy." As if it was my fault I wasn't? It was no good protesting I had always wished I had been one; it did not help matters at all.

I came to the conclusion there were too many women in England. If I had only been a Boche girl now I might at least have had several Donnington Halls put at my disposal! I was finally sent to Brighton, and thanks to Lady Dudley's kindness, became an out-patient of one of her officers' hospitals, but even then it was a nuisance being a girl.

Another disadvantage was that all the people treated me as if I was a strange animal from the Zoo; men on crutches had become unfortunately a too familiar sight, but a F.A.N.Y. was something quite new, and therefore an object to be stared at. Some days I felt quite brazen, but others I went out for about five minutes and returned, refusing to move for the rest of the day. It would have been quite different if several F.A.N.Y.s had been in a similar plight, but alone, one gets tired of being gaped at as a *rara avis*.

The race meetings were welcome events and great sport, to which we all went with gusto. I fell down one day on the Parade, getting into my bath chair. It gave me quite a jar, but it must be got over some time as a lesson, for of course I put out the leg that wasn't there and went smack on the asphalt! One learns in time to remember these details.

It was ripping to see friends from France who ran down for the day, and when the F.A.N.Y.s came over, how eagerly I listened to all the news! The lines from one of our songs often rang through my brain:

On the Sandy Shores of France
Looking Blighty-wards to sea,
There's a little camp a-sitting
And it's all the world to me—
For the cars are gently humming,
And the 'phone bell's ringing yet,
Come up, you British Convoy,
Come ye up to Fontinettes—
On the road to Fontinettes
Where the trains have to be met;
Can't you hear the cars a-chunking
Through the Rue to Fontinettes?

On the road to Fontinettes
Where the stretcher-bearers sweat,
And the cars come up in convoy,
From the camp to Fontinettes.

For 'er uniform is khaki,
And 'er little car is green,
And 'er name is only FANNY
(And she's not exactly clean!)
And I see'd 'er first a'smoking
Of a ration cigarette.

173

And a'wasting army petrol
Cleaning clothes, 'cos she's in debt.
On the road to Fontinettes, etc.

I longed to be back so much sometimes that it amounted almost to an ache! This, and the fact of being the only one, I feel sure partly accounted for it that I became ill. According to the doctor I ought to have been in a proper hospital, and then once again the difficulty arose of finding one to go to. Boards and committees sat on me figuratively and almost literally, too, but could come to no conclusion. Though I could be in a military hospital in France it was somehow not to be thought of in England. Finally I heard a W.A.A.C.'s ward had been opened in London at a military hospital run by women doctors for Tommies, and I promptly sat down and applied for admittance. Yes, I could go there, and so at the end of November, I found myself once more back in London. I was in a little room—a W.A.A.C. officers' ward, on the same floor as the medical ward for W.A.A.C. privates. I met them at the concerts that were often given in the recreation room, and they were extremely kind to me. I was amused to hear them discussing their length of active service. One who could boast of six months was decidedly the nut of the party! We had a great many air raids, and were made to go down to the ground floor, which annoyed me intensely. I hated turning out, apart from the cold; it seemed to be giving in to the Boche to a certain extent.

I loved my charlady. She was the nearest approach to the cheery orderlies of those far away days in France, I had struck since I came over. Her smiling face, as she appeared at the door every morning with broom and coalscuttle, was a tonic in itself. I used to keep her talking just as long as I could—she was so exceedingly alive.

"Do I mind the air rides, Miss? Lor' bless you no—nothin' I like better than to 'ear the guns bangin' awy. If it wasn't for the childer I'd fair enjoy it—we lives up 'hIslington way, and the first sounds of firing I wrap them up, and we all goes to the church cryp and sings 'ims with the parson's wife a'plying. Grand it is, almost as good as a revival meeting!"

(One in the eye for Fritz what?)

I asked her, as it was getting near Christmas, if she would let me take her two little girls (eight and twelve respectively) to see a children's fairy play. She was delighted. They had never been to a theatre at all, and were waiting for me one afternoon outside the hospital gates, very clean and smiling, and absolutely dancing with excitement. I was of course on crutches, and as it was a greasy, slippery day, looked about for a taxi. It was hopeless, and without a word the elder child ran off to get one. The way she nipped in and out of the traffic was positively terrifying, but she returned triumphant in the short space of five minutes, and we were soon at the door of the theatre.

I had to explain that the wicked fairies leaping so realistically from Pandora's box weren't real at all, but I'm sure I did not convince the smaller one, who was far too shy and excited to utter a word beyond a startled whisper: "Yes, Miss," or "No, Miss." There were wails in the audience when the witch appeared, and several small boys near us doubled under their seats in terror, like little rabbits going to earth, refusing to come out again, poor little pets!

In the interval the two children watched the orchestra with wide-eyed interest. "I guess that guy wot's wyving 'is arms abaht like that (indicating the conductor) must be getting pretty tired," said the elder to me. I felt he would have been gratified to know there was someone who sympathised!

Altogether it was a most entertaining afternoon, and when we came out in the dark and rain the eldest again slipped off to get a taxi, dodging cabs and horses with the dexterity of an acrobat.

Christmas came round, and there was tremendous competition between the different wards, which vied with each other over the most original decorations.

At midday I was asked into the W.A.A.C.'s ward, where we had roast beef and plum pudding. The two women doctors who ran the hospital visited every ward and drank a toast after lunch. I don't know what they toasted in the men's wards, but in the W.A.A.C.'s it was roughly, "To the women of England, and the W.A.A.C.s who would win the war, etc." It seemed too bad to leave out the men who were in the trenches, so I drank one privately to them on my own.

As I sat in my little ward that night I thought of the happy times we had had last Christmas in the convoy, only a short year before.

CHAPTER 18

Roehampton: "Bob" the Grey, and the Armistice

After Christmas it was thought I was well enough to be fitted with an artificial limb, and in due course I applied to the limbless hospital at Roehampton. The reply came back in a few days.

Dear Sir, (I groaned),
You must apply to so-and-so and we will then be able to give you a bed in a fortnight's time, etc.
             Signed: Sister D.

My heart sank. I was up against the old question again, and in desperation I wrote back:

Dear Madam,
My trouble is that I am a girl, etc.

. . . .and poured forth all my woes on the subject. Sister D., who proved to be an absolute topper, was considerably amused and wrote back most sympathetically. She promised to do all she could for me and told the surgeon the whole story, and it was arranged for him to see me and advise what type of leg I had better wear and then decide where I was to be put up later. He was most kind, but I returned from the interview considerably depressed for, before I could wear an artificial leg, another operation had to be performed. It took place at the military hospital in January and I felt I should have to hurry in order to be "doing everything as usual" by the time the year was up, as Captain C. had promised.

For some reason, when I came round I found myself in the big W.A.A.C.s' ward, and never returned to my little room again. I did not mind the change so much except for the noise and the way the whole room vibrated whenever anyone walked or ran past my bed. They nearly always did the latter, for they were none of them very ill. The building was an old workhouse which had been condemned just before the war, and the floor bent and shook at the least step. I found this particularly trying as the incision a good six inches long had been made just behind my knee, and naturally, as it rested on a pillow, I felt each vibration.

The sheets were hard to the touch and grey in colour even when clean, and the rows of scarlet blankets were peculiarly blinding. I realised the meaning of the saying: "A red rag to a bull," and had every sympathy with the animal! (It was so humorous to look at things from a patient's point of view.) It had always been our ambition at Lamarck to have red top blankets on every bed in our wards. "They make the place look so bright and cheerful!" I daresay these details would have passed unnoticed in the ordinary way, but I had already had eight months of hospitals, during which time I had hardly ever been out of pain, and all I craved was quiet and rest. Some of the women doctors were terribly sarcastic.

We were awakened at 5 a.m. as per hospital routine (how often I had been loath to waken the patients at Lamarck), and most of the W.A.A.C.s got up and dressed, the ones who were not well enough remaining in bed. At six o'clock we had breakfast, and one of them pushed a trolley containing slices of bread and mugs of tea from bed to bed. It rattled like a pantechnicon and shook the whole place, and I hated it out of all proportion. The ward was swept as soon as breakfast was over. How I dreaded that performance! I lay clenching the sides of the bed in expectation; for as surely as fate the sweeping W.A.A.C. caught her brush firmly in one of the legs. "Sorry, miss, did it ketch you?" she would exclaim, "there, I done it agin; drat this broom!"

There were two other patients in the room who relished the quiet in the afternoons when most of the W.A.A.C.s went out on pass. One of them was a sister from the hospital, and the other a girl suffering from cancer, both curtained off in distant corners. "Now for a sleep, sister," I would call, as the last one departed, but as often as not just as we were dropping off a voice would rouse us, saying: "Good afternoon, I've just come in to play the piano to you for a little," and without waiting for a reply a cheerful lady would sit down forthwith and bang away virtuously for an hour!

We had had a good many air raids before Christmas and I hoped

Fritz would reserve his efforts in that direction till I could go about on crutches again. No such luck, however, for at 10 o'clock one night the warnings rang out. I trusted, as I had had my operations so recently, I should be allowed to remain; but some shrapnel had pierced the roof of the ward in a former raid and everyone had to be taken down willy-nilly. I hid under the sheets, making myself as flat as possible in the hopes of escaping. I was discovered of course and lifted into a wheel chair and taken down in the lift to the *padre's* room, where all the W.A.A.C.s were already assembled. Our guns were blazing away quite heartily, the "London front" having recently been strengthened. Just as I got down, the back wheel of my chair collapsed, which was cheering!

We sat there for some time listening to the din. Everyone was feeling distinctly peevish, and not a few slightly "breezy," as it was quite a bad raid. I wondered what could be done to liven up the proceedings, and presently espied a pile of hymn-books which I solemnly handed out, choosing "Onward Christian Soldiers" as the liveliest selection! I could not help wondering what the distant F.A.N.Y.s would have thought of the effort. In the middle of "Greenland's spicy mountains," one W.A.A.C. varied the proceedings by throwing a fit, and later on another fainted; beyond that nothing of any moment happened till the firing, punctuated by the dropping bombs, became so loud that every other sound was drowned.

Some of the W.A.A.C.s were convinced we were all "for it" and would be burnt to death, but I assured them as my chair had broken, and I had no crutches even if I could use them, I should be burnt to a cinder long before any of them! This seemed to comfort them to a certain extent. I could tell by the sound of the bombs as they exploded that the Gothas could not be far away; and then, suddenly, we heard the engines quite plainly, and there was a terrific rushing sound I knew only too well. The crash came, but, though the walls rocked and the windows rattled in their sockets, they did not fall.

Above the din we heard a woman's piercing scream, "Oh God, I'm burning!" as she ran down the street. Simultaneously the reflection of a red glare played on the walls opposite. All was confusion outside, and the sound of rushing feet pierced by screams from injured women and children filled the air. It was terrible to sit there powerless, unable to do anything to help. The hospital had just been missed by a miracle, but some printing offices next door were in flames, and underneath was a large concrete dug-out holding roughly 150 people. What the total casualties were I never heard. Luckily a ward had just been evacuated that evening and the wounded and dying were brought in immediately. It was horrible to see little children, torn and maimed, being carried past our door into the ward. The hum of the Gotha's engines could still be heard quite distinctly.

Sparks flew past the windows, but thanks to the firemen who were on the spot almost immediately, the fire was got under and did not spread to the hospital.

It was a terrible night! How I longed to be able to give the Huns a taste of their own medicine!

The "All clear" was not sounded till 3 a.m. Many of the injured died before morning, after all that was humanly possible had been done for them. I heard some days later that a discharged soldier, who had been in the dugout when the bomb fell, was nearly drowned by the floods of water from the hoses, and was subsequently brought round by artificial respiration. He was heard to exclaim: "Humph, first they wounds me aht in France, then they tries to drown me in a bloomin' air raid!"

There was one W.A.A.C.—Smith we will call her—who could easily have made her fortune on the stage, she was so clever at imitations. She would "take you off" to your face and make you laugh in spite of yourself. She was an East-ender and witty in the extreme, warm of heart but exceedingly quick-tempered. I liked her tremendously, she was so utterly alive and genuine.

One night I was awakened from a doze by a tremendous hubbub going on in the ward. Raising myself on an elbow I saw Smith shaking one of the W.A.A.C.s, who was hanging on to a bed for support, as a terrier might a rat.

"You would, would you?" I heard her exclaim. "Sy it againe, yer white-ficed son of a gun yer!" and she shook her till her teeth chattered. I never found out what the "white-ficed" one had said, but she showed no signs of repeating the offence. I felt as if I was in the gallery at Drury Lane and wanted to shout, "Go on, 'it 'er," but just restrained myself in time!

A girl orderly was despatched in haste for one of the head doctors, and I awaited her arrival with interest, wondering just how she would deal with the situation.

However, the "Colonel" apparently thought discretion the better part of valour, and sent the sergeant-major—the only man on the staff—to cope with the delinquent. I was fearfully disappointed. Smith checkmated him splendidly by retiring into the bath where she sat soaking for two hours. What was the poor man to do? It was getting late, and for all he knew she might elect to stay there all night. He knew of no precedent and ran in and out of the ward, flapping his arms in a helpless manner. I felt Smith had decidedly won the day. Imagine an ordinary private behaving thus!

There were sudden periodical evacuations of the ward, and one day I was told my bed would be required for a more urgent case—a large convoy was expected from France and so many beds had to be vacated. Three weeks after my operation I left the hospital and arranged to stay with friends in the country. As it was a long railway journey and I was hardly accustomed to crutches again, I wanted to stay the night in town. However, one comes up against some extraordinary types of people. For example, the hotel where my aunt was staying refused to take me in, even for one night, on the score that "they didn't want any invalids!" I could not help wondering a little bitterly where these same people would have been but for the many who were now permanent invalids and for those others, as Kipling reminds us, "*whose death has set us free.*" I could not help noticing that at home one either came up against extreme sympathy and kindness or else utter callousness—there seemed to be no half-measures.

In March I again hoped to go to Roehampton, but my luck was dead out. I could still bear no pressure on the wretched nerve, and another operation was performed almost immediately.

The W.A.A.C.s' ward was all very well as an experience, but the noise and shaking, not to mention the thought of the broom catching my bed regularly every morning, was too much to face again. The surgeon who was operating tried to get me into his hospital for officers where there were several single rooms vacant at the time.

Vain hope. Again the familiar phrase rang out, and once more I apologised for being a female, and was obliged to make arrangements to return to the private nursing home where I had been in August. The year was up, and here I was still having operations. I was disgusted in the extreme.

When I was at last fit to go to Roehampton the question of accommodation again arose. I never felt so sick in all my life I wasn't a man—committees and matrons sat and pondered the question. Obviously I was a terrible nuisance and no one wanted to take any responsibility. The mother superior of the Sacred Heart Convent at Roehampton heard of it and asked me to stay there. Though I was not of their faith they welcomed me as no one else had done since my return, and I was exceedingly happy with them. It was a change to be really wanted somewhere.

In time I got fairly hardened to the stares from passers-by, and it was no uncommon thing for an absolute stranger to come up and ask, "Have you lost your leg?" The fact seemed fairly obvious, but still some people like verbal confirmation of everything. One day in Harrod's, just after the 1918 push, one florid but obviously sympathetic lady exclaimed, "Dear me, poor girl, did you lose your leg in the recent push?" It was then the month of June (some good going to be up on crutches in that time!) Several staff officers were buying things at the same counter and turned at her question to hear my reply. "No, not in this last push," I said, "but the one just before," and moved on. They appeared to be considerably amused.

How I loathed crutches! One nightmare in which I often indulged was that I found, in spite of having lost my leg, I could really walk in some mysterious way quite well without them. I would set off joyfully, and then to my horror suddenly discover my plight and fall smack. I woke to find the nerve had been at its old trick again. Sometimes I was seized with a panic that when I did get my leg I should not be able to use it, and worse still, never ride again. That did not bear thinking of.

I went to the hospital every day for fittings and at last the day arrived when I walked along holding on to handrails on each side and watching my "style" in a glass at the end of the room for the purpose. My excitement knew no bounds! It was a tedious business at first getting it to fit absolutely without paining and took some time. I could hear the men practising walking in the adjoining room to the refrain of the "*Broken Doll*," the words being:

> *I only lost my leg a year ago.*
> *I've got a 'Rowley,' now, I'd have you know.*
> *I soon learnt what pain was, I thought I knew,*
> *But now my poor old leg is black, and red, white and blue!*
> *The fitter said, 'You're walking very well,'*
> *I told him he could take his leg to —— ,*
> *But they tell me that some day I'll walk right away,*
> *By George! and with my Rowley too!*

It was at least comforting to know that in time one would!

Half an hour's fitting was enough to make the leg too tender for anything more that day, and I discovered to my joy that I was quite well able to drive a small car with one foot. I was lent a sporting Morgan tri-car which did more to keep up my spirits than anything else. The side brake was broken and somehow never got repaired, so the one foot had quite an exciting time. It was anything but safe, but it did not matter. One day, driving down the Portsmouth Road with a fellow-sufferer, a policeman waved his arms frantically in front of us. "What's happened," I asked my friend, "are we supposed to stop?" "I'm afraid so," he replied, "I should think we've been caught in a trap." (One gets into bad habits in France!)

As we drew up and the policeman saw the crutches, he said: "I'm sorry, sir, I didn't see your crutches, or I wouldn't have pulled you up." The friend, who happened to be wearing his leg, said, "Oh, they aren't mine, they belong to this lady." The good policeman was temporarily speechless. When at last he got his wind he was full of concern. "You don't say, sir? Well, I never did. Don't you take on, we won't run you in, Miss," he added consolingly, turning to me. "I'll fix the stop-watch man." I was beginning to enjoy myself immensely. He regarded us for some minutes and made a round of the car. "Well," he said at last, "I call you a couple o' sports!" We were convulsed!

At that moment the stop-watch man hurried up, looking very serious, and I watched the expression on his face change to one of concern as the policeman told him the tale.

"We won't run you in, not us," he declared stoutly, in concert with the policeman.

"What were we doing?" I asked, as he looked at his stop-watch.

"Thirty and a fraction over," he replied. "Only thirty!" I exclaimed, in a disappointed voice, "I thought we were doing at least forty!"

"First time anyone's ever said that to me, Miss," he said; "it's usual for them to swear it wasn't a mile above twenty!"

"A couple o' sports," the policeman murmured again.

"I think you're the couple of sports," I said laughing.

"Well," said the stop-watch man, lifting his cap, "we won't keep you any longer, Miss, a pleasant afternoon to you, and (with a knowing look) there's nothing on the road from here to Cobham!"

Of course the Morgan broke all records after that!

Unfortunately, in July, I was obliged to undergo an operation on my right foot, where it had been injured. By great good luck it was arranged to be done in the sister's sick ward at the hospital. It was not successful though, and at the end of August a second was performed, bringing the total up to six, by which time I loathed chloroform more than anything else on earth.

Before I returned to the convent again, the king and queen with Princess Mary came down to inspect the hospital.

It was an imposing picture. The sisters and nurses in their white caps and aprons lined the steps of the old red-brick, Georgian House, while on the lawn six to seven hundred limbless Tommies were grouped, forming a wonderful picture in their hospital blue against the green.

I was placed with the officers under the beautiful cedar trees and had a splendid view, while on the left the different limb makers had models of their legs and arms. The king and queen were immensely interested and watched several demonstrations, after which they came and shook each one of us by hand, speaking a few words. I was immensely struck by the king's voice and its deep resonant qualities. It is wonderful, in view of the many thousands he interviews, that to each individual he gives the impression of a real personal interest.

I soon returned to the convent, and there in the beautiful gardens diligently practised walking with the help of two sticks. The joy of being able to get about again was such that I could have wept. The Tommies at the hospital took a tremendous interest in my progress. "Which one is it?" they would call as I went there each morning. "Pick it up, Miss, pick it up!" (one trails it at first). The fitter was a man of most wonderful patience and absolutely untiring in his efforts to do any little thing to ease the fitting. I often wonder he did not brain his more fussy patients with their wooden legs and have done with it!

"Got your knee, Miss?" the men would call sometimes. "You're lucky." When I saw men who had lost an arm and sometimes both legs, from above the knee too, I realised just how lucky I was. They were all so splendidly cheerful. I knew too well from my own experience what they must have gone through; and again I could only pray that something good would come out of all this untold suffering, and that these men would not be forgotten by a grateful country when peace reigned once more.

I often watched them playing bowls on the lawn with a marvellous dexterity—a one-armed man holding the chair steady for a double amputation while the latter took his aim.

I remember seeing a man struggling painfully along with an above-the-knee leg, obviously his first day out. A group of men watched his efforts. "Pick it up, Charlie!" they called, "we'll race you to the cedars!" but Charlie only smiled, not a bit offended, and patiently continued

183

along the terrace.

At last I was officially "passed out" by the surgeon, and after eighteen months was free from hospitals. What a relief! No longer anyone to reproach me because I wasn't a man! It was my great wish to go out to the F.A.N.Y.s again when I had got thoroughly accustomed to my leg. I tried riding a bicycle, and after falling off once or twice "coped" quite well, but it was not till November that I had the chance to try a horse. I was down at Broadstairs and soon discovered a job-master and arranged to go out the next day. I hardly slept at all that night I was so excited at the prospect. The horse I had was a grey, rather a coincidence, and not at all unlike my beloved grey in France. Oh the joy of being in a saddle again! A lugubrious individual with a bottle nose (whom I promptly christened "Dundreary" because of his long whiskers) came out with me. He was by way of being a riding master, but for all the attention he paid I might have been alone.

I suggested finding a place for a canter after we had trotted some distance and things felt all right. I was so excited to find I could ride again with comparatively little inconvenience I could hardly restrain myself from whooping aloud. I presently infected "Dundreary," who, in his melancholy way, became quite jovial. I rode "Bob" every day after that and felt that after all life was worth living again.

On November 11th came the news of the armistice. The flags and rejoicings in the town seemed to jar somehow. I was glad to be out of London. A drizzle set in about noon and the waves beat against the cliffs in a steady boom not unlike the guns now silent across the water. Through the mist I seemed to see the ghosts of all I knew who had been sacrificed in the prime of their youth to the god of war. I saw the faces of the men in the typhoid wards and heard again the groans as the wounded and dying were lifted from the ambulance trains on to the stretchers. It did not seem a time for loud rejoicings, but rather a quiet thankfulness that we had ended on the right side and their lives had not been lost in vain.

The words of Robert Nichols' *Fulfilment*, from *Ardours and Endurances* (Chatto & Windus), rang through my brain. He has kindly given me permission to reproduce them:

Was there love once? I have forgotten her.
Was there grief once? Grief yet is mine.
Other loves I have, men rough, but men who stir
More grief, more joy, than love of thee and mine.

184

Faces cheerful, full of whimsical mirth,
Lined by the wind, burned by the sun;
Bodies enraptured by the abounding earth,
As whose children we are brethren: one.

And any moment may descend hot death
To shatter limbs! pulp, tear, blast
Beloved soldiers, who love rough life and breath
Not less for dying faithful to the last.

O the fading eyes, the grimed face turned bony,
Open mouth gushing, fallen head,
Lessening pressure of a hand shrunk, clammed, and stony
O sudden spasm, release of the dead!

Was there love once? I have forgotten her.
Was there grief once? Grief yet is mine.
O loved, living, dying, heroic soldier
All, all, my joy, my grief, my love are thine!

CHAPTER 19

After Two Years

My dream of going out to work again with the F.A.N.Y.s was never realised. Something always seemed to be going wrong with the leg; but I was determined to try and pay them a visit before they were demobilised. On these occasions the word "impossible" must be cut out of one's vocabulary (vide Napoleon), and off I set one fine morning. Everything seemed strangely unaltered, the same old train down to Folkestone, the same porters there, the same old ship and lifebelts; and when I got to Boulogne nearly all the same old faces on the quay to meet the boat! I rubbed my eyes. Had I really been away two years or was it only a sort of lengthy nightmare? I walked down the gangway and there was the same old rogue of a porter in his blue smocking. Yet the town seemed strangely quiet without the incessant marching of feet as the troops came and went. "We never thought to see you out here again, Miss," said the same man in the transport department at the Hotel Christol!

I went straight up to the convoy at St. Omer, and had tea in the camp from which they had been shelled only a year before. This convoy of F.A.N.Y.s, to which many of my old friends had been transferred, was attached to the 2nd army, and had as its divisional sign a red herring. The explanation being that one day a certain general visited the camp, and on leaving said: "Oh, by the way, are you people 'army'?"

"No," replied the F.A.N.Y., "not exactly."

"Red Cross then?"

"Well, not exactly. It's like this," she explained: "We work for the Red Cross and the cars are theirs, but we are attached to the second army; we draw our rations from the army and we're called F.A.N.Y.S."

186

"'Pon my soul," he cried, "you're neither fish, flesh, nor fowl, but you're thundering good red herrings!'"

It was a foregone conclusion that a red herring should become their sign after that!

The next day I was taken over the battlefields through Arcques, where the famous "Belle" still manipulates the bridge, and along by the Nieppe Forest. We could still see the trenches and dug-outs used in the fierce fighting there last year. A cemetery in a little clearing by the side of the road, the graves surmounted by plain wooden crosses, was the first of many we were to pass. Vieux Berquin, a once pretty little village, was reduced to ruins and the road we followed was pitted with shell holes.

It was pathetic to see an old man and his wife, bent almost double with age and rheumatism, poking about among the ruins of their one-time home, in the hope of finding something undestroyed. They were living temporarily in a miserable little shanty roofed in by pieces of corrugated iron, the remains of former Nissen huts and dugouts.

In Neuf Berquin several families were living in new wooden huts the size of Armstrongs with cheerful red-tiled roofs, that seemed if possible to intensify the utter desolation of the surroundings.

Lusty youths, still in the *bleu* horizon of the French Army, were busy tilling the ground, which they had cleared of bricks and mortar, to make vegetable gardens.

My chief impression was that France, now that the war was over, had made up her mind to set to and get going again just as fast as she possibly could. There was not an idle person to be seen, even the children were collecting bricks and slates.

I wondered how these families got supplies and, as if in answer to my unspoken question, a baker's cart full of fresh brown loaves came bumping and jolting down the uneven village street.

Silhouetted against the sky behind him was the gaunt wall of the one-time church tower, its windows looking like the empty sockets of a skull.

Estaires was in no better condition, but here the inhabitants had come back in numbers and were busy at the work of reconstruction. We passed "Grime Farm" and "Taffy Farm" on the way to Armentières, then through a little place called Croix du Bac with notices printed on the walls of the village in German. It had once been their second line.

In the distance Armentières gave me the impression of being almost untouched, but on closer inspection the terrible part was that only the mere shells of the houses were left standing. Bailleul was like a city of the dead. I saw no returned inhabitants along its desolate streets. The Mont des Cats was on our left with the famous monastery at its summit where Prince Rupprecht of Bavaria had been tended by the monks when lying wounded. In return for their kindness he gave orders that the monastery was to be spared, and so it was for some time. But whether he repented of his generosity or not I can't say. It must certainly have been badly shelled since, as its walls now testify. On our right was Kemmel with its pill-boxes making irregular bumps against the sky-line. One place was pointed out to me as being the site of a once famous tea-garden where a telescope had been installed, for visitors to view the surrounding country.

We passed through St. Jans Capelle, Berthen, Boschepe, and so to the frontier into Belgium. The first sight that greeted our eyes was Remy siding, a huge cemetery, one of the largest existing, where rows upon rows of wooden crosses stretched as far as the eye could see.

We drove to Ypres via Poperinghe and Vlamertinge and saw the famous "Goldfish" Château on our left, which escaped being shelled, and was then gutted by an accidental fire!

I was surprised to see anything at all of the once beautiful Cloth Hall. We took some snaps of the remains. A lot of discoloured bones were lying about among the *débris* disinterred from the cemetery by the bombardments.

Heaps of powdered bricks were all that remained of many of the houses. The town gasometer had evidently been blown completely into the air, what was left of it was perched on its head in a drunken fashion.

Beyond the gate of the town on the Menin Road stood a large unpainted wooden shanty. I wondered what it could be and thought it was possibly a Y.M.C.A. hut. Imagine my surprise on closer inspection to see painted over the door in large black letters "Ypriana Hotel"! It had been put up by an enterprising Belge. Somehow it seemed a desecration to see this cheap little building on that sacred spot.

The Ypres-Menin Road stretched in front of us as far as the eye could see, disappearing into the horizon. On either hand was No-man's-land. I had seen wrecked villages on the Belgian front in 1915 and was more or less accustomed to the sight, but this was different. It was more terrible than any ruins I had ever seen. For utter desolation I never want to behold anything worse.

The ground was pock-marked with shell-holes and craters. Old tanks lay embedded in the mud, their sides pierced by shot and shell, and worst of all by far were the trees. Mere skeletons of trees standing gaunt and jagged, stripped naked of their bark; mute testimony of the horrors they had witnessed. Surely of all the lonely places of the earth this was by far the worst? The ground looked lighter in some places than in others, where the powdered bricks alone showed where a village had once stood. There were those whose work it was to search for the scattered graves and bring them in to one large cemetery. Just beyond "Hell-fire Corner" a *padre* was conducting a burial service over some such of these where a cemetery had been formed. We next passed Birr Cross Roads with "Sanctuary Wood" on our left. Except that the lifeless trees seemed to be more numerous, nothing was left to indicate a wood had ever been there.

The more I saw the more I marvelled to think how the men could exist in such a place and not go mad, yet we were seeing it under the most ideal conditions with the fresh green grass shooting up to cover the ugly rents and scars.

Many of the craters half-filled with water already had duckweed growing. Words are inadequate to express the horror and loneliness of that place which seemed peopled only by the ghosts of those "Beloved soldiers, who love rough life and breath, not less for dying faithful to the last."

We drove on to Hooge and turned near Geluvelt, making our way back silently along that historic road which had been kept in repair by gangs of workmen whose job it was to fill in the shell holes as fast as they were made.

As we wound our way up the steep hill to Cassel with its narrow streets and high, Spanish-looking houses, the sun was setting and the country lay below us in a wonderful panorama. The cherry-trees bordering the steep hill down the other side stood out like miniature snowstorms against the blue haze of the evening. We got back to find the Saturday evening hop in progress (life still seemed to be formed of paradoxes). It was held in the mess hut, where the bumpy line down the middle of the floor was appropriately called "Vimy Ridge," and the place where the shell hole had been further up "Kennedy Crater." The floor was exceedingly springy just there, but it takes a good deal to "cramp the style" of a F.A.N.Y., and details of this sort only add to the general enjoyment.

The next day I went down to the old convoy and saw my beloved "Susan" again, apparently not one whit the worse for the valiant war work she had done. Everything looked exactly the same, and to complete the picture, as I arrived, I saw two F.A.N.Y.s quietly snaffling some horses for a ride round the camp while their owners remained blissfully unconscious in the mess. I felt things were indeed unchanged!

That evening I hunted out all my French friends. The old flower lady in the Rue uttered a shriek, dropped her flowers, and embraced me again and again. Then there was the *pharmacie* to visit, the paper man, the pretty flapper, *Monsieur* and *Madame* from the "Omelette" Shop, and a host of others. I also saw the French general. For a moment he was puzzled—obviously he "knew the face but couldn't put a name to it," then his eye fell on the ribbon. "*Mon enfant*," was all he said, and without any warning he opened his arms and I received a smacking kiss on both cheeks! *Quel émotion!* Everyone was so delighted, I felt the burden of the last two years slipping off my shoulders.

Quite by chance I was put in my old original "*cue*." I counted the doors up the passage. Yes, it must be the one, there could be no doubt about it, and on looking up at the walls I could just discern the shadowy outlines of the panthers through a new coating of colour-wash.

The hospital where I had been was shut up and empty, and was shortly going to become a Casino again. How good it was to be back with the F.A.N.Y.s! I had just caught them in time, for they were to be demobilised on the following Sunday and I began to realise, now that I was with them again, just how terribly I had missed their gay companionship.

It was a singular and happy coincidence that on the second anniversary of the day I lost my leg, I should be cantering over the same fields at Peuplinghe where "Flanders" had so gallantly pursued "puss" that day so long ago, or was it really only yesterday?

France,
May 9th, 1919.

A Nurse at the War

EARLY DAYS WHEN WOMEN COULD GET TO THE FRONT

Contents

CHAPTER 1

The Road to Lierre

The F.A.N.Y. Corps is not well known, because since the 14th September, 1914, they have been too busy over in Flanders and France to talk of their work. But the F.A.N.Y. Corps that started on active service in the person of one woman is increasing steadily, and at present over 50 members are working in the zone of the armies, and a few more are busy in the centre of France in a big convalescent camp. Their work is varied: motor ambulance work in the actual firing line has now given way to motor ambulance work at the base; the first-aid work behind the trenches has changed to first a clearing hospital and now a base hospital, and the excursions to the front with what were then much-needed comforts have given place to running a big canteen for 700 convalescents. Now the F.A.N.Y.'s have fought their way to recognition, a few of the experiences one of them underwent may be of interest.

Those were strange days when I was alone in little Belgium. Antwerp was fiercely fought for, and for weeks we worked from morning till night caring for the men who were brought in, broken and torn and shattered. Ah! it made my heart ache and my eyes wet, but I did my best. They were heroes, these men: they did not cry nor grumble nor complain; they smiled, they called me "*Petite soeur,*" and nothing I did failed to please them—though in much I was clumsy and unskil-ful. There were so many of them—in all the hospital about 200; but on the floor I worked on 64, and some would die and be carried out on a stretcher with a sheet over them, and some would rise and dress and walk out; but what hurt one most were the evacuations.

An evacuation means to empty the hospital, and it was done when news came that the Germans were coming very near. Then men's faces would turn white with horror and with fear, women would tremble and turn faint; and we, who had to work, would spend every ounce of our strength in dressing those poor fellows—pulling shirts over their shattered bodies, wrapping dressing gowns or coats or what we could round them in their weakness and suffering. We carried them down long stairs on stretchers, even on camp beds if there were not enough stretchers; we ran down stairs with mattresses and lifted them off the stretchers on to the mattress, for we had to take the stretchers to bring down others; and to some of these men each movement meant agony. This used to happen once a week at least! And then very often, after having been taken to the station on a tramcar, the men would all be brought back and have to be carried upstairs again and put back to bed.

Then one afternoon I went out with a motor ambulance to just behind where fighting was. We met a cyclist who said he wanted help at a lonely trench to take men away and so we went. There was a little brick hut or stables, and there the car stopped, and before I got out from inside, the chauffeur and the cyclist and the owner, who was with us, were running hard along the road. It was flat country, and the road was alongside a deep ditch; and a few little thin trees were along the roadside. Far away I could see cottages here and there, and there was a lot of noise all round. I was running after the men, when suddenly something made my heart stop and then thump hard. I slowed down and looked all round, and the sun glittered on a silver medal on my breast and held my eye. I put the medal into my pocket, and a feeling of awful loneliness came over me. I was alone, quite alone—there was nobody English near me.

At that moment I longed for an Englishman. Then I looked behind—the ambulance looked safe and stolid, somehow; then I looked ahead. The men who had come with me were jumping down into a trench. I had never seen a trench, but I felt it was one, and into my heart and brain came something I had never felt before, I looked up at the little clouds of smoke breaking in the sky; I looked ahead and saw great clouds of smoke bursting from the ground; and I suddenly felt a great exultation, and I ran—ran my hardest—and stood on the edge of the trench and looked in. There were three or four figures there, very still, in big blue coats, but I hardly noticed them. Two men were lifting a man out and putting him across a third man's back, and a man wearing a heavy uniform coat, with a ragged, untidy moustache, and a white face was trying to climb out of the trench. One of his legs was

196

all torn,—clothing and blood and bandage, and I leapt down beside him.

Then, with his hand in mine and his arm drawn round my neck, I pulled and pushed and struggled, and we got out and slowly reached the road. In front of me two men were struggling along, each with an unconscious man hanging over his shoulders, and a group of soldiers who looked tired and were limping. Then suddenly came a terrific noise, so loud it dazed me, and all my sense of thought seemed gone. I stood quite still, and on my left a cloud of dark smoke rose, and a horrid smell. I looked all round—I was alone. My poor man with the shattered leg!—where was he? I wheeled slowly round, blinking my eyes, and there in the ditch was my sufferer, and all the other men. Then, in a flash, I knew! It was a shell that had burst close beside us. I dashed to the ditch and sat down. The men were looking at me with stolid unconcern, they were rising—going on. I went too.

Along that bare road we ran at a sort of loping trot. Then through the cloud of deafness that still held me I seemed to hear a wailing scream, and the three soldiers nearest stopped and held on to a little thin tree. I stopped too, facing them, looking in their faces to question them. To me it was all new. I did not understand; *I* had had none of the horrors they had passed through. All *I* saw was three white scared faces, with fixed eyes,—in them a sort of dumb appeal. They were gasping, their lips were black, their clothes dirty and stained. A demon of mischief woke in me. I thought of a cinematograph, of what we must look like—four hefty people hanging on in fear to a little thin tree! I laughed; and their white faces and troubled eyes glared at me, but they ran on. I followed at their heels, and so we reached the ambulance and found the chauffeur already there.

Two men lay on the ground—one very white and still unconscious, the other, with wide eyes, moaning. I had some brandy with me and gave him some. We lifted him up, put him on the car—it was a beautifully-fitted car; the side came down and outwards, and the first stretcher was fitted in its place: then we turned a handle, and the stretcher was raised without any jolting and the other stretcher placed on the board on rails that slid inwards, and so, with no jolting, each sufferer was safely fixed. Inside were two or three folding chairs, and on these we put all the men with wounds that permitted them to sit down. There were three or four, and then there were places for two outside, and still there was one man left.

The owner of the ambulance looked at me, but I shook my head and looked at the man who remained; then the owner leapt aside, told the chauffeur to go on, and waited with me. There were lots of men here, ragged and unwashed heroes, but all cheery and brave and smiling. To them I was a strange being; to me they were a new revelation. They took me inside and showed me the holes in the roof—in the walls, in the floors; the bar, where broken glass and china lay scattered still; the yard behind, where a dead pig raised a stench of protest to the sky. One lad went to where the shell had burst and brought me a piece of it, a long, thin, jagged bit of iron with cruel edges. He gave it me with a smile, and his fellows watched me and wondered.

"You are not afraid?" one man asked, and seemed to wonder when I laughed.

"You are brave," said another; but I laughed and shook my head vigorously.

"But you were really not frightened?" a sergeant had to ask, and when I looked up at him and said, "Yes, I was really frightened, terribly frightened, for a little time," he shook his head and shrugged his shoulders.

Then the car came back, and we got the *blessé* inside; I sat outside with the driver, and the owner sat beside us. We left the wounded in a hospital in Antwerp. After this we drove to the English headquarters, and there we found cars and cars, dozens of them, and soldiers and a few sailors. A staff officer looked surprised to meet me, but we got the directions we wanted and went on.

This time it was another lonely *poste*, empty houses by the roadside, and crowds of soldiers; plenty of wounded, too, but most of them already bandaged. We filled the car and sent them in, and I waited for its return. This time the owner could not wait; he had to go, and so I was left alone. The men were curious, but very courteous; they all wanted to talk—to know if I was an officer, to ask if I had helped many wounded, to know why I left England and my home to come and help the Belgians.

One man picked me a bunch of flowers; another took me to see the inside of a little cottage: the room was empty, tables and chairs thrown on the floor, a few little china ornaments, cheap and tawdry, still stood in a cupboard in a corner of the room, and there was a hole in the wall high up—a great gaping hole ....

Outside on the road men galloped past, or motor cars whizzed by, and heavy wagons trundled along. Artillery rolled past, the men all turning to salute the Englishwoman in khaki in their midst. The sun was setting, and far away the loud roar of guns cut the evening stillness. This was war! Up the road slowly came two men on horseback—they stopped to ask the way; they had a message for the British lines: behind them where a hedge jutted on to the road came a man in khaki afoot. My eyes brightened—one of our own men. I felt suddenly proud. The men round me pointed him out. I nodded; they said to the two men on horseback, "Why not ask *him?*" The two men replied in Flemish and rode off. He came slowly, very slowly. My pride at seeing him began to wane. He started every few steps, and looked fearfully behind him—he dragged along. I went to meet him; my heart was burning. The men round me were watching him, and something within me resented it. He wore khaki—he was a British soldier.

I stopped and waited; he had seen me. Every Belgian soldier saluted and smiled every time I met them. This man—in khaki like myself—did not salute; he shambled up to me—hardly even stopped.

"Are you hurt?" I asked.

"No."

"Where are you going?"

"To ——" naming the nearest English trenches three kilometres away).

"Are you tired; wouldn't you rather ride or go in a car? I'll ask a lift for you if you like!"

"No; I'm safer walking. I've been in with a message, and I'm going back."

"Do you know the way?"

"Oh, I'll find it!"

He refused a ride in a car. Two or three of the men I had been talking to spoke to him, but he just stared at them and did not answer.

He was in no hurry to go on. He told me suddenly that he never wanted to ride in a car again. He had seen a Belgian officer driving a car, with a priest beside him, just a short time before; then a shell burst, and the officer's head went into the road, and the car and the priest went on a few yards before the car swerved and came to a violent halt. He looked for sympathy. I returned his look coldly, for I was too new at the game to realise what nerve-strain those gallant fellows had to undergo. Many a time since have I regretted my hardness, my stupid lack of understanding, for the poor lad had been through hell!

"It was an awful sight," he muttered, still staring over his shoulder.

"It was; I saw it," I said quietly.

He went on down the road, walking beside a Belgian on horseback—a good-natured fellow, who promised me he would show him the way. I wished the car would come; I felt suddenly depressed. The cheery crowd of Belgian soldiers were too cheery. I resented it. I knew what they had gone through—weeks of weary warfare in the trenches, their country in danger, their homes ruined, their women and children murdered and tortured. And they smiled and talked and spoke with wonder of the courage, of the devotion, of the English! And I saw that shambling figure in khaki, starting at every shadow, looking fearfully over its shoulder.

CHAPTER 2

Malines, Bucherout, and Vieux Dieu

One day I was out as usual. The car came for me at 9.30, and we went out to the collecting stations, loaded up, sent the men in, and I waited, doing dressings, for the car to return. One day we went to an old church in the centre of Malines; the beautiful cathedral was desolate and shattered, the windows knocked out, parts of the wall fallen in. All round were houses and cottages battered and rent, empty rooms and broken furniture; it was a sad sight. And out there in the convent church were sadder sights! The sacristy was filled with packets of cottonwool and bandages, bottles of iodine, and a precious—very precious—bottle of chloroform. In here I went to find two men who had just been carried in: one we took off the stretcher and laid face downwards on a table; he was shot through the buttocks, and lay without murmuring.

The other—poor fellow!—was a big, strong man about five and thirty; he was tenderly laid on a table, his feet and legs propped up with chairs, his shirt cut off as gently as possible. One arm hung by a thread of flesh from the shoulder, and bled—always bled—though the tourniquet was as tight as possible; the dark blood oozed through steadily and fell with a constant drip, drip. He was shot through the diaphragm, too, and, although I was not well acquainted with death then, even *I* could tell his days were numbered. His face, livid and twisted with pain, looked towards us; he cried in a strange voice and a strange tongue, for in those days I knew no Flemish.

A surgeon was there, a tall, clever Englishman, and he injected saline. His quick, deft movements fascinated me—I longed to help. Once he looked me full in the eyes, and it seemed to me he wondered what I felt, and I think the pity in my eyes must have answered him. A nurse was there, an English nurse. She was crying as she held the man down, for he was struggling—and to me that, too, was strange; and suddenly she ran away sobbing, so I slipped up and took her place. The surgeon glanced at me keenly and was apparently satisfied, and so, as the poor fellow struggled and twisted, we held him. I had one arm and side; a priest held the other, and two Belgian women, in while overalls and caps with big red crosses on them, stroked his face and bent over him, speaking to him soothingly in his mother tongue. He shouted and writhed, and at last his head fell back: then, with a mighty effort, he raised himself and opened his mouth to speak; but only a stream of blood rushed forth, and a brave soul had gone to its God!

The chapel was empty as I knelt to whisper a prayer for the dead, and passed on into the outer chapel, where, to my horror, I saw three English women in weird and wonderful costumes having tea, laughing and talking; it was like a tourist party attending a funeral. Something of what I felt was, perhaps, shared by an English doctor. He looked at the women inside; he took a long breath of fresh air and gasped out:

"My God, there's too much joy-riding about this to please me!"

At that moment a stray shell landed in the courtyard, far away from us, but very near a sturdy little English chauffeur who had just entered! However, it did no harm beyond churning a hole in the yard.

From there I went to a little barricade at a small village, Hofstade; and here were Belgians who had that very morning at 3 a.m. driven the Germans out of the ruins they now held. (That night the Germans took it again—to hold it for good.) From a steep embankment one could see the woods where the Germans were in hiding, and see the country burning all round, for both Belgians and Germans were trying to burn all woods and any sort of "cover." It was a desolate scene. Here was a fine young priest with a brassard on his arm, and a haversack with "First Aid Dressings" on his shoulders; he had been busy all that night and all that early morning succouring his brothers-in-arms spiritually and physically. He was a powerfully-built man, and I said to him, did he find it a very hard life?

"Not hard enough," he replied, "if only I could kill too!"

He spoke with simple regret; for he, too, had looked upon war and its horrors. He was the minister of the Lord Christ, and he burned to revenge the devilish deeds that had been perpetrated.

I wandered behind one cottage, and saw a strange heap; the chauffeur looked at me and held his nose.

"It is not healthy to be here," he said; but I did not answer, and he came to see why I looked with an awful horror in my face. The smell

MASS IN THE TRENCHES

DURING THE FIRST WINTER, 1914

was enough to knock one down in ordinary times, but in those days, mentally and physically, I could endure tremendous strain. . . .

A *gendarme* followed and joined us, and we all stood with our eyes fixed on the charred and blackened body that lay there. I had never known a human skeleton would look so small when the flesh was gone round it. Then involuntarily we looked at the tiny cottage, of which the walls still stood; and little tawdry gilt figures were on the shelves inside; even a child's cradle lay there—broken, it is true.

The chauffeur showed me brass candlesticks he had looted. I looked at him in wonder; I could not think of such things then, with this little village of ruined cottages under my eyes. With him I made a tour of the other houses: everywhere hurried preparation for flight—beds with the blankets still thrown down; china and glass scattered everywhere. One little cheap figure of a child I slipped into my pocket, wondering sadly if it had been some child's treasure. Then in one house the chauffeur hesitated—said I had better not come in; his face was white and his lips shook. I looked past him; and the colour left my cheeks too, and tears came to my eyes.

A baby lay there.—a tiny waxen form with a cruel bayonet-thrust through its tender flesh. I looked all round. There was only a rough blanket, so I laid that over the little martyr, and into my heart swept a fury of black passion. I thought of the Germans I had known who had children, huge families of children, and had professed to love children; and on that day I cursed Germany and all its people, and I cried to Heaven to avenge the blood of the innocent and defenceless. Cruel it had been to stand by whilst a strong man went out in agony, but crueller was it to think of this tender babe foully murdered, to picture the mother perhaps; but no . . . . I rushed out in a panic; I must have air—must get away from this accursed spot.

Round Antwerp were miles of barbed wire cunningly twisted into an impassable barrier; moats filled with deep water; earthworks, barricades; it was a wonderful sight; and little did we dream then how futile all these would prove.

One day, after forty-eight hours I rain, we dashed past a stretch of country close to the waterworks: the stench was terrible, thick and heavy, and too horrible for words; the soft earth was wet and heavy, and disturbed. Others said they saw human limbs sticking upwards, protruding from the earth as if in appeal to Heaven. I did not look closely—I could not. I knew only that 300 corpses had been hastily covered with earth after a fight a week or two before.

One day we were at a line of trenches in an entirely opposite direction—towards Lierre; there had been many wounded, and the little car had made many journeys. Loaded up inside and with one man between me and the chauffeur, we started homewards as the sun was setting. I was tired; as usual, I had given my sandwiches to the men who needed them more than I, and suddenly I felt very hungry and feeble inside. Then to my amazement I saw sailors—English sailors— drawn up in a big group, and an English doctor in naval uniform barred our way. He was about as surprised as I was! He held my hand and asked if we could load up one more Belgian who was complaining of bad pain in the side, and his hand lay on mine as he spoke. His face was tired, and his eyes had dark shadows under them; and he was so pleased to see an English girl! We made the Belgian sit where I had been, and I stood on the footboard, holding on with one hand to the roof of the car. On we sped, and the sky was flaming red, and suddenly our road lay clear and straight through long lines of English bluejackets and marines—miles of them—all marching forth with steady tramp and resolute, kindly faces. How my heart went out to them; and how their ringing friendly cheers brought the blood to my face and a great joy to my heart! No more hunger—only pride—as these lines of men—my men—went out gaily to fight for *me* and all the women of the Empire.

In the town that night I had to go to six hospitals before getting my load out of the car. That made me think as I went to sleep that night.

Next morning we started off again. This time we got to Bucherout, a small village; and here were English naval doctors working against time, and an Irishwoman and her little four-seater just arrived to interpret for them. Orders for retreat were out, and all the wounded were being packed off as quickly as cars or carts passed within hail. I had only jumped out, when I had to dress a man with a bullet in his arm—I could feel the bullet. The wounded were lying everywhere— on the pavement, propped against the walls. My little car was quickly loaded and sent off: then came a naval ambulance from the front with a man shot to pieces on one stretcher; a shattered thigh on the stretcher underneath; a broken arm and a shrapnel in the head opposite.

The doctor, the same whom I had met the night before, looked very weary; he could only give morphia to the top man, and from there we went to an A.S.C. cart just arrived with six more. We had to unload them, as the cart had to go on for ammunition and go back.

One man was very bad; a dear old Scotchman carried another on his back to the doorway and set him down. I was raiding the empty houses for blankets, pillows, mattresses. Then the Irishwoman went off full speed with her car and chauffeur to get St. John's men and a motor 'bus. She shoved some sandwiches into my hand.

"Make the doctors eat something," she said, and I cornered one—asked him if he could spare two minutes inside the doorway. He looked at me with tired surprise—imagining, probably I was feeling faint!—and acceded. He followed me inside and I slipped round and barred the doorway by standing against it.

"Eat that," I said firmly—"quick!"—and, laughing, he did so when I assured him there were more for the other doctors. He had been working all night, and he couldn't remember having had anything to eat; he *thought* he'd had a cup of coffee "somewhere about 6 o'clock"!!

The motor 'bus arrived at length with twenty St. John's men—fine workers and skilful. We helped all those who could go upstairs, and many who were not fit to go on top; one, a St. John's man and I carried up between us—no easy job on a 'bus stairs! There was one very badly wounded man on the pavement. I begged the doctor to let him be, but he shook his head. "He *may* live some time," he said, "and we must get him out of the way." Shells were not far off and shrapnel everywhere near, so I suppose he was right, and I helped to arrange the poor fellow on the floor of the 'bus. I had a presentiment he was going, and I knelt by him till the 'bus was ready to start. He was struggling. A nice St. John's man who had been helping me was to accompany that load.

"I think he is beginning to die," I said; "couldn't we put him out and let him go in peace?"

The man bent over him.

"It looks like it," said he, "but we'd better take him."

Later on that same bearer came to me to tell me the man had died ten minutes after the 'bus started. It seems a dreadful nightmare, the memory of these men tortured and suffering, British and Belgian; but all that day there was so much to do I could not grasp the horror of it. One load came in with a Belgian boy, quite young, with a broken leg; he was shrieking with pain. The doctor put it in splints; he wanted to give him morphia. I begged the boy to have morphia, but he refused violently, and so with piercing screams and racking sobs of agony we had to load him on to a motor 'bus and let him go; his terror of morphia was greater than the agony he endured.

A gallant English marine was brought in with his jaw shot away and one arm pierced; he was quite conscious and must have suffered horribly, but he lay quiet, with never a murmur. They were all heroes; they would find time in the midst of their pain to say "Thank you, Sister," when I gave them something to drink or slipped cushions under them. Many a journey my little car made that day—filled each time. A big bread wagon came along and I commandeered it; the sergeant at first demurred, but he quickly entered into the spirit of it. We spread a big blanket in a gateway and turned out all the bread. I climbed into the cart and passed the huge loaves out! Then I dragged the sergeant to an empty house, and we got mattresses and blankets and cushions, and made the bottom of that cart comfortable.

The doctor came along and was delighted. "That's splendid," he said; and soon we loaded in wounded and the cart went off.

All this time we were watching the signal to emit. If the artillery went down a certain road, we had to go, Troops were passing in all directions. Winston Churchill—then First Lord of the Admiralty—rushed past in a car many times with Colonel Seely, going backwards and forwards from Vieux Dieu to the trenches. For an hour and a half there came a lull, and lots of St. John's men and a few soldiers in khaki joined us. Suddenly a call came for a car to go to an outpost to bring in three wounded, it was a matter of four kilometres, and the road was being shelled all the way. Luckily my little ambulance was waiting, and off we went. There were one or two other cars on the road, and we passed an open car with a stretcher slung across the back seats.

We got to the outpost, a lonely building, and there was an Englishman with a little Belgian cap on his head! He was attached to the Belgian service: a brave man he was; I met him again and again, and always where there was danger, but he had no fear. We ran the car alongside, and then we all bolted for our lives round the corner of the house, and with an ear-splitting skirl a shell came on the roadway and ploughed a huge hole and brought a tree down. It stopped short of the car by less than a dozen yards. We waited quite a long time before the priest and the soldier who had gone to carry back the wounded appeared, and the Englishman showed me an enormous shrapnel case he was going to take away as a trophy.

When we drove back to the dressing station at Bucherout the St. John's men cheered, and one came up to me and gave me a pear. I wanted him to keep it, but he looked so hurt I took it and thanked him; then another man gave me an apple, which I put in my pocket. A soldier in khaki came up to me shyly with a little bunch of mignonette; it almost brought tears to my eyes, for it suddenly made me think of a quiet garden with one corner overrun with mignonette, and my mother in a shady garden hat leaning on her stick, for it was her favourite plant.

In the evening our work grew lighter, and at last I myself stood on the footboard to accompany the last load in. The Belgian Military Pharmacy had arrived before I left—a big caravan drawn by two horses, and stocked with every possible medicament, also bandages and thousands of first field dressings. I had been busy interpreting too, for none of the doctors spoke French. Before I left I was commissioned by the senior medical officer to get a complete list of all the British wounded in Antwerp, for no records had been kept; they were put in all and any passing vehicles, and by them dropped at any hospitals in the town. It is true cars were given the names of the hospitals to go to, but these were often full, and the cars had to go on to others turn by turn till they could leave the men. My Belgian friend, the owner of the ambulance, undertook to get the returns for me; and sure enough next morning he had it all ready for me, and sorry I am I did not keep it!

We ran out early towards Bucherout, but what was my amazement to find Vieux Dieu deserted, the English headquarters empty, and shells bursting in the streets!

A big car with British staff officers came towards us and stopped, and I ran round and asked them whether Bucherout was still the collecting station, and where the wounded were. The man I spoke to first was very worried. He said he did not know where the wounded were; he added: "Go back at once; this is no place for an ambulance. The firing line is 200 yards from here."

The man opposite him, a clean-shaven, strong-faced officer, did not seem so agitated, so I appealed to him, but he knew nothing either. So we drove on to some Belgian soldiers we saw in the distance, and they said there must be wounded, but they didn't know where; anyway, the road wasn't too dangerous if *mademoiselle* stayed behind!

Mademoiselle laughed and went on; and there was Bucherout, so busy yesterday, deserted!—not a sign of life, nothing but two black dogs who came to me for sympathy. There, too, we met a little group of marines wheeling a wounded Belgian in a barrow; they had stopped to replace the bandage on his leg, which had got swamped with blood.

I jumped out, and one sailor said to the man who was bandaging, "Let Sister do it."

They were a very forlorn little band—had no idea where they were going nor where Antwerp lay, and knew no French. They had saved six stretchers, which I slung upon the roof of the car. I told them the way (straight forwards) and one boy—he was perhaps seventeen—said to me, with a quiver in his voice, "We couldn't help it, Sister; we had to go. We were shot down and couldn't help ourselves; we had no guns."

It was the first time I heard that pathetic cry—"We had no guns." The next day and the next, and for many a week afterwards, I was to hear it—the unspoken lament, the mute reproach; and many a time when wounded men have turned to me for strength, and dying men have held my hand in an anguished farewell to life, and women have clung to me sobbing, and I myself have felt courage and hope and faith break within me over the cold faces of the best-beloved and the nearest of kin, these words have leapt to life again and struck me across the eyes—"We had no guns."

What happened to the Belgian in the barrow? He was helped inside the ambulance, and we ran further on to look for wounded. We met a few Belgian soldiers—fourteen, I think—and they were all excited, and some had held to their rifles and some had thrown them away, and one, a non-commissioned officer, told us a long tale. He spoke of the English who had come to save Antwerp; he spoke of these men in their trenches and the great German guns that swept them like a scourge. He spoke of the Marine Light Infantry, and the handful of them that started to charge the German guns across three miles of country, and he even muttered something of the harvest these guns reaped—because the English had no guns.

Then he ended up with the tale of the English throwing down their cartridges and rifles. . . . Retreat is an ugly tale to hear—an uglier thing to come to grips with. My chauffeur tried to check the narrator, and tried to show his sympathy with me. He had seen me come tearless and dry-eyed from many a pitiful sight—he had been with me when death seemed certain—so now he turned away from the suffering in my eyes and the mist that would blot everything else out.

Then came the wounded—four of them—and a man who spoke of Englishmen in a trench with no one to help them, and he wanted to go to English headquarters to tell them where to send help; so back we sped, and stopped to take up one marine to look after their stretchers.

Later on we ran out another road to the Château de Troyenhem, and near here we found an English doctor with everything ready. He was calm and confident, and quite amazed to think outside help was offered him! His preparations were complete—his "dugout" shelters shell-proof; he was very confident. Yet next day he was gone, and only his shellproof shelters remained for the Germans! So back we went to Vieux Dieu, and there found English soldiers and sailors making trenches and building a big barricade across the road to Bucherout. The chauffeur looked ahead and asked if *mademoiselle* were afraid to go. *Mademoiselle* said there was no question of fear, but of wounded; if there were wounded the car must go. And so it went, and inside I cast a frantic look back at the khaki and bluejackets—there I felt lay safety.

Then overhead the singing filled the air—*Whizz-zz-zz*.....*boom*. ...*Whizz-zz*....*boom* ...*ei-ei-ei-ei-yah*; and I felt so lonely. I crouched down in a corner, and then I wrote a note on a slip of paper with my mother's address on it and slipped it into my tunic pocket; and then I knelt down and prayed, and with the prayer my imagination lost its force, and I could look calmly out on the bare road, and not feel desolate, because there was no other living thing there. The dead horses were sad, and at Bucherout the houses battered and fallen, were sad; and I called and whistled and searched for the two black dogs, but got no reply.

We drew up for a few minutes. The intense stillness was rather terrifying, and I think our nerves were strung up, for a whiz of shrapnel that came very close made us jump violently, and my companions bolted like rabbits and crawled under the back of the car! I followed them blindly, but there was no room for me; I could only crouch down, wondering what was going to happen. Then the crash of falling masonry at very close quarters relieved the tension, and up we got, and I think the chauffeur broke all speed records on that return trip! It was a wonderful thing to get back inside that barrier, to run in with only a quarter-inch to spare between sandbags piled high, and the moment we were through to see that gap filled up. I reported to the medical officer there, and he took me to his "hospital" in the fort—great stone cellars they looked like, all these rooms so carefully guarded with the earth all round them.

The doctor had no dressings (someone had forgotten to supply them!),and so I sent my car in to Antwerp with a chit to get more

RUINS OF A CHURCH

WHERE A BOMB FELL

dressings from the Belgian Red Cross. Also I gave the chauffeur all the money I had with me, and told him to bring white bread and butter and cheese; then I was offered some sandbags for a seat, and watched the men building. That was interesting and amusing.

There were Belgian soldiers who stood round watching the British building and strengthening the barrier; then a Belgian sergeant came and ordered them to take bags and build too. Some of them smiled; some of them winked at each other. One man winked at me, as much as to say, "Our brave sergeant; he's showing off!" The sergeant seized bags himself and swung them into place. Outside the ever-growing barrier a marine officer was directing his men. He was swinging the heavy bags into place himself—pointing out weaker places; he was a good officer. Once he paused to wipe the perspiration off his brow, and leaned against the wall of sandbags, and, so leaning, discovered me watching him. His eyes opened wide. Doubtless in his heart he said "What the devil is a woman doing here?" but he merely smiled and saluted.

I, too, swung a sandbag into place—laid one tiny bit of the wall that was to keep the Germans out—but did not. Along to the left the marines and the Naval Brigade were toiling, making beautiful roofs to their trenches—dragging heavy wooden beams into place, and on them supporting hundreds of sandbags and big sods of earth. Soon the trench became like a long hut—comfortably screened from rain and wind, and shell-resisting. For hours they worked, these big, strong men of ours, all looking good-tempered and jolly. Close to and behind one end of the trench were two stone houses, high and narrow, and towering over the barriers. I asked one of the officers if they were going to blow them up, remarking that if a shell hit them they would collapse in the trench and kill the men there.

He absolutely exploded:

"We have been asking all day to have that house taken down—and we can't."

"Why not?" I asked, astonished. "Can't you do it?" (He wore three stars.)

"No, it's all red tape; a fussy old staff officer came along and said they were not to be touched."

Instance of red tape that made me gasp at such a time. Never had I realised what victims it claims; and that evening, when I left these particular forts, I was witness of another distressing example of it. The same old "fusser" came along and ordered all the splendid roof to be taken off the trench; the protection these men had worked hour after hour to build was condemned because the supports were solid tree trunks (all the material available) wedged in with sandbags and earth; and the text-book said *iron* supports should be used, as wood might catch fire! My heart ached for them; it was already dusk, and instead of warm covered trenches they would have to pull down their sheltering roof and live in the open trench, for there was no iron to be got. The men were disheartened and furious, and many a curse fell on that staff officer's head, and personally I think he deserved them.

However, to return to the earlier hours of the afternoon.

My chauffeur returned armed with loaves and two huge cheeses and butter, and a big scaled drum of sterilised dressings. The doctor loaded up some men with the food, and I carried a big cheese, and we made a quaint procession following the winding footway that led through wire entanglements to a narrow plank bridge and so into the fort itself.

When I got back one of the young naval division stretcher-bearers came to me. It was the same boy whom I had met near Bucherout—with the little party who had lost their way and had the Belgian in the barrow. He explained on behalf of the little band that they had no rations, as they belonged to —— Company, which they could not find, and were now with —— Company (one being "Collingwood" and one "Drake"), and so, as only strict rations were issued, they had no food. He was a nice lad; I hope he got safely through what followed.

Whilst all this work was going on the blue sky above was very peaceful, and up there floated placidly a large captive balloon, furnished with a wireless telegraphy apparatus. The Germans were calmly surveying all the English preparations, and sending down to their artillery the new range of distance! I demanded to know why we couldn't shoot the balloon or send an aeroplane to attack it and drop bombs on the German guns, but was told all the Allies' aeroplanes had left for Ghent two or three days ago, to avoid possibility of capture!

Suddenly about 5 o'clock a new noise made itself heard—a deep *boom-boom*; this was the one and only Long Tom, which had been out of action since 5 o'clock in the morning owing to the cement having given way.

Shortly after this I left with a young Naval Brigade officer carrying despatches for the Commodore. Running through Vieux Dieu, we were stopped by a mob of people—weeping women and gesticulating men. Two poor women were alone in their house, and a man had started looting it, a rough civilian of the working class. Heedless of the two women he carried chairs and clocks and wine from the house to a little cart. A few yards farther on some soldiers and some civilians were drinking coffee and beer outside a little restaurant. We stopped whilst the owner of the ambulance scolded the thief, comforted the women, fetched two soldiers from their coffee to guard the house, and handed the man over to their charge.

About two miles beyond we met a Belgian regiment bivouacking for the night, fetched the *commandant*, drove him back with two military policemen; he arrested the looter, ordered him to be shot, and returned with us to his regiment. At last we arrived at the commodore's headquarters. The gallant despatch-bearer had told me a moving tale of his long day without food, and I had proudly presented him with a pear which a St. John's man had given me the day before and which I had kept for emergency; also I found a last scrap of chocolate. I forgot to tell him I had had one slice of plain bread and a chunk of cheese since 8 o'clock that morning, nor did he ask. True he was a little reluctant to take the pear, and ate the chocolate slowly without undue display of hunger.

When, therefore, he had disappeared up the long dark avenue with his despatches, I stamped about the road to keep warm, and then saw a light in what seemed a cottage in the grounds. I hesitated, then went boldly in, and knocked on the door to ask for a cup of hot coffee for the poor lad when he came out. To my astonishment, a big bluejacket appeared, and was as delighted to see me as I was surprised to see him. He overwhelmed me with offers of chicken broth, but I begged for a cupful for my despatch bearer; however, I was induced to accept coffee and biscuits, and thankful I was to have them. I was taken into a parlour with what had once been beautiful furniture, and whilst I was having my coffee a sturdy, sailorly-looking man came in, and we chatted. He was full of an expected division that must have taken the wrong roads, and looked worried to a degree.

Then he retired, and I curled up on a sofa in a corner, feeling terribly sleepy and tired; in fact I was just dropping off to sleep when an *aide-de-camp* entered. We had a long talk, and amongst other things I told him of the despatch-bearer's long day without food, and to my surprise (also relief) I learnt that the starving officer had already been for lunch at headquarters at noon! He entered himself after long delay, and felt rather shamefaced, I think, about his little desire to appear a romantic figure suffering pangs of hunger. He was very young, and I chuckled over his discomfiture many a time.

Meantime the *aide-de-camp* had entrusted me with his sword (for repairs), and armed with it I clanked back to the ambulance, where the chauffeur was much impressed by my appearance with the wonderful sword at my side.

(He returned to his *confrères* later with a great tale of his English miss, who had been presented with a sword for her gallantry!!!)

After reconducting our naval officer to his fort, we returned to Antwerp, and I swung into the hospital with great swank—sword clanking! To my dismay, appeared the head doctor.

"Oh, Miss So-and-So; take off that sword; we mustn't have weapons in a hospital!"

I gasped, and quickly explained I was only in charge of the sword.

However, to return. After supper I was filling some big jugs of water for the night nurses from the well (the waterworks having been shattered a few days earlier when Walhem was taken), and a young officer of the *Garde Civique* was helping me. To him I mentioned that the people whose hospitality I had enjoyed all the time I was in Antwerp had left, and I had nowhere to go for the night. He promptly fetched his mother, who lived two doors away, and with whom another nurse was billeted, and she begged me to sleep in their cellar, which was furnished as a bedroom. I accepted gratefully, and retired there about 10 o'clock, very weary. After the usual "*indaba*" with my hostess and her family, I washed in the kitchen sink, and got into bed and wrote up my diary. That took some time, and as midnight was striking I closed it, turned off the electric light (which was actually in the cellar), and was snuggling down in my pillows, when, *whizz-zz-zz* . . . *boom*, came the first shrapnel over Antwerp.

Chapter 3

Antwerp the Bombardment and Flight

That was a terrible night. For two and a half hours we worked carrying men downstairs—the top floor first, with its 69 beds to clear (for that night there were extra beds in the corridor), then the second floor, and lastly the fracture wards on the first floor, though to me that seemed a mistake. It was down slowly with a heavy stretcher, and up rapidly with an empty one. I made slings for myself with a bandage, but even then my wrists and legs ached after the first ten men.

One dresser I helped time after time—I think we two carried down 30 cases alone. Into one ward on the second floor I went to see if I could help, but found the London surgeon (who did all the worst operations there) with another doctor and two dressers in consultation over a very bad case. I turned to go out, when the great man saw me and called cheerily: "Ah here's Miss So-and-so; *now* we'll be all right!"

I swallowed a lump in my throat; at that time when I was alone a friendly greeting meant very much to me.

Down below, the scene was a terrible one. The kitchen was in the basement, also many offices (scullery, wash-place, passages), and these were now a mass of helpless men—some on mattresses, some on rugs—all exhausted with suffering and want of rest, racked by the pain of their wounds, but brave as the gods of old.

No murmurs, no complaints—although many a broken cry for water made one's heart ache. One poor sailor lay on the landing of the staircase to the basement; he had had an eye shot out and was half delirious, and his cry for water was very pitiful. Another man, very badly wounded in the side, caught my eye: he was lying on the stone floor with no mattress; I got him some cushions. One man with broken legs yelled with pain as we lifted him on and off the stretcher. Some of the men tried to cheer the others up. Gradually the lights were lowered and the stretcher-bearer's work finished, and I slipped upstairs and brought a mattress down for the man with the bad wound in the side.

Upstairs coffee and bread and treacle were going; and most comforting it was. Then the hospital showed a strange sight. Down in the entrance hall lay silent figures. On a bench behind the door sat a doctor and the sister-in-charge: the steps were crowded with doctors, dressers, and nurses, all huddled together, with a few patients in between. Outside there was a clear moon and pure air, and outside I went with my Burberry on, dragged a wooden bench to the middle of the courtyard, and lay down. *Whizz-z-z . . . boom.* At steady intervals came the shrapnel through the air, cutting the silence like a knife— once or twice coming so near I leapt up and ran to the wall, crouching down with bitten lips. Then back to the bench. Dr. Hoyle came out with blankets; but the horror of dirt was more to me than the cold of the night, bitter though it was, and, finding me set on this point, he kindly fetched newspapers and spread them over me. As he was talking the night sister joined us; she sent me out her own big coat to cover me. It was very good of her. Once she came out with a utensil in her hand, and called a greeting to me, when the whizz-z-z came between us, and she dropped her china and we met under the shadow of the wall, both breathing rather hard.

"Why don't you come in?" she pleaded; "it's awful being alone out here."

But I shook my head obstinately. If I were to die, I would rather it were outside, with God's moon to bear me company.

I closed my eyes resolutely and tried to sleep—tried, at least, to control myself and not run to cover. One shrapnel—two, three, eight, nine, ten. I began to feel proud of myself when eleven came; the loud hissing of it seemed to go through my brain. In wild, unreasoning terror I bolted to the wall and crouched there, holding my breath, praying madly; and the great boom was followed by an appalling crash—part of the house next door had gone. Several people came to look out— Dr. Hoyle to see if I was safe, Nurse Mitchell and Sir Bartle Frere to discuss the damage; and with the last two I went upstairs to the very top floor, and there, by climbing a long ladder, we could see out of a skylight, one at a time. It was a weird sight. Dawn was coming—very slowly—and here and there broken laps of flame told that some shells had found a mark. Housetops everywhere, and a few heaps of broken masonry (not many), and the great, quiet sky, and the *whizz-z-z* . . . *boom* as a shrapnel sped overhead on its deadly errand.

I was not sorry to climb down and return to my bench in the yard. About 4 I went in and lay on a sack of potatoes behind the front door,—the night sister's coat over me, Dr. Hoyle, big and kind and protecting, sitting on the bench; but sleep was not for that day! Soon the sounds of hurrying footsteps drew us to the door. Men and women were passing carrying odd bits of furniture and little bags of clothing. Two men passed, carrying a little girl in a chair. Three women passed, sobbing, a bundle tied up in a tablecloth in their hands. The day was come—this strange day of terror!

Very early an Irishwoman attached to the hospital and a Miss —— prepared to go; they had motorcars. They offered to take two nurses; only one said she would go, and she was suffering from a long strain. They took two English officers who were wounded, and insisted on one of them leaving his revolver behind—the other had none—professing to be afraid the Germans would catch them and shoot them all if they had firearms on board!

I got an early message from the house next door to remove my sword; the people indeed offered to bury it in a rubbish heap with the *Garde Civique* uniform belonging to the son of the house! He was very much perturbed about his future. I urged him to enlist; I urged his duty to his country—vengeance on the Germans. His parents urged his duty to them (they had four sons) and would give none of them to fight for their country.

Events followed fast. Mrs. St. Clair Stobart and her secretary came down to ask for help in getting away: they had 40 patients in a convalescent home at the top of the *boulevard*. Lots of wounded came in—one man a horrid sight of burns and blood, his face practically gone! The man who brought him in said there were crowds of wounded and no one to bring them in. It was already long past the Place de Meir to the Belgian Red Cross headquarters. The streets were empty. Once I passed some weeping women beside their house, of which two storeys had fallen in, and I had to whistle to myself and hum snatches of a song as I walked to keep my courage up, and every shrapnel that whizzed over my head made me wonder if anyone would find me if I got knocked out then. It was a weird walk, and one I have no longing to repeat, although I wish sometimes I had been more observant of

218

LIFE IN THE FRONT LINE

DIVISION BEING REVIEWED ON ITS RETURN FROM THE TRENCHES

the damage wrought around.

At last I reached my goal, but found hardly a soul there—only an *ambulancier* I had already met, who wrung my hand, muttering "*Bonne chance, mam'selle*," and dashed out. Nobody knew of the car, the owner or the chauffeur, and as the committee-room door was open and the president and two other members were there, I asked them. As I went out, with a message to take back to the hospital, the London surgeon and the hospital head walked in, and as I stopped to scribble a message on a sheet of paper, a terrific crash outside smashed all the windows. I hurried to look out; a shell had killed two people. At that instant the three members of the Belgian Red Cross walked out and vanished, and the two English doctors called to me to jump into their car to return.

With them I went to the English headquarters, and later to the hospital, entrusted with the fact that three motor 'buses were to come for the wounded and three of the nurses and a doctor. I took it on myself, therefore, to slip up to the top floor and pack boxes full of dressings and bandages, scissors, and other necessaries.

The first detachment was leaving in charge of an American doctor, and to him I entrusted my suitcase, as everyone expected a "*Sauve qui peut*" later. I took my precious charge the sword out also, but to my amazement a general outcry was raised, and the doctors and nurses would not hear of a sword going. However, I felt I should lose it if I kept it, so I wrapped it inside the Union Jack and so carried it out to one of the 'bus drivers, a sailor, giving him a few shillings to see it through!

It got to England long before I did, but my suitcase got lost, with many valued possessions.

Later on four other motor 'buses came, thanks to the efforts of Dr. B——, and into these the poor sufferers were crammed; and on the tops a few patients and all the doctors and nurses had seats. The chauffeur of a gallant Englishwoman who had done a lot of splendid rescue work round Antwerp helped me to break into the store cupboard and pack boxes of provisions—simply because it seemed nobody's business to see to it!

Off we started, and stopped outside Mrs. Stobart's hospital to offer help, but it was empty—not a soul was left; and then, dodging the broken electric wires of the tramway which were hanging across the road in places, we went slowly through the deserted streets. Every window was shut and barred; here and there a stolid woman would watch us pass, a child raise its hand in greeting.

Down by the *quai* the crowd was appalling—men and women and children; 'buses, carts, barrows, *limousines*, taxicabs marked "*Service Militaire*" or protected by Red Cross flags: everywhere people pushing and shoving or waiting stolidly; women sobbing and women calm and smiling; babies, dozens of them, piled on to carts and barrows the parents doubtless somewhere in that dense throng of humanity. The guns were booming in the distance—shrapnel falling on the town. Thank God! they had not yet got the range of the *quai*—a shell falling in the midst of that crowd did not bear thinking of. Then at last, after an hour or an hour and a half of weary waiting, whilst officers restrained and controlled the people and kept their own irritation in check—and it must have been intense!—the order came to move, and slowly the four 'buses, packed with sufferers, rolled over the pontoon bridge, and all around the yellow sky and the setting sun seemed to cast a halo on the forsaken town. It was then that Sir Bartle Frere, who shared the back seat of the 'bus with me, rose.

"I can't leave Antwerp like this," he said, and went down the steps slowly.

"Good luck!" I called; and;

"Goodbye!" he responded.

Miles and miles of long roads, and hunted. Weary people staggering along; bundles of goods, carts with chairs and tables! all their humble and valued possessions; little children trying to keep up, their eyes big with fear, their little legs weak with walking—how one's heart ached for them! And suddenly behind us a great sheet of flame lit up the dusk the petrol tanks were ablaze.

Gradually the night darkened and the cold became bitter to a degree. It: was early in October, and I had hastened to Antwerp from a hot country with very little clothing. I ached with cold and with sitting erect on that little narrow seat. A Scotch boy-dresser had taken Sir Bartle Frere's place; we had a blanket apiece, so we sat on one and held the other over us round our necks; but the blankets were thin, and it got colder and colder.

One nurse broke into helpless sobbing; she had gone down earlier to help the nurse inside with the wounded. She was a brave and splendid woman, and this was our second night without sleep, and the days had been filled with hard work. Every now and then the 'bus would stick in the mud; often we had all to get down and shove to get it out of the ruts, and the jolting and jarring were terrible.

One patient in the 'bus in front, a young Flemish boy, screamed with agony, moaning and yelling; that in itself was nerve-racking. A man was propped up against the windows of the 'bus, his head rolling from shoulder to shoulder with the rough motion; he had been trepanned two days before.

Once we stopped, and I helped an American nurse and two others to get hot water and make soup by throwing dozens of tabloids into huge cans of hot water; and a Frenchwoman, whose husband was a Belgian, made tea. Every man had a drink. It was St. Nicholas. One man was dead, but for some reason the doctor in charge of that 'bus refused to let his body be handed over to the Belgian regiment in the town. The nurse refused to travel with a corpse, and so another nurse was put in beside the body, being left to discover the ghastly truth after the start. To me that always stands out as a needless piece of cruelty.

So the long night went on, endless and terrible: the cold was bad enough, but the jolting and jarring seemed worse, and sleep was impossible. I turned to the boy beside me, whom I scarcely knew, and said I must put my head on his shoulder. I was too tired to feel almost; and I was strong, very strong. What that night of hell meant to some of the nurses and to the wounded God alone could witness. Better to let the veils of silence drop.... To me in the past war had meant romance and heroic deeds, not the awful hell of agony it is.

CHAPTER 4

Ghent

The grey light of dawn had scarcely broken when the heavy 'buses rolled into Ghent, and so along endless streets of tall, narrow houses with shuttered windows to the Hotel Flandria, an auxiliary hospital opposite the big station of St. Pierre. Here the doctors arranged for twelve of the wounded to be taken out, the wounded officer particularly, as there were English doctors and nurses attached to this hospital with ambulance cars. Whilst they were unloading, a London hospital nurse and myself found the kitchen and a big pan of hot milk, and, securing a few cups, we made the round of the 'buses. In No. I 'bus was a terrible scene—every man was livid, with a drawn face, and lines of agony were stamped on every mouth. Yet when we held out the first cup of hot milk and I offered it to a young English boy of eighteen, who had been one of the cheeriest and pluckiest in the whole hospital, he twisted his mouth into a smile and said: "Give it that chap up there, Sister, he needs it more."

And each man passed it on to his neighbour in misery. That boy's smile broke through my calm, and I was crying bitterly whilst we finished our round. My companion was the same; it was one of the saddest moments in life.

Then the 'buses moved on to a big convent, and here 32 were unloaded; six or eight of them were English, and the good nuns were at the door to welcome them, and us, with hot coffee and English tea!

It was indeed a comfort to be fed with hot, strong coffee by those gentle, kindly nuns, and when the mother superior asked for an English nurse to stay and help them, as they spoke no English and had no nurse amongst them, I held my breath in fear lest a trained nurse would offer to stay; but none did, and I rushed to the reverend mother and begged permission to remain. It was at once granted, and with a great joy in my heart I remounted the 'bus to go and find the doctor who had charge of my suitcase.

The next halt was at the Hospital Civile, a big forbidding-looking place, and here the remainder of the loads were deposited. Then the 'buses went to a *café*—a rendezvous; but here a sort of rush commenced, and at length, finding it hopeless to get any information, I took a cab and drove to the house of a Belgian doctor whose address had been given me.

To my relief Dr. Hoyle was expected there for breakfast, and the doctor's wife, who spoke English well, made me come in and wash, and was very kind to me. Dr. Hoyle appeared later, but not my suitcase, which had been sent in error to Bruges and then to Ostend. However, it was a pleasure to see the good doctor himself, and he tried hard to persuade me to go on with them. At last he left, and Madame —— and her daughter offered to take me back to the convent. They did so, calling at the English Consul's *en route* to tell him where I was and that there were English wounded there. His daughter was much interested, and promised to come and see us. I was more than half asleep when I reached the convent door; it had been a long walk, and after two days and two nights of excitement and no sleep I felt very near the end of my tether. Above all things I longed for a hot bath, but though that was impossible, it was a luxury to get off my clothes and tumble into bed. I slept at once, and an hour later a nun came hurrying to waken me.

The motor 'buses were at the door taking away the English patients!

I dressed hurriedly, but I was too tired to be very quick, and stumbled downstairs to find the 'buses had gone, taking all the English but three!

I was at once called upon by the doctor, who had just arrived, to get the dressing-wagon ready and go round with him. It took two hours to do the men. There were about 50, and some of the wounds of the new arrivals were in an awful state. The men themselves were worn out with the suffering of their night in the 'bus and the sleepless night of the bombardment. The doctor was very capable, and extremely clean in his methods. There was a bevy of fair lady helpers to accompany us, and they all had special duties allotted them. One very pretty girl had to hold the patients' hands and head and fondle them to take his mind off the pain of his dressings. One held the bowl of swabs, one the pail for dirty dressings, etc., etc., and not one of them was allowed to touch the dressings and bandages prepared for use. This was my work, and I had to undo all the dressings and syringe the wounds that required it, etc.

I had lunch with a little Belgian girl, whose relatives were all killed at Louvain, and she had been in Antwerp some weeks at the hospital there. She was a good little worker, and was very helpful. After lunch I had to take temperatures, etc., at the doctors' special request, as he was returning at 3 o'clock. However, it was 5 when he came, and many of the dressings had to be done again. At 6.30 I got permission to go to Madame —— to see if my bag had arrived. There were lots of English soldiers at the Gare St. Pierre, and in the streets people ran to offer them chocolates and cigarettes and fruit. . . . It was told me as a fact that when the English marched in to Ghent the poorer people gave the soldiers all they could to eat and drink, and spent all their ready money for the purpose.

I had supper at 7.30, and fell into bed more dead than alive, but even then burnt my candle low jotting the events of the day in my diary in case of forgetting what occurred; and so, very wearily, I went to sleep. The tiny cubicle amongst a dozen others was a haven of peace, and I had slept perhaps an hour and a half or two hours when cries awoke me. I leapt out of bed, slipped on my coat, and blindly groped my way to the place from whence the noise came. My head was confused—my brain a mass of chaotic thoughts; in another cubicle I found a big figure in white groaning and stamping and yelling.

To me came the thought it was strange to have a wounded soldier amongst the nun's cubicles, and then that this was a thief . . . or a German. . . . I seized the figure and pushed it on to the bed, and wondered vaguely if I could overcome it or if I would be killed; and suddenly the mists of sleep cleared away and I realised it was a woman and she had cramp in her leg. I knelt beside her and rubbed, rubbed with a sort of hopeless energy, wondering a little bitterly if I would ever get a night's sleep again, for that night, an hour earlier, a messenger on horseback from the medical officer of the English division had brought a note for me, and heard with surprise I was in bed; but the nun brought up the note, and that was about 10, and I was awakened then to read it. The outcry had at length awakened the rest of the sleepers, and the good woman's maid appeared, and I left her to rub and slipped back to bed, falling asleep to the sound of voices crying:

"*Qu'es-ce que c'est donc!*"

"*Mon Dieu! qui arrive . . . .*"

Morning came, and I was duly called at a quarter to 6! The morning was a busy one—the dressings took a long time. Every quarter of an hour one of the English sailors sent for me to ask "if his girl would love him now he'd lost an eye." Poor soul! it was he who sat on the staircase at Antwerp all that night of bombardment, suffering from thirst as well as physical agony.

That afternoon I had an hour off and went to the "Government House," the headquarters of the English division. There I left a note and there I saw lots of our men—big and strong and confident; it is wonderful the moral effect conveyed by a big Englishman in khaki. . I returned to the convent feeling less lonely, and no longer a waif in a foreign town.

When I returned I found that the *erysipelas* case was to be moved at 8 o'clock, and as no one but myself was allowed to touch him, I got him ready and waited. . . . Nine o'clock came and 10 o'clock, and still he was not fetched. At 10.30 we got a man who knew something of first aid (or said he did) to go out and make inquiries. At 11 o'clock a van with one horse came. The driver refused to touch the stretcher or help in any way—he was afraid of infection; and so, with the first-aid man to help me, I had to get the poor fellow on to the stretcher and carry one end myself and lift the stretcher into the van. The nun on night duty came to help, but her long sleeves and cloak made it difficult for her to come near. The poor fellow had 105 degrees of fever, and it was a very cold night, but orders had to be obeyed! (He was returned a few hours later, as the fever hospital would not take him in!) Then I had to swab all the bed and the floor with disinfectant and put the sheets, etc., into solution. It was 1 o'clock when I got to bed.

Next morning was Sunday, and I rose at 5.30 to go to mass. It was a moving sight. I knelt in the background in my khaki with the nuns and the wounded who were able to get up. . . .

Unfortunately for my chance of breakfast, the doctor had gone to mass also, and I was at once requisitioned to start work. He was quite annoyed because the temperatures were not taken! And then we started at once on the dressings. Then one of my Englishmen had to be prepared for an operation, and was taken away in a horse van, and it was 11 o'clock before the doctor took his departure and I could go and get some breakfast. Later on in the afternoon the consul's daughter called, and when she heard how difficult it was to get anyone for night duty she offered to come on, if her people would consent, and let me go to bed.

THE MORNING WASH

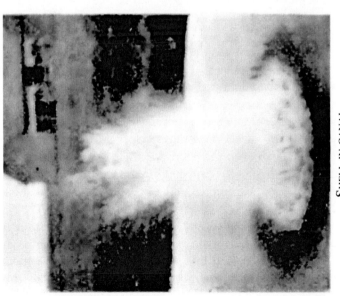

SHELL IN CANAL

So I got permission from the Reverend Mother to go out with her. She took me to the Flandria Hotel first to see the English wounded there, and she made inquiries for the officer we had brought from Antwerp. It was then a little lady with St. John's Association badges met us, and she told us gently she was then in charge for the afternoon of the officer in question, and he was far from well. We had an interesting chat; she was a novelist whose name is well-known, and she made a note of my name and promised to come to the convent and see my wounded. (She came sooner than either of us dreamt!) Then when we reached the consulate, and Miss Lethbridge explained the situation and that she would gladly come for the night, their telephone bell rang. It was an order from Ostend that the consul was to leave at once.

I returned to my convent and told the Reverend Mother what had happened, for many wild rumours had been abroad all day. Later on that evening the little lady from the Flandria appeared. . . . It was late and very dark, and the streets were lonely, but she had come herself to tell me her party were leaving before dawn and would take me and my English wounded at her request. It was very good of her to think of a stranger, and I explained to the Reverend Mother. Already we had had orders for all the Belgians to go at 8 o'clock in the morning!

So then I helped one of the nuns to make little bundles of all the available clothes, and I warned the stronger of the two Englishmen to be ready; the other man was bad and had to get medicine every hour, so the other Englishman lent me his watch to keep me right. I was sitting there in the dim light with all that ward of suffering men—some of them groaning, some snoring, some twisting and turning. Then of a sudden one poor fellow took a bad attack of pain, and I was attending to him when outside came the heavy tramp, tramp of hundreds of feet. . . . The man near me fell to the floor in a dead faint. I lifted him up and put him on his bed and hurried out to call the nun. We had rather a job getting him settled, and ever outside went that tramp, tramp, tramp.

As soon as I could in decency I rushed to the next room (the surgery), threw open the window, and leant out into the night. Dimly could I discern the moving mass, the seemingly endless throng, and the heavy tramp, tramp, tramp drowned my cry of "Good luck, boys," for all my soul seemed drawn from me. So the English Army marched from Ghent. . . . The tramp died away in the distance—I still stood there; but of a sudden I felt desolate and very much alone, and because such thoughts are not good I shut the windows and returned to the ward.

It was an hour or two later when Miss Sinclair came with her car. The nuns were very sad; and I, too, felt my heart heavy, for they had been the kindest of friends, and I loved them. One of my men was dressed in white flannel trousers, a khaki tunic, and a khaki cap, and he moved us to laughter even then by his solemn anxiety. . . .

"I came here a sailor and I'm going away a soldier," he remarked gruffly. "Funny, ain't it?"

Outside the Flandria other cars were loading, and at last we started. There were four or five other women in the car and two men, and I tried to keep awake, but to no purpose. The narrow seat, the hard bar where I rested my head, the intense cold, were barriers to sleep, but Miss Sinclair put a blanket round me and drew my head to her shoulder, and then I knew no more. Discomfort and cold and fatigue vanished, for I had the gift of the gods—sleep. I was wakened to descend on a road white with frost, and everyone went up to a house where a big fire burned in a comfortable English-looking room. Beds were offered to the ladies; but they were a democratic crowd, and chauffeurs, doctors, a parson, and the women all sat round together.

Someone made room for me close to the fire; I felt dazed with sleep and cold. Miss Sinclair seemed to be in great distress; she was half-crying. A handsome woman was fiercely arguing some point with her. It appeared that they had left an English officer in Ghent, at the Flandria, as he was too ill to move. I went outside and was joined by Miss Sinclair and the parson, and to them I explained I was going back to Ghent to try and find the officer, who was dying, and to stay with him till the end. They tried to dissuade me, as I would have to go alone.

Miss Sinclair and the young clergyman walked beside me until we came to a station, and there I learnt a train for Ghent was due. The two of them saw me off. Poor Miss Sinclair was terribly upset, and was very sorry she was not a trained nurse, as if that had been the case she would have returned also. The frost was intense and the country white. I walked up and down the dirty match-strewn compartment to keep my temperature and courage up. The guard came, and laughed when I owned I had no ticket; he wanted to warn me Ghent was already full of Germans.

"Go back, *mademoiselle*," he said. "The 'Boches' are brutes; it is not for an English lady to go there now."

But when I told him there was an Englishman there badly wounded, tears came to his eyes, and he pressed my hand. Two old Flemish men came to offer me a big pear for "the devotion of the Red Cross."

At the station people were dashing about in wild confusion: many rushed up to me to ask if the English were coming back! Men and women and children were staggering about carrying and dragging heavy trunk?—the hated "Boches" were coming.

At the Flandria was wild confusion: people were packing rapidly. I got a doctor to take me to the poor English lad. He looked very white and tired, and wanted to know where "they" had all gone. He could not understand why nobody had washed him, nor why he was alone. It was hard work finding water, and the gas-ring to boil it on, and basins, cup, etc. The other bed in the room had to be made: all the adjoining rooms were dirty. Once a Belgian girl looked in. "Oh," she said, "you will stay with him! I am going: my father and my mother are ready." She tore off cap and overall and gave me them.

A kinder-hearted, more thoughtful patient I have never come across: he was a hero, this slip of a boy, wasted with suffering. I went to tell the nuns I was there. I met a man with a big beard, and asked him how I could send a message.

"I am not the porter." He said gruffly.

Shortly afterwards the same man entered the room.

"Oh." I said, "are you the doctor? I can find no charts nor treatment book. What does he get?"

"I am not the doctor," he replied shortly, and went away.

Then a Belgian lady came, and after asking her a question five times, I found she was deaf. She was very kind. As soon as I spoke through her trumpet she went to make arrangements. Then we carried the poor boy to a Belgian nursing home on a stretcher. It was a weary task, for the stretcher-bearers were not trained and wanted many rests. At last I took the front handles myself.

We went to the operating-room, and by this time I had broken down hopelessly, and when I found myself at a table with a cup of hot coffee I sobbed for sheer relief; and to crown all the wonderful comfort came another Scotch girl, a nurse in the home! In a haze of warm gratitude I saw a clean room, a comfortable bed; and I slept for four hours just as I was—tunic and belt and boots I was wakened by a loud explosion, which was said to be the Belgians blowing up a bridge.

Then a German regiment marched past—little men, all of them;

and I watched them in a fury of despair from the window. That night Germans were quartered on the home: they were quite civil, indeed two of them, common soldiers, went about on tiptoe in the corridors when they heard there were "*maladies*" there (they were not told there were wounded). The first two nights were rather nerve-racking, as I sat by my patient wondering if the Germans would come in and kill him. However, morning came and the next night passed. Then Death came bringing freedom in her hands, and after that a sad little ceremony on a wet, dismal day, and a gallant British officer was laid to rest unmolested by the enemy to the end. There was no Union Jack and no "Last Post," and only three nurses to lay him to rest and I to read the Burial Service, but his was a hero's death—gallant and patient to the end.

The Germans were rather astonished at my khaki uniform; indeed, as I followed the coffin out we met a party of 18 Germans coming in who were newly billeted on the home. One of them ran to inform his officer of my coming, and for a moment I feared a scene; but the officer saluted gravely, and I got into the carriage with the two nurses. We drove through lines of soldiers, and passed many regiments—well-fed, sturdy men, with brown stubby beards and little eyes.

Later that afternoon I drove to the German headquarters, having vainly appealed to the American consul and to the Spanish consul for assistance. The sentries at the gates eyed me with amazement, and the corporal of the guard came to ask my business and conducted me to the general. As he threw open the big glass doors into a sort of ante-room filled with officers, there was a dead silence for a moment. Every head turned towards me; for a moment I think they took me for a man. One or two saluted, and I saluted gravely and looked round for a likely interpreter. I had just caught the eye of a jolly-faced old general or colonel, with twinkly eyes, when a very dapper A.D.C. asked my business. I stated it quietly:

"I am English. The officer I have been nursing is dead; I want to return to England."

A little crowd gathered round me; they all spoke perfect English. They would not permit me to go, I must indeed go to Brussels, and from thence I would be sent to Germany, and perhaps from there to England!

I pressed the point: I was a nurse. I would not nurse Germans: I must go to England! They were polite and very sorry, but inflexible. I was ordered to present myself at 9 o'clock the following morning, and my papers for Brussels would be ready. One young puppy even warned me it would be a long walk to Brussels. I told them if they wished me to go to Brussels they would have to send me; for myself, I was going to England. So with many salutes we parted, and I swanked out through that courtyard filled with Germans as if khaki had never before been fittingly worn!

At 9 o'clock next day I breakfasted in bed; and at the same hour the day after I started for Holland, and England.

The Germans were friendly on the whole.

A picket was drawn up by a sergeant to salute me. Sometimes the men made friendly remarks about the "worthy English *Frau*-lieutenant." Once a man made rude remarks about the "English swine," and I told him off sharply and in execrable German threatened to report him! He took it meekly, and the Belgians round nearly embraced me. Once in a shop a German officer was buying a pencil and I a writing-block. The woman brought me one "made in Germany." I told her to take it away and see if she had English or Belgian paper, and then, as if by accident, knocked the offensive article on the floor. The officer went away without buying his pencil, and the good woman in the shop beamed with delight!

In other shops they would bring out their best for me, and ask if I were not afraid. Once I ran down the stairs of the home and came suddenly on a German sentry: his eyes bulged; he jumped violently and grabbed his rifle. I laughed aloud with great delight, and he got very red. He thought I was a man at first.

One night a big banquet was arranged for 150 German officers, but was cancelled owing to the death of General von Besslaer, who was shot through the right lung on the road to Bruges when some of our infantry were hidden in a wood to stop the German advance.

What a blessed relief it was to leave the last German sentry behind and be greeted by the friendly Dutch sentries with smiles of welcome, and to unfurl the Belgian flag on our car! Ternhuisen was full of refugees from all parts, and many an interesting yarn went round the big table where everybody dined *en famille*. The little boat was well loaded, and there were two Englishwomen on board who were working amongst refugees in Holland. A Dutch officer asked permission to take my photograph, and he, too, had strange tales to tell. Since the war began the strangeness of truth over fiction has been demonstrated over and over again.

The crowds outside the steamer offices at Flushing were enormous. I managed to get there amongst the first six, and was given a ticket for England for next day's boat and a chit for a berth on board a refuge boat! I found I was expected to share a cabin with a fairly big boy and his mother; so I explored the boat, noted the number of a tiny cabin with one bunk in it, and went back to the office, where they at once made the exchange for me. When the steward came on in the evening I got clean sheets from him—for, indeed, the sheets in use looked as if many a strange being had inhabited them!

I had supper at the only hotel—a poor meal for an exorbitant charge; and there again were crowds of homeless wanderers. One poor woman with a baby in arms had come from Hamburg. Her husband, a sea captain, was a prisoner, and she and her babe had been ordered on to the prison boat, where 70 men and 20 women were imprisoned. However, the American consul intervened on account of the child and got her away.

A St. John's nurse came to ask me something: she was there with wounded, and they had all slept in a hayloft for a week.

The morning came at last and the boat started; but never shall I forget the interminable weariness of that crossing. I suppose it was the reaction after the constant work, but as the hours went by I felt almost sick with the endless monotony of it all. People all talked to each other: many thought I was there, in case the boat might be sub-marined, to render aid to the passengers. We caught sight of a torpedo and other boats, and once we had to stand-to whilst someone on a little minesweeper harangued the bridge through a megaphone. Then came Folkestone, and the dragging past of the hours until we got to Victoria. By this time I was in a fever of impatience, although none of my people were in England, only friends, to whose flat I hastened, and as I ran out of Earl's Court Station I wondered wildly if I would find them out; but that blow was spared me. As for them, they greeted me almost as one returned from the dead . . . and very pleasant it was!

And that was the first chapter of the war for me; and the second is, perhaps, stranger still, for Providence led my comrades and myself into as strange places as ever women went before. This at least the Great War has done—it has proved to men that women can share men's dangers and privations and hardships and yet remain women.

PART 2: FRANCE

CHAPTER 1

How the Corps Came to Calais

Out of the grey mists of the past rise shadowy forms that come and go—some have deeper tints and stronger outlines than others; all are shrouded in silence. These are the women who formed what we called in jest "The Band of Hope." For it was no light task to take from safety to a troubled land those who had not already been there. I myself came back purged temporarily by the pain I had witnessed— all selfish considerations swept away for the time by the sight of suffering; and I had a brief glimpse into the real glory of life—a life where money was not thought of, where the future lay in stronger Hands, and only the need of the moment could be considered. So it was that money and friends and love itself proved no bar, and away I went light-hearted, taking on me willingly the responsibility of eleven other beings, mostly older, some younger, than I. Wise counsels of parents, the cautious teachings of friends, were listened to and lightly disregarded.

Came the whisper, came the vision, came the power with the need,
And the soul that is not man's soul was sent us to lead.

Exactly seven days sufficed to order a Unic motor ambulance, watch it building, sell stock to pay for it, get the necessary permits, and leave England. With twelve pounds in the bank then, and no promises of work, no definite destination, we sailed from England merrily. It was even difficult to depart; obstacles blocked every step of the way— officialism, red tape, active enmity, all these had to be pushed aside; and infinite patience, much bluff and more blarney had to back up the steadfast purpose of our going.

What was the next scene! Calais the cruel, the pitiless; Calais swept

234

by storms of rain and wind, cold and wet, and cheerless; the Calais along whose *quais* one never-to-be-forgotten night rows of wounded lay—in the darkness, and the cold, and the rain. The wind was shrill and the heavens screamed their protest, but the great hotels remained closed; hospitals, with rows of beds and hot-water bottles, stood empty, the people slept in their warm beds and digested their heavy meals.

Yes, fathers of sons who were fighting, mothers of men who were wounded! they listened from their warm houses, and, perhaps, shivered at the howling of the wind; and along the *quai*, with sometimes a blanket to cover them, lay the heroes who had saved France. Hundreds of them came to Calais the cruel—men whose own country was lost to them; men whose mothers and wives and children had been murdered and outraged; Belgians who had been taken by surprise by a well-prepared foe and given their life and strength to keep that foe from seizing France. So the wind and the rain mourned over them, and with the dawn came English ships and doctors, and the 40 who had not the courage to deny to the wind and the rain the lives they had refused to the Germans were borne aside. As for the others—well, a few got better. After all, this is only a little part of what war means.

There was a side-light on war, too. Shall I raise that veil also? I remember two French *piou-pious* coming to tell me there were sick children down by the docks. I remember a little hut—a species of rough tram-shelter—where 30 women and children were striving to keep warm and dry round a little stove, and on the bare boards three tiny children lay flushed and fever-stricken. The eldest was possibly six: Belgian children are small for their age by English children. Her little eyes were very brilliant; her cheeks burnt my hand; her throat was horrible to examine. Her temperature was 104. The other two were not quite so bad—their temperatures were 102 and 102.2; and in a broken perambulator in the corner a babe of sixteen months had the same symptoms. It took us five minutes to clear that hut, open the windows, and get some air in to purify the place; and then Nurse Jordan absolutely devoted herself to the children. Till 10 o'clock that night she swabbed their throats and tended them. My task was to get them taken to a hospital; and I failed.

It is a memory that will never cease to rankle—it is a regret, a remorse, that will never cease to trouble my heart. It is true there were difficulties—would you believe them, I wonder? Listen

The people at the nearest hotel could not give any help: they knew of no civil doctors no fever hospital, no institution to help. . . . There was an English nurse passed across the *quai*, a woman with ambulance cars and orderlies to meet her. I told her of the children—the little children. She said she was here for wounded, and she passed by...There were English officers—medical officers. I told them of the children— the little children. They asked with great superiority if I were there for the refugees. . . . My reply made them say they would see to it. Yes, they would see to it; and little children were lying on hard boards, with no milk and no pillows. We could only get *so* little milk. . . . There were others who sent me a message "to leave the children alone or I would get quarantined"; and we were there for the wounded. . . .

Then came a Belgian general and a French officer, and to them at first the matter seemed of no importance; but by this time I was desperate, and they came to see for themselves. By this time also two of the others of our little band had spent two hours trudging through the streets and found a doctor. And all these good men promised to see what they could do! Then came two other men—one a reporter to an English paper; and they, too, undertook to "do something" to help. And meantime there were orders to go and transport wounded, and this we did, and after many journeys in the darkness and rain, our motor ambulance barged into a man with a hand cart, and broke our radiator and his cart. He himself escaped with a cut, and so it was very late before we had found a garage,—and returned on foot to the *quai*.

It was 10 o'clock when we collected a cab and all our hand luggage, and Nurse Jordan and Nurse Dunn, both worn out by the long day and their efforts to help the children with scarlet fever. It was a struggle to go and leave these children alone with their mothers; but we were very tired, and none of us had eaten since 12 o'clock midday, and so we went, the two nurses in the cab and the rest of us on foot tramping through the wet endless streets to find our different billets. It was like a funeral. . . . The first billet was filled, but a kindly old man offered to put up one of us; my brother was decided on. The next billet took two, the third took three, and the fourth drew blank, which left two out of a shelter—it was an empty house! Then we got four into a billet for two, and three into another billet, and there still remained the three men of our party and myself. My billet was a single one, and I had left it to the end purposely, and arrived to find it filled by two men refugees. The old woman put her head out of the window and volubly explained the position, and in the end, relenting, offered to let me share her bed, which was a converted sofa in the back parlour of a tiny tobacco shop.

Weary as we were, we could still enjoy the situation, although it was now 11 o'clock. Then the old gentleman who had come to my brother's rescue said he would also find room for me. He was indeed a good Samaritan, for he piloted us all that evening. So we bade farewell to Elizabeth Smith (for such was the homely name of the French tobacconist) and trudged along to deposit the two medical dressers. We rang the bell of their billet—no response; we rang, and rang; and gradually the truth came to us—it was another empty house! And again our good Samaritan rose to the heights and said he would somehow manage to put us all up.

So behold us arriving at his dear little home, with an anxious housekeeper suddenly confronted with four English strangers who were homeless. She too behaved "like a Briton," and I helped her to cut bread and butter and make coffee, and on that, and an apple each, we feasted royally. Bed was very welcome that night, and my passing regret for turning the good Samaritan out of his room was soon lost in the thoughts—tearful thoughts, I admit—of the little children who lay on bare boards, and even that passed swiftly into sleep.

We were early afoot next day, and early at the docks, but the hut was empty. The fever-stricken children had gone, with 600 fellow-creatures, aboard the refugee ship that had sailed for England.

Calais recalls another memory—another glimpse of the way we treat each other in war time. We were still in our shelter of a glass roof and stone floor—the part of a disused corridor in the station waiting-rooms. We were making tea with a little spirit lamp, and in walked two men carrying a stretcher with a boy scout on it, and a woman walking with them who wore a Red Cross armlet and a white cap with a red cross on it. They laid the lad down and departed, merely stating he was ill and needed rest, that he had come on a boat from England. The boy seemed to be in a stupor—we could not diagnose it; and there was no doctor to be got. We finished our tea (which was also supper) and asked the hotel people to take the boy in. Impossible I—there was no place, but he must be moved. I examined his papers. He was a Belgian hero, decorated for taking prisoners, singlehanded, three *uhlans*. He was sixteen.

His photograph adorned the front cover of the *Daily Mirror*. Two of us went to a Belgian boat, and there found the Red Cross armlet lady having a meal with the skipper. I told them we were bringing the boy on board for the night. Impossible! Why? There was no room.

I looked round the empty boat. There was no room for sick people. Not even for their own countryman—a boy, alone in a foreign country? No, not even for him. Then I do not know if my temper or my French was worse. Anyway, there could be no doubt left in either of their minds as to my opinion, and I asked that woman how she dared wear a red cross, and I ended by telling them they had refused shelter to a hero, honoured by their king for his bravery; and so I swung down their gangway mad with rage.

A Belgian officer had joined the group as I left. Then we went to the English ship and explained to the doctor, and he at once told us to bring him, and we carried him on board and left him; and as we passed the Belgian boat with the empty stretcher the officer and the woman called out: "We will take him; you can bring him now;" and with huge pleasure I hurled back at them: "You won't get him; the English will take care of him."

Then came our hospital of 100 beds, and the cleaning and the scrubbing, and the dying; and hardly were things in order when the typhoid scourge developed. From the first we had two patients, and they grew to eight and to 20 and to 50, and Sister Wicks and her little staff were busy day and night fighting the worst fight of all—grappling with death at very close quarters, fighting against heavy odds; for milk and eggs were hard to get, and our Belgian adjutant had his work cut out to get supplies, and some days these supplies gave out. And there were other things to overcome—insanitary conditions and foreign prejudices.

And in the other building a steady fight went on with wounds—ghastly injuries; and shortage of dressings and lack of instruments and a hundred and one odd things had to be thought of and appealed for and found. For ten days we had to cut sheets in half to have sheets for each bed; we had to wash shirts and socks and use them next day; we had to go on with the work when some were ill and the staff at a minimum, and all these first months we kept a dressing station going at Oostkirke, a mile behind the trenches.

Up there, little Walton, with her constant smile and little fragile face, stayed with another girl for a fortnight—sleeping on straw by night, shelled out of the "*Poste de Secours*" by day, up to the knees in mud, going to and from the trenches, shrapnel bursting everywhere. Walton, Sayer, and Bond, they all went through it, and a Belgian girl was with us for a time. Some days we had no butter and plenty of bread; and we sent to Calais for butter: it came, tins of it, and we had no bread! Potatoes and black coffee were the staple items of diet, and "*plâtre*" a sort of bully beef in tins that we stewed and fried and boiled and made into potato mash. And once from the troop kitchen we got five packets of "Little Mary Custard Powder," and as milk was an unheard-of luxury, we made custard with water, and it tasted better than the best custard ever made at home!

It was a strange world—the world of men, where no women ever crossed our path, and where conventions had ceased to exist. Conventions indeed were unnecessary. Chivalry was the outstanding characteristic of the men, and up there alone in the midst of the Belgian Army we were as safe as in a London drawing-room. One night there were only two "rooms" available, so on one side on straw we slept, and on the other the doctors and their orderlies, and in the other room 40 soldiers spent the night. Up in the trenches it was amusing to see the utter unconcern of the men—their quiet drollery, their games of cards, their delight at getting newspapers, and there were several who used to fry potatoes in little pots.

Once it was most thrilling. Commandant T——, an officer who was promoted and got the Legion of Honour for an exceptionally brave deed, took us along his trenches. It was a lovely November morning, bright and clear, and more like a picnic than anything, and suddenly a hare crossed the ploughed field behind, and two soldiers jumped out and chased it with sticks and others threw stones, and everyone watched with laughter, and then the Germans recalled us to reality. *Whizz-z-z* . . . *boom* came the cloud-balls of shrapnel, and the men were chased back to the trenches by the officers.

How well I remember it all, even now: the fields with the trenches thrown up, and the happy faces looking over—for the Belgian soldier is as gay as he is brave; and here and there in the earth, just above the trenches and very close to the edge, little wooden crosses caught the eye. Ahead of us lay more fields, and about 50 yards from us five figures lay, very still, with a queer contorted look. And in one corner was a farmhouse and an old mill where there were Germans, and that was why the five figures lay there unburied: it was death to go to them, for the guns from the farmhouse had the range—had tried it five times effectively! A doctor had braved the death that was certain, and returned unscathed, worming his way there and back, and with a clear conscience certified they were dead and beyond man's aid. Then the river went past, broad and blue, and sometimes dark things bobbed up and down, and through glasses one could see arms and legs and Ger-

239

man uniforms. And beyond the river was an artificial bank, and there, entrenched, lay the to worship—the Heaven that heard the prayers of Allies and enemies, and ordered all things as it thought best.

There is another picture of the trenches a week later. It was raining—hard, steady rain—and we had a long tramp; the railway line was broken up with shell-holes and the fields were swampy. We scrambled along communication trenches and zigzag trenches. My field boots were lost in the mud, my skirt tucked up to my knees, and my buckskin breeches were soaked through at the knees with slimy, greasy mud. The trenches were closed up with straw and grass-sod roofs, and a wet and dreary officer welcomed us. He clapped his hands, and the grass-sod roots were cautiously shifted a few inches, and out popped dozens of heads like rats in a hole. The cigarettes and shirts and seeks brought shouts of delight, and grimy, happy faces peered at us curiously from the earthen burrows. From there we trudged along to a battery of artillery. They were so cold, poor fellows! standing about, soaked; to the skin, with only mud to sit down on; they had branches and bushes stuck on their guns to look like a line of trees from afar.

The day before a passing observation car had halted by our *poste*, and a red-headed kindly sailorman (with an Aberdeen accent that rivalled my own) had shared our simple meal of soup and potatoes. He had been so touched by hearing of our little bundles of comforts for the men he had torn off his own mittens and thrust them into my hands, saying: "They may keep some poor devil warm; I can get others." The point of this digression is that one gunner had hands purple with cold, and to him I gave the warm-hearted sailor's mittens. Tears came to his eyes; the brave fellow looked at the mittens, then at me, then at his gun.

"The English are always good," he said simply; "I shall fire my gun better now."

On our way back with empty pockets we found some French soldiers in stables and a Sénégal acting as cook, so we hunted in our coats for one or two odd cigarettes. The Sénégal was so touched that he fumbled round his neck, beneath his tunic, and offered me, as a little souvenir—a German ear! It was said that the Sénégals cut off the ears of dead Germans and made necklaces of them. The French soldiers seemed to relish that tale—so did my companions!

One day we wandered into a lonely Flemish farmyard. Dead cows with their legs in the air made one long for *eau de cologne*; beside one ungainly corpse a little party of soldiers were cheerily cooking their

240

A Trench in the Sand.

Guns Hidden in Branches.

midday meal. . . . Inside the farmhouse an old bent man was crouching over the stove; opposite him sat an aged woman; and three soldiers and a wounded officer on a mattress completed the party. The window had never been open all the years the farm had been built. Over the stove, on a narrow shelf, were ten priceless willow-pattern plates in excellent condition. From the window we could see the little garden enclosed in a field, and then a plank, and beyond that the trenches and the blue line of the Yser. In the field we had crossed to reach that farmhouse were 300 shell-holes. . . . All through the preceding week the Battle of Dixmude had raged round this humble-home.

Thousands of killed and wounded had covered the ground with their blood and agony, and all through that scene of slaughter and horror the old bent man had sat by his fireside, and the aged woman had walked to Furnes, about 16 miles away, and on this very morning she had returned. Poor old Darby and Joan!—the war had burst in fury round them, but they only looked on with a sort of childish wonder. I longed to get one of these plates, but I could not bear to ask for it; I knew that at any moment one of the shells splitting the air outside might for ever end the plates, but to ask seemed sacrilege. So we shifted the wounded down to the roadway, and at length to the *poste* and into the ambulance. It was dark by the time the car started—it was safer to work in darkness—and so, piloted by a French officer in his car, we ran back to Furnes without lights. Furnes itself was in darkness, and it was hard to drive and find the hospital in streets where never a lamp was lit, because it was within reach of those dreaded German guns.

Next day we were shelled out of our *poste*. Walton was cooking the breakfast, when a shell burst outside and smashed all our windows. We went out to examine the hole it made, when another came. They were shelling the road and the railway near. In a big field hundreds of men were drawn up for roll-call, and each shriek made us close our eyes, expecting to see a great gap in their midst. But the officers proceeded calmly, and then the men fell in, company after company, and marched away, falling into single file as they went. The "system" of shelling was explained to us. The enemy always shelled first one spot, then farther on, and farther on again; so it is really safer to stay where the first shells come than to run backwards.

All this time—which was not long as days count—the car kept in constant touch with Calais. Some days I went back there to see that all was well; some days I stayed where I was. At Calais the work went on quietly, steadily—day after day of steady rain and raw cold and bad smells. We were all ill in turn. The water was bad, the work was hard; our food was at first rather a makeshift. One after another suffered from severe dysentery, and there was little comfort for the sick. The hospital, our base, was little more luxurious than the trenches. But now I will try and describe it more fully. Comfort was a mere detail,—a forgotten trifle belonging to a previous existence; and never a grumble betrayed that any of us noticed its absence. War was work, and we looked for nothing better. We still lived on the few pounds I had brought for emergency, and we had not time to write and tell those at home of our needs. All we could spare went to our *blessés*, and overtime was never thought of. Someone was ill—that meant a night on duty to follow a day's hard work, but that was nothing. To us all war spelled work, and work spelled war; and we never looked beyond.

CHAPTER 2

The Hospital in Early Days

What was our hospital to look at? Well, it had not an impressive appearance. That never-to-be-forgotten day when I marched a squad up the yard to "take over" we all noted with interest the air of the place.

A large gateway led into a dirty courtyard where two long ungainly buildings lay parallel with each other. Opposite the doorways were rows of latrines, and the odour from these made one shrink back in disgust. Inside the old schoolrooms looked dirty and untidy, and men lay on straw *palliasses*; one or two had beds—three wooden planks supported on iron legs: these were *châlets*. In one room next the door two doctors and six nurses were cooking or boiling water on a little stove—an old-fashioned iron thing like a drainpipe. There was one table and a wooden bench in the room. Opposite this was a ward. An ugly wooden staircase with a sharp narrow turn led to another ward where were 16 men, some of whom seemed very bad; then there was a dirty room, with one or two wooden benches in it, and that led into a third ward. Above that we were told not to go.

A second staircase led downstairs into the private rooms of the headmistress, who also owned rooms above.

Outside one had to go round the courtyard to get to the second building, but it, we were told, was empty. It took very little time to give everyone a job. Our packing-cases arrived; the three men carried them in, and emptied four and made a cupboard. The nurses attended at once to the patients, many of whom had very bad wounds; two were very ill with septic pneumonia, and their wounds had been left without fresh dressings for two days because there was not much hope for them! Three of us scrubbed the upstairs room and two the kitchen, and the Belgian orderlies watched us, at first resentfully, then curiously, and at length one of them came and took my bucket and scrubbing cloth from me and himself washed the floor and stairs.

The others followed suit; they were convinced the "English mees" could work, so they worked too.

We scrubbed desks out, to have places at once for bandages and dressings; we invented all sorts of shelves; and that evening at 6 o'clock, when the two former doctors called to offer their help, they exclaimed with surprise at the changes wrought.

We were exceedingly fortunate, too, in our Belgian quartermaster: he was a kindly, simple soul who made his staff work. All that afternoon he kept them busy filling mattresses with straw—arranging dozens of *châlets* he had managed to secure. To him I went in despair over the question of cooking. "*Mademoiselle*," he said, "*tout est possible*."

Two days later the kitchen had a good range, a cauldron for hot water, tables, chairs, cups, and plates. This first day he watched us, and we, when we had time, watched him. But by night everything was clean. The "theatre," as we dubbed the empty upstairs room, was stocked with desks; each desk labelled, and containing bandages, dressings, bottles of iodine, chloroform, peroxide, etc. Walton got us a nice little supper from our stock of tinned meats, etc., which was now carefully arranged in a cupboard made from empty packing-cases. Linen and shirts and socks were also packed neatly in the shelves, and when Sister Wicks appeared, having gone to rest at once like a good nurse, she was immensely surprised. It was 9 o'clock when they left to walk to their billets. I stayed to help Wicks, as there were a lot of bad cases. We had a busy night: a little lay brother was downstairs in the kitchen, and one of the men dressers slept on a stretcher in the theatre.

There was lots of work. We had to boil all our water on a little stove with a small kettle. The night wore slowly on, and I was sitting in the upstairs ward when the lay brother came to beg us to do something for the "*infecté*." The who? The "*suspecte*," who was alone. He had been alone all day.... Could nothing be done for him? ... By degrees we learnt that a typhoid case had been left by the out-going doctors in the opposite building—alone. They had told me they had had a typhoid case, but had moved him. Perhaps they had meant to, and forgotten. Let us hope so!

Wicks went over to him at once, and I remained in the upstairs ward, where six men had pneumonia, two septic ... Twice I had to force the clothes off a man who was delirious and kept dressing himself when I was busy elsewhere; and then one big man suddenly got out of bed and stood shouting;

245

"Let me go; open that door!"

I went to him to put him back to bed, and he raised his great fist and threatened me. I tried to coax him, but he glared at me furiously. I tried to order him like a soldier, but I did not know the words of command. Still he wavered, and then, again rearing himself up, hit out at me.

"Open the door. Why is the door shut?" And I backed to the door, watching him, opened it, and darted through to the theatre.

"Wake up—quick, there's a man raving," I said to the dresser, who was very sound asleep, and rushed back to the ward and again tried to put the man back to bed.

The dresser came, and, telling him to be ready, I darted downstairs, called to the *frère*, and he came up too. But the man's violence increased. He wanted to hit us; he was mad, and we were all a little nervous, I think. Then Wicks came back, and she marched boldly up to him to take his arm, but he struck out wildly and held us at bay. Then I slipped away, wakened a sergeant downstairs with a hand-wound, and asked him to come up and give the man sharp orders. He did, and the soldier instinct won; the madman obeyed the sharp voice of authority, and sat down on the bed. Next moment he was under the blankets and the dresser was sitting on the bed ready to hold him down.

One of the men with septic pneumonia was very bad—so bad I sent for a priest and a doctor. The priest came first, hurrying up the stairs, serious and quiet. He bent over the poor fellow, whispering in his ear, and even as I turned back the blankets for the priest to make the sign of the cross on his feet his spirit went. The doctor came next, but merely agreed that the man was dead and departed.

It was all Wicks and I could do to carry the body to an empty landing where we could lay him out. Then I went down and made cocoa, and we had bread and jam, and up again to the ward; this time to the other septic pneumonia, a fine boy, who said to me gently: "I am going to die, *mademoiselle*, and I feel a little frightened; do not leave me."

So I stayed by him as much as possible, and told him he must get well, and bathed his head with cold water; but he smiled and repeated always: "Thank you, *mademoiselle*, but I am going to die." Then he would lie quiet, smiling, and once he said: "I cannot sleep, but I shall soon never waken."

Then dawn came, and washings and dressings and breakfast, and after breakfast I went back to Antoine. Of course it was absurd and sentimental, and I ought to have gone quickly back to a billet and slept, but Antoine was lonely and begged me to stay. "Do not leave me, *mademoiselle*; I am a little lonely." He got so bad about 10.30, the priest was sent for and gave him extreme unction. He was very simple and brave, and kissed my little ivory and silver crucifix and held it in his hand. He told me of his mother and his little brother José; he did not know where they were—he thought they would be in England. He spoke English well himself. Aladdin came to his other side, and we moistened his lips with wine and held him while he coughed, for his cough came in spasms and tortured him. I went down to lunch, but the Belgians looked at my red eyes and white face, and I couldn't eat.

The afternoon wore past. Aladdin and I knelt beside him, and he was very splendid. "Do not cry for me, *mademoiselle*," he said once. "I am a soldier, and I am glad to die like one. I am not afraid to die. God is good.

"Tell my mother, if ever you can see her, that I was happy when I died and thought of her.

"*Mademoiselle*, what devotion for you English ladies to come and nurse us! My only regret in dying is that I cannot live to show you how grateful a Belgian can be.

"Do not weep, *mademoiselle*; I am better dying here with you to care for me than many of my comrades who died away from everybody."

He was very beautiful. His face was as noble and fearless as his words; and he was such a boy to die, such a child for all his strong limbs—he was only nineteen. His coughing fits were piteous, but he always smiled gently when they were past and said, "I am not afraid to die."

Walton brought me tea to the door, and I gulped it down. Later they came and begged me to go for supper, but food is impossible to think of sometimes. At last I could bear the fatigue no longer. My knees were cramped, my back aching, and so, lest I should faint, and so distress the poor lad, I kissed his forehead and bade him farewell, and so stumbled from the room. Aladdin and Franklin stayed by him till release came at dawn. The pity of it!—these brave young lives lost to us. The worlds beyond this must be very full of heroes now.

There were many sufferers to think of and care for in those days. One day a stretcher case was carried in unconscious, a gaping head wound healing badly—the body thin and wasted—the legs mere skin and bone. I could span the ankle with my finger and thumb—yet the lad must have been about twenty-four, and formerly of splendid physique. His mouth was full of solid food—gone wrong;—his back already broken in a gangrenous bed-sore. The doctors examined him, shrugged their shoulders, and walked out. Later an officer came with two men to remove him to a "head" hospital—in spite of his absolute exhaustion, aggravated by his removal from another hospital—because he was Belgian, so must be in a Belgian hospital. Here we fought red-tape and won—and for many weeks the poor lad was kept alive by the whole-hearted devotion of Nurse Jordan. She slaved for him; he needed more constant (and unpleasant) work than any other in the hospital, but her care told.

Gradually, to the amazement of all, "Harry" came back from the Land of Shadows. His eyes opened: in them interest and intelligence began to flicker. Lady Baird brought a water bed from England for him; the bedsore, bad as it was, grew cleaner. "Harry" ate oranges, smoked one cigarette a day, could sit up at length, and month followed month until one day he was carried on board the hospital-ship for England. That was a transformation, a solid proof of what care and devotion could do. The doctors never treated him, never examined him even; yet from the half-dead, lifeless thing they brought in evolved the bright-eyed, rosy-tinted face, and a stronger, though still pitifully weak, frame that was sent to England. There, I regret to say, we lost sight of him; a solemn promise to let us know where he was sent was broken by someone, and the work rolled on. "Harry" became a memory—a name.

Then the typhoid scourge grew. We had one case the day we took over; a week later we had ten. A whole building was given up to them, and all day long the typhoid staff worked. At first the coffin-cart rolled in and out of the yard with daily regularity, then its visits became less frequent, and gradually ceased altogether. And those who nursed the typhoids were not nurses whose long training and life-work was spent in nursing. They were gently-bred, high-spirited girls, who heard the call of misery and answered it. Under the supervision of "Sister-Sergeant Wicks," they went about their monotonous, dull, unpleasant duty, and to it pave their hearts and their high courage and their patience and unselfishness. The weeks passed—the worst and most disagreeable part of the winter—but their courage and their enthusiasm never faltered.

The scarcity of milk, eggs, and brandy was a problem that had to be tackled many times, and our Belgian quartermaster showed a wonderful energy in getting larger than the other hospitals could obtain. Beds too, were one of our unfulfilled ambitions. The men were more fortunate in many other hospitals in not having to lie on mattresses on the floor, but the planks on iron trestles that made their beds left much to be desired; but here, again, the gods were kind.

One weekend our English chaplain came to Calais, and on Sunday evening a few of us dined with him at the hotel on the *quai*; and good fortune (to call by the lowest name the force that guides all) sent hither also the S.M.O. of Calais—a gallant and kind-hearted officer, who never threw us a crumb of praise when inspecting out hospital, but who made ample amends for that in his official reports to England. It sent, also, General Sir Arthur Slogget, kindliest and cheeriest of Directors-General, and Mr. Stanley, the most broadminded and generous of men. Despite the importance of the conference that brought them to Calais, they had time to remember out little efforts to help, and three days later their interest was materially shown in the arrival of a splendid supply of spring beds, bedding, blankets, sheets, etc., etc. I did wish that the kindly donors had witnessed the delight of the patients!

All this time the staff had many hardships to go through, the chief being the necessity of changing their billets every few days, and of going to different houses at night after a hard day's work. We sent the ambulance with them when possible, but it added to the administrative work greatly, for it meant going to the *mairie* to get new billets, then going round the billets to inspect them, and very often returning to the *mairie* to report empty houses, or inhabitants who flatly refused a room, or workmen's houses which were quite unsuitable. Taciturn and almost insolent clerks had to be propitiated, and personal feelings had to go to the wall when one was confronted with the possibility of seventeen or eighteen English girls being left homeless—without beds to sleep in!

Many an afternoon has run into evening, and supper been relegated to a late hour, in this disheartening, thankless job. How I hated it!—the endless explanations, the necessity of keeping one's temper under insulting remarks, the visits to strange houses, the rudeness of many of the proprietors, the constant red tape that sent me backwards and forwards from one official to the other. Unluckily it was a job I had always to do myself, as the other officer of our little band did not speak French.

It was the same with the arrival of stores—all the fuss and worry attendant on getting them off the *quai* fell to me, as it meant more arguments and more French officials to cope with. Then I tried to get a house given us for sleeping accommodation, and, after endless refusals met with persistent new applications, after endless arguments and explanations and pleading, and stormy scenes, I was sent to see the owner of an abandoned shop that had been offered as an overflow hospital. Bare rooms and dirty walls, one table, five chairs, and 20 beds composed the furniture, but it was rent free, and it was available at once. A little flattery and coaxing soon brought good-humoured assent from the owner, and the F.A.N.Y. had a "flat."

What a relief it was to have a home to go to at night! We painted the walls where the paper was hanging in shreds; we cut out pictures and put them up round the room; we got a few cushions—there was no more endless worry about billets. Four of us slept at the hospital in camp-beds—a trained nurse, the housekeeper, a chauffeur, and myself. We had a lumber-room behind us and slept in half our living-room. At night, if cases came, we were on the spot to decide if they could be kept or sent elsewhere. We had our meals in the kitchen, and picnic teas to which the English officers in Calais came occasionally. There was eternal hubbub and noise, but we enjoyed it. For a few weeks an airwoman cooked our suppers and baked cakes and jam tarts. There was constant commotion. At night we fell into bed with a sigh of relief. The wounded loved us. When evacuation orders came these men would burst into tears, refuse their food, beg to be allowed to stay. We sent them off with heavy hearts. We were spokes on a tremendous wheel—orders must be obeyed. And so the days wore to Christmas, and that is a tale by itself.

CHAPTER 3

Convalescents and Christmas

It was ten days before Christmas, and the surgeon-general looked worried. His kindly smile was vague, his eyes wandered.

"What is the matter, my general?" I ventured to inquire; and he looked at the colonel, then at me.

"Ah, *mademoiselle*," he said, "we can find no place for our typhoid patients who are past the worst, and we must make room for many others who arrive."

"My general," I said half in jest, "I will find you a place."

He and Colonel F. laughed.

"Thank you, *mademoiselle*. Can you, then, succeed where we fail?"

"You shall have your convalescent home as a New Year's gift to the Belgians from the F.A.N.Y.s," I retorted.

All that afternoon I was very silent. It was true I had spoken on the spur of the moment; but the need was very great, and when the need is great there is always a way if one can but find it. That evening a sad story was brought to me. Four of our poor typhoids had been so far on the road to recovery they were taken from us to make room for worse cases. They were sent to another hospital, where they slept on straw and got little food and less milk. The die was cast.

Next day, with Billy and Bond and the old Unic, I went along the coast. We tackled a hotel at Sangatte, but the proprietor was in Paris, and we could get no authoritative answer to our demand that we should take it over as a convalescent home. So then Billy and Bond remembered a *château* on the road to Boulogne, where Belgian soldiers had been billeted. It was very cold, but we raced along and came to the *château*. Leaving the car at the gates, we walked in, and were received in the hall (which was evidently in use as an orderly-room) by a major.

"*Monsieur*," I said blandly, "we are English nurses in the service of the Belgian Army. We have a hospital at Calais of 100 beds. We want this *château* to send out convalescents to. How soon can you find your men other accommodation?"

To say that the poor man was surprised would be hardly adequate. His mouth opened, his eyes bulged, and at last he gasped:

"But, *mademoiselle*, we are using this *château*; it is ours. And it is not suitable for sick men; it is cold and damp, and there are only three rooms left open."

So we amicably visited the kitchen and the other rooms. I had to admit it was not all one could desire for convalescents. But I would not give up hope.

"If we find nothing better we shall return. *Monsieur* would not let the sick suffer for want of the *château*, I am sure."

As we stood at the gate we saw an elderly priest climbing the hill towards us. With a sudden instinct, Bond and I tackled him.

"Good evening! *Monsieur* is perhaps the *curé* of the village?"

Monsieur not only was *curé* but replied in fluent English. He not only was a French priest, but had an Irish mother. He loved us on the spot. He had an empty hall that he kept for church entertainments; it would hold 25 convalescents. He mounted the car. We escorted him home; we inspected and accepted the hall; we talked of drainage, and accommodation, and everything possible. Next morning, with triumph in my heart, I told the general, in a casual voice, that the convalescent home was found and would be ready on Christmas Eve. Thereafter followed the question of beds and blankets. A hurried visit to England four days before Christmas included a rush to the British Red Cross, and the generous grant of 25 more beds for our typhoids from Mr. Stanley.

So the old wooden beds were disinfected and went out in an ambulance to St. Ingilvert; the blankets and mattresses followed, and then the patients and two girls to look after them, cook and cater, and keep them in order. And then the authorities woke up to the fact of what had happened, and even spoke of withdrawing passes for the cars to St. Ingilvert, and vaguely protested that they had not consented to convalescents going there. But possession generally ensures victory, and the convalescents remained until they were cured.

The enterprise was unique. The staff consisted of only two girls—a mistake, perhaps, viewed in the light of later experiences; but they worked nobly, and not till long afterwards did I realise that they had been doing the work of four. Anyhow, the patients grew fat and rosy-cheeked.

They used to rise at 6, have roll-call, and breakfast; then they made their beds and tidied up, under supervision of one girl, whilst the other got the dinner ready; then after a good meal they were taken *en masse* for a walk, had coffee and biscuits on entering, played games, read, and smoked till supper time; then after washing up they went to bed. The two F.A.N.Y.'s slept in an adjoining farmhouse; the *curé* would willingly have provided them with a room, but the laws of his Church made it impossible unless they had both been over forty, whereas their joint ages did not reach fifty!

The *curé* has been a staunch friend ever since, and he and his old housekeeper nearly wept when after three months the Belgians secured Camp du Ruchard for their convalescents, and St. Ingilvert knew us no more.

Christmas came at Calais, and we got trees with great difficulty, and candles and ornaments, and spent a busy Christmas Eve preparing all things. At midnight we went softly round each ward and placed a complete outfit of new clothes (*i.e.*, shirt, vest, pants, socks, scarf, mittens, and handkerchief) by each man's bed. Every bed was full, and we had two extra.

The general came, and received a little lucky pig off the tree. Tears came to the dear old man's eyes, and for a moment he was choked with emotion. The Belgian heart is very easily touched, and shows the generosity of the Belgian character.

Everyone got a present from the trees. Wards 2 and 3 had a tree in the operating theatre, and all came round it. Ward 1, where all were helpless cases, had a tree to themselves, and wards 4, 5, and 6 had a large tree where all could see it.

What a spread we had too—cakes and shortbread and sweets! And all the orderlies and patients, and many officers and doctors besides our own, and an English naval officer, were the guests. We dragged the piano to the head of the stairs; and how the men loved the songs and the choruses! The pianist-in-chief was an orderly who had been a professor of music at Louvain. A week before Christmas he had a nervous breakdown, and on Christmas morning his temperature was 101; but his sole obsession was to play the piano for the "Miss," and so he worked himself into such a frenzy the doctors said it would be safer for him to get up and play than to be kept in bed by force. How happy he was, too! His cheeks were flushed; his long, thin nostrils quivering;

his eyes dilated. He played on and on. Poor lad! he has been in bed ever since. For weeks after his case puzzled the doctors, and then he was sent south with tubercular disease.

After the tea was over (it lasted till 7 o'clock) an English Tommy came and sang to the men in the different wards. Then we had dinner in the kitchen, with plum-pudding and turkey, and at last, very weary, we dragged ourselves to bed about 11 o'clock. As most of us had been to early church at 6 that morning we were thankful to turn in.

A week later came the Belgians' turn. They asked us to come into the kitchen at midnight on New Year's Eve. We were greeted by the whole staff, who made long speeches about "the English misses and their devotion, and how we had left our homes to care for their home-less wounded." And they all wept, so much did their speeches touch their hearts; and I tried to reply suitably, and assure them that we were honoured in helping the heroes who had saved Europe from the hordes of the Hun. Then the adjutant kissed the cook (an old soldier, I had better explain), and the cook embraced the sergeant, and in fact the Belgian staff all wept and embraced each other.

Then the cook and the *chef de service* insisted on executing a weird and wonderful dance, and sang all the time a Flemish ditty that we did not understand. Then we all joined hands and sang "Auld Lang Syne "which *they* did not understand, and then we bade them farewell and went off in the Unic to "first-foot" the British Senior Medical officer and the Naval Transport officer. Alas! the former fiery Irishman was in bed, and did not understand Scotch customs, and the porter whom we sent to waken him returned hastily, swearing that nothing would induce him to go near the colonel's door again.

So we wound up at a far-off hospital where there were British doctors and nurses; but alas! the four Scotch doctors were teetotallers, and looked sleepy and bored, and so we returned to our own quarters to snatch a few hours' sleep before morning.

So passed our first Christmas at Calais, and had anyone told us then that we should spend our next Christmas in France we should have treated them with scorn.

CHAPTER 4

Life at a Regimental Aid Post

When the battalion doctors chose an abandoned cottage on the roadside they only asked for shelter from the rain and cold and mud—comforts were there none. Picture, then, our little *poste*. The door opened into a small square room, with two chairs and a table; off this were a tiny room (which held a small round table about the size of a card-table and two chairs) and the kitchen, in one corner of which was the well which supplied the house with drinking water: overhead was a long, low loft, where 40 to 50 soldiers slept on bare boards. Here, then, we established ourselves.

The outer room was used by all and sundry. Every morning from 8 to 9 large numbers of men came from the trenches half a mile away to report sick, or get slight wounds dressed. They stood in a mass in the doorway and entered two by two. Dr. Hannsens and little Dr. L——— examined them, and we stood by ready to put on a fresh dressing or administer a dose of medicine. To each one we put the same question: "Have you a good shirt and good socks?" And the necessary articles were ready. Most of the men did not stand on ceremony, Their eager "*Merci beaucoup, mam'selle,*" was followed by a dirty ragged shirt being thrown on the floor and the new one hastily donned, Socks, too! . . . One lad told me he had worn his socks two and a half months, and truly they looked like it! Their simple gratitude was very touching.

Then the men went out and fresh ones entered, When the morning "out-patients" was over, Sayer and I usually accompanied the doctor to some part of the trenches. Once the way lay along the railway, where large shell holes made the going difficult. Shrapnel whizzed over us, and we stood to watch the result. In a field at the corner some troop horses were tied up.

Poor beasts! When we returned 15 of them lay with their heels in the air. The doctors considered the railway too unhealthy, so we struck off across a held. It was heavy going, and we were clinging to the usual bundles of shirts and socks and cigarettes. To add to the difficulty, rain came down in torrents. We reached a communication trench, and Dr. L—— and I fell into this and stumbled along. My field-boots were up to the knees in mud, my skirt was turned up round my waist, my overcoat thick with slush. It was a tiring journey, and we were glad to climb out and cross a held under cover of a straggly hedge. We came on a draggled but cheery officer. He greeted us joyously, and accepted for himself some handkerchiefs, then guided us to what looked like a badly-turfed bank. He clapped his hands, and the bank heaved; large pieces of turf were cautiously pulled aside, and rows of jolly faces appeared.

"What will you have, *monsieur?*"

"Ah, but a clean shirt, *mam'selle*, but a thousand thanks! The English are always kind."

Then another cheery face would peer out like a rabbit from its hole:

"If *mademoiselle* had a pair of socks! . . . Oh, but the English are good!"

And so on till we wore left with empty arms and apologies for the stock giving out and assurances that more would come.

No casualties had occurred—the weather was so bad the Boches were keeping under shelter. So we went back, dirty and muddy, to our hut, where Walton had a hot and steaming lunch to welcome us. Rations included tins of "*plâtre*," a sort of corned beef, and this chopped up and mashed with potatoes formed our usual meal. Then we had bread and coffee—very black and very strong—and washed up for the afternoon. This afternoon we were invited to coffee at 4 p.m. with the doctors of another battalion.

They were celebrating the fact that Dr. Van de W—— had received the Cross of the Legion of Honour. He had carried two wounded gunners to safety, and then returned to a trench just as the Germans reached it to care for a wounded officer. Later on he escaped from the Boches and came back to his work. He was a smart little man, with a keen, alert face, and his comrades had drawn with coal on the walls imaginary and wonderful incidents of his career, closing in reality, and showing the rescue of the gunners and his intrepid return to the trench as the Germans arrived! They had made him a wreath of laurel, which they clapped on his head despite his protests. That morning an orderly had gone ten miles on his bicycle to fetch champagne for the occasion!

We were a merry party—six doctors, a *commandant*, a colonel in a green coat, a stray Englishman who blew in from the storm of wind and rain: and the champagne and biscuits and coffee were passed gaily round. Speeches were made, and the cheery scene was strange indeed. We could hear the guns outside. The little, long stove was white hot. The presence of English girls staggered the Englishman. He was very much taken aback: to him it was an unheard-of adventure!

Then in the midst of our merriment came a loud knocking on the door, and next moment it flew open and a drenched figure stumbled in, dazed and white of face, clinging to a rifle with one hand, and the other hand in its shabby blue sleeve tied up with bloodstained rags. After him came a man carrying a stretcher, and the second stretcher-bearer.

Back went our chairs and coffee cups, and in a moment the hero of the feast was ripping the trouser leg of the moaning figure and we were bandaging the shoulder and hand of the other man. The leg was an ugly sight, and before it was dressed another stretcher was carried in, and a lad with half his head shot off lay at our feet. Outside a lull came in the storm, and as the rain ceased the clouds cleared and a dull red sunset flamed across the sky.

As the ambulance rolled off with its burden of pain Sayer and I stood for a moment to watch the sky. Up came an armoured train— quite near us over the rails we had walked along that morning. It rolled up, cumbersome, quaint and wicked-looking, and came to a standstill a few hundred yards away. Fascinated, we stood watching. From the sides a mass of figures seemed to clamber and rush round, and then boom, boom, and a cloud of smoke melted into the twilight. *Bro . . . oom—broo . . . oom, boom—boom*, growled the angry guns at Dixmude, where the Boches had received the shot.

Bom-bom, spat the train, and *boom—boom*, came the answer. It was an unforgettable thing. Up here alone, far from civilisation, very far from the homes where perhaps our people thought of us, but certainly did not imagine our surroundings—here we were, girls of the twentieth century in this atmosphere of storm and war living what surely few women ever dreamt in their wildest fancies until this war began. This was life! My ears tingled; I breathed in long, deep breaths. Had I spoken, a sort of wild war song would have come from my lips. The Highland blood in me bubbled and frothed; I wanted to run for

257

miles—to race, to climb—action at all costs. And then . . . well, along the came weary, stumbling figures, and most of them carried stretchers or long strange bundles. There was no romance or triumph here, no wild war cry and exaltation—just these men, dirty and muddy and footsore, bringing in their comrades, broken and maimed and moaning . . . or very quiet. . . .

The sunset and the tight between the armoured train and the German guns at Dixmude lost their glamour. War was no romantic heroic this dreary reality of gaping wounds and quivering flesh. These men were far from their homes. They had left their wives and children, all they loved—their lives of comfort and good food and warm firesides; and their rewards were not laurels and the plaudits of a rejoicing and grateful crowd, No, their rewards were shrapnel and torn limbs, hours of pain and misery, mud and cold and wet, and much tossing from place to place; bar they smiled and said "Thank you!" when a painful dressing was finished. These were the men of the Yser—shorn of romance and poetry, pitiful and human and noble beyond all words; heroes indeed, and heroes of the world.

It was late that night when we passed into the darkness to grope our way back to our own post—so dark, that when I slipped and my foot came to rest on the body of the man who did not live to go on in the ambulance the others did not *see* why I was silent, nor why my voice was shaky for a few minutes, nor that my thoughts rested with the poor corpse who lay there alone under a thick blanket.

A diversion occurred that caused much amusement. In our absence my brother had arrived from Calais with the Unic, and we found him, black with mud, mending a tyre in the roadway. His task completed, he came through to wash in the kitchen, and I left him getting off layers of mud into a bucket of warm water. Later he joined us.

"Have you emptied your bucket?" I asked, as I had not heard the heavy outer door open.

"Oh, yes," he replied; "I emptied it down the sink in the kitchen."

A horrid thought came to me.

"There is no sink," I exclaimed, "only the well of drinking water in the corner."

Sure enough it was there the dirty water had gone, and someone even murmured that the coffee that night had a flavour all its own.

We had a hot meal of coffee and bread and syrup, and then we girls drew our straw from the pile thrown in by the orderlies, and covered the floor of the tiny room and folded our tunics to make a cushion for our heads, and got our blankets out, one for each. In the big room the doctors slept on straw also, and in the little kitchen twelve soldiers were snoring and grunting. The guns boomed; the smells from the backyard were overpowering; the cold was horrid; our damp stockings did not keep the straw from pricking our feet; my poisoned finger was throbbing. This was war! And the wounded! Yes, there were wounded—where? Somewhere . . . and this was sleep.

CHAPTER 5

A Day of Odd Jobs

One day in the spring of 1915 Chris and I started off for the front with "Flossie," the little Ford ambulance. It was a perfect day, a cold wind blowing but a blue sky overhead. The road between Calais and Dunkirk flew past; the walls of Gravelines and the narrow winding streets were left behind. Dunkirk itself was gay with *zouaves* in their baggy red trousers. Along by the canal we raced—past ponderous convoys toiling up with their loads. Many a staff car and "*ravitaillement*" wagon met us and sped on their ways. And so to Furnes, no longer the busy centre of activity it had been earlier, but a desolate town with one or two large shell holes in the square. No shops, no *cafés*, except in the side streets—all was quiet and deserted. So we left Furnes, too, behind. Along the straight bare road we whizzed, and now not far off we heard the old familiar booming. We passed the picket at Pervyse, and there drew up to make inquiries.

As we halted we caught sight of two Englishmen pacing slowly along a side path, looking at the rows of damaged houses—the streets of ruin—and on recognising one as Major G——, a familiar figure in Belgian lines, we hailed him. He introduced his companion, Lord Curzon, and on learning our errand they made further inquiry, and let us know that the fighting was in the neighbourhood of Oostvleteren. We ran on past the field with its 300 shell holes that had formed our first landmark in November. Our old "*poste*" at the cross-roads was occupied by strangers, who hailed us with delight, and with them we left a few hundred cigarettes and some socks for the —— Division.

A shell, mistaking its direction, came crashing to earth on the roadway near by, so we hastened our farewells and shot off past the little church that had been bombarded steadily for months. It was still standing, but the troops once quartered in the cottages round about had been withdrawn. The canal bridge, where the morning washing parade was held regularly in December, was deserted. No life seemed to exist in that once busy spot; and the shrapnel whizzing over us in the sky, directed against the railway to our right, was a sign of the times. We slowed up at Lampernisse, and sadness seized us. The church was down. I recalled its friendly tower—the throng of soldiers that had surrounded it, the gay faces of the little blue Belgians that had met one cheerily on every side. Today there was quiet and stillness, and the outer walls of the church were represented by heaps of loose stones. Inside the pillars stood—broken wall, broken altar; fragments of glass and melted lead from the windows that had been. As we watched, the *curé* appeared, sad of face. He came to us simply, and at our few faltering words tears came to his eyes.

"There were 40 wounded inside," he said gently; "we saved all we could." A grave at my feet was churned up—broken bits of wood stuck upright in the earth; a heavy stone monument had turned sideways and lurched forward like a drunken man; and something else lay near, thrown out of the earth to which in happier days the priest had committed it. I shuddered involuntarily. The *curé* asked if we could take one of his remaining parishioners to safety: she was old and bedridden; her cottage was there in the shadow of the church. Shells came daily and at any time one might strike the roof that sheltered her. We took a stretcher up the tiny path, and in at the little door. There on the floor on a mattress lay an old withered woman. We carried her out gently, the *curé* helping. General J—— passed—a brave and kindly man, adored by the soldiers. He remembered us, and approved our action. Then he asked us to lunch with him on our return journey.

We started off slowly and evenly and reached Alveringhem, where the *curé* had told us a convent of nuns took in such old and helpless peasants. Alas! the mother superior refused. Nothing would shake her decision; she would have no more—her hands were full. I looked round the large waiting-room, and begged her to let the poor old thing lie there. But it could not be. So we went on several miles farther, and were directed to a home kept by an Englishwoman for refugees. We sent messengers on every side to find her—unsuccessfully—so we left the old woman in the house in charge of the other refugees, as we could find no one with authority. We left full particulars and departed. We were late, as the difficulty in finding shelter for our charge had been greater than we anticipated.

We lunched off sandwiches *en route*, and explained our non-appearance for lunch at Divisional Headquarters. General J—— was very charming, and gave us tea and invited us to lunch for another day.

We had arranged to dine at an artillery mess at Ramscappelle, and so hurried on there. Things were fairly lively, and after a wonderful dinner we had some music, and then in the darkness went up to the trenches. The rockets and flares were fascinating. Viewed from afar they are strangely remote, but very friendly here, when one crouched down amongst all these gallant men—soldiers and heroes whose country had been torn from them, whose wrongs cry out for vengeance, whose simple response to honour saved the whole of Europe from being overrun by the barbarous Boches.

We made sure the doctors had no cases to dispose of, and returned to the brickyard, where "Flossie" waited patiently. The flares and a pocket flashlight were all the light we had, and we got of! across bumpy roads—in and out of shell holes. Once we nearly had a nasty smash, but that was near Furnes. A convoy of great heavy wagons had been left on the wrong side of the road, and as lights were not permitted and the night very dark Chris was driving slowly and warily—peering into the shadows. She brought "Flossie" to a violent halt, our bonnet touching the first of these unwieldy monsters!

Three days later General J—— sent his motorcyclist to bring us out to lunch. The courtesy was indeed great, as the lad had 50 miles to come, if not more. Unluckily he had a smash, and rode back on the step of our car. He was a type of the modern Belgian youth. Well-bred, clever, with frank, humorous eyes, and the adorable smile of a "*Parisian gamin*," he kept us amused all the way. His comments were racy, and always gallant.

"I am no longer a simple soldier; I am corporal. The general has done that—because of you others, there is no doubt."

And his merry eyes challenged us to disbelieve that a simple soldier would not be good enough. As escort.

"Yes, we are all gay," he would say: "yes, but it is sad too. I am *fiancé* and I have no letter from her—no, not from the day the war broke out, I have written, yes, but she not answer. It is gay the war, *n'est-ce pas, madame?*"

And a little later, with his childish pout: "I have had a letter from my mother. She is in Brussels: she does not find the war gay. She cannot see me and she loves me."

His shrill whistle, prolonged on a certain note, took as past sentries and barricades.

"You see, the Belges are musical. There, hear me whistle like a bird, and say '*Passez! Pasez! Les oiseaux!*'"

The wind was keen and the roads greasy, but Chris sat steady as a rock, her great grey eyes, fixed on the future, her mobile face calm and tranquil. Jean was piqued.

"Look, *mam'selle*, Chris is absorbed. She drives, yes; but she will not listen to our chatter. She has no time to smile then. Oh, these ladies who drive cars!"

Chris (who had danced and shared in peaceful days with the little cyclist) turned her ready smile in his direction, and he forgave.

We arrived at length, at the farmhouse where Divisional Headquarters were. The general was busy, but greeted us warmly. He sent for liqueurs, at the appearance of which Chris edged diplomatically nearer the coal-scuttle. The general produced his mascot, a woolly dog sent by a lady from England. He showed us also his grand chain and Order of Leopold Premier given him for his gallantry at Dixmude. Then we had lunch—and such a luncheon as any London restaurant would have been proud to serve. Suddenly the telephone rang. Taubes were bombarding a village near at hand. Even as the adjutant rang off and reported to the general we heard the engine throbbing overhead. We all ran out to the yard to watch the graceful death-dealing machine circling in the clear sky. Then it flew on and glided out of sight. The general showed me his two horses lying down in a little shed near.

I forgot to mention that before lunch he took us up to his bedroom to wash, and displayed with simple pride the bed he shared with his major and the other bed which two captains occupied. Accommodation was limited! He also produced a bottle of scent for our use!

Then he sent for his car, and with Major —— we set off for the nearest battery. The chauffeur cared not for speed limits, and a wild rush landed us in a very short time at the corner of a field. We walked across this to inspect a battery of small guns. Then we went on, carefully avoiding the wire of a field telephone to an advanced gun position. As we neared what looked like a ridge of trees we saw that these also were cunningly contrived to conceal the guns. This was a new battery of which the officer in charge was very proud. He told us what good work they had done within the last ten days. They had only been sent up then. In another hour he suggested we might judge for ourselves; but General J——did not deem it prudent, so we thanked

WHERE THE HUN HAS PASSED.

WAYSIDE GRAVES.

the officer and the cheery gunners for all the trouble they had taken. Here, too, the dugouts were beautifully finished off—even little panes of glass were let in as windows.

The general then took us to a bridge on the canal where fishing was occasionally indulged in. The doctor who had lunched with us appeared, and with great glee produced a hand-grenade which he flung in the water. The explosion was followed by a geyser-like rising of the water, and then hundreds of dead fishes floated to the surface and were caught in a net and safely landed!

Just then an officer joined us to ask if we could take away from the nearest village four little children and their mother, who was shortly expecting another baby. The village was being bombarded, and the little family were in terror. We gladly acquiesced, and the general took us back in his car; we got *Le Petit Camerade* (our second Ford ambulance) into action and departed, Jean, the motorcyclist, being sent by the general to see us on our way. We collected the poor little mother and her four sturdy little boys, wrapped them well up in scarves and balaclavas, and took them to the English lady's refugees' home. Again, unluckily, we failed to find her. Jean ran round himself to look for her, and at last, after waiting for an hour, we left the little family there and departed.

The relief of the good woman was touching. She was not like the other woman with nine children, a husband, and a pig, whom we tried in vain to rescue. The doctors of a certain division were perturbed by the danger run by the nine children (whose ages were from two to eleven), who had to lie in a damp trench for four hours every day whilst their village was bombarded. After much argument, the woman consented to leave, and we arranged with the Refugee Committee in Calais to take them over, and we sent a big car out to fetch them. However, when it came to the point, the mother refused to leave the pig; all persuasion was useless, and the car took the father and the nine to Calais. Two days later he got permission to take his nine children for a walk; and they never returned. News was heard of them walking back the 50 miles to rejoin their mother and the pig!

Having left the four little fellows waving to us from the doorstep, we retraced the road and arrived at Pervyse. Here we said goodbye to Jean and took the road to Ramscappelle. The sentries at first refused to let us pass, as the road was being shelled, but we were in a hurry, so they yielded. We left the car at one point and took shelter in the ruins of a cottage, but a shell also landed there, knocking one of the shattered walls to pieces, and so we deemed it more prudent to rejoin the "*Petit Camerade*" and race for our lives. A burst of derisive laughter followed us. Unknowingly we had been on the edge of a Belgian trench!

As we neared Ramscappelle a soldier leapt towards us with a warning cry. We heard the cold shriek above our heads that denoted trouble coming; and Chris set her mouth a trifle sternly, rammed her foot on the accelerator, and we were past just as the house staggered towards us and fell, blocking the road behind us. We glanced round; the soldier who had shouted waved reassuringly, and we turned into the old brickyard. A few fresh shells had fallen, and beside the path were two little graves marked with wooden crosses that had not been there last time we passed. We found a suitable place to leave the "*Petit Camerade*" against a wall of bricks piled high. The ground was rough and greasy. We hurried to the cottage where the artillery mess was, and the whizzing and whistling overhead denoted "activity on the front." In fact we ran at top speed up that garden path and hammered on the door. Friendly faces greeted us, and we were soon inside and the table was being laid.

Our hosts got us a jug of cold water and a basin, and we proceeded to wash on a chair in the corner of the room, the commandant and three other officers being interested spectators. Then we sat down to dinner and had soup and fish and meat; and then, ye gods! asparagus and cheese and fruit—a right noble repast. The windows were barred and shuttered, but all around we heard the heavy boom of big guns, the angry screaming of shells. As the meal drew to an end the two telephones in the room got busy. There were, I think, fifteen officers and ourselves, and two of the subalterns were at the receivers:

"Yes, my wife is in England. She is so happy there; she loves the English, and there is no sign of war." The *commandant* was interrupted in his peaceful picture by the sharp voices of the telephonists.

"'*Allo, 'allo, 'allo!* Find the trench major. '*Allo!* What? No, the major, find the major; I would speak with the major. No—the major . .*"

The wild glare of the exasperated man who wanted the major met the equally ferocious stare of the man who held the other wire, and whose voice had all this time been cutting through his.

"'*Allo, 'allo!* Yes, this is the Artillery; yes, he is here. '*Allo!* What? When? At what hour? What? Speak up! *Cré nom de Dieu*, speak clearly! *Pardon, mon Colonel.* Tonight towards eleven hours. Yes, *mon Colonel.* It is understood."

By this time the table talk had risen—something was under discussion . . . Our voices rose; the two telephonists voices rose also. My eyes met Chris's; we could not help laughing—this was like a scene from a pantomime.

"*Sapristi!*" The man who still wanted the major could not forbear longer.

"Silence—I beg of you. Silence. Be quiet, you with that telephone. '*Allo, 'allo!* Find the trench major."

From the other side of the room the other man spoke:

"Be quiet with your own telephone. '*Allo, 'allo!* Yes—yes. Gentlemen—ladies—I pray you be silent. '*Allo!* Yes—*mon Colonel*. Oh, what is then—Lieutenant who?"

And so on! We were asked to write our names in the pocket-books of all our hosts. Then someone said "Music," and in a moment we were all round the piano that had been brought from a shelled farmhouse in our honour. The telephones were still busy, and one young lieutenant got orders to go to the top of a very tall chimney that remained standing "to observe, as there was a certain movement along the front." His comrades mocked him, crisping their fingers, as if climbing hand over hand up the long iron ladders.

"You make a good target, George," one wit said soothingly.

George bade us goodnight, looking annoyed. We heard him in the passage directing his sergeant to go up the chimney and waken him if necessary!

Chris played and sang song after song; every chorus caught up and re-echoed. Then in a lull we heard steps outside and a heavy banging on the shutter, and as we listened a pure tenor voice lilted:

"*Goodbye, Piccadilly,*
Goodbye, Leicester Square;
It's a long, long way to Tipperary,
But my heart's right there."

"De —— de ——!" everyone shouted, and Captain de —— entered, smiling.

"Where have you come from?" we asked, for we had last seen him at Calais.

"My battery is seven miles from here, and they telephoned to me you ladies were here, so behold me!"

We had more songs, and then the Belgian National Anthem. It was a fine and inspiring thing to hear—sung from their hearts by these big, strong men who were offering their lives daily for their king and country, and sung as it was to the tune played by Chris, with her lovely girlish face, and the deep booming of the guns to render it still more effective. I shall never forget it.

Then out in the darkness we groped our way to our car, thinking the day's adventures were ended. Along the sky the rockets and star shells blazed and spluttered, lighting us for the moment, and then leaving the darkness still more oppressive around us. It took much pushing and shoving to get the "*Petit Camerade*" on to the roadway, and our hosts bade us goodbye heartily, though in whispers, as we were very near the "movement along the front."

CHAPTER 6

A Night in Nieuport

It was very dark that night on leaving Ramscappelle as we halted at the "*infirmerie*" at the cross-road to ask if they had anyone to send in. The doctor was out—in the trenches probably—but the orderly reported there were wounded in Nieuport. After a few minutes' discussion we left the car beside the *infirmerie* door, and, laden with the big field haversack, started off on foot. The road was lonely, and we groped our way, crossed the bridge, and held on to the right. We spoke little, for we were tired, and so came along the side of a wood to where another road branched off. We were brought to a quick stop by a high-pitched voice shouting, and discerned a sentinel, his rifle pointed in our direction, his voice agitated. I yelled "*Officiers*," Chris yelled "*Croix Rouge*," and together we shouted at him "Liège," or whatsoever the word was that night. If the wood had been full of Germans they would have heard us; as it was, our good sentinel repeated his challenge, and we hurled the word at his head with all the breath in our bodies, for we liked not that rifle pointed full at us. He hesitated and at last had a brainwave.

"Advance one and give the word," he said, and hand in hand we tiptoed towards him and whispered in his ear the word we had hurled at him from afar. The effect was magical!

"Pass, *mesdemoiselles*—pass; it is cold, is it not? Ah, these roads! I like them not."

"Horrid work for you," we ventured sympathetically, and got the information that he was a volunteer, and did not join the army with the thought of lonely nights at windy cross-roads. It was nervous work; but what would one have, after all? It has to be done; and some day, why some day, the war will end and the German swine be driven from poor little Belgium. A packet of cigarettes won warm gratitude, and we walked on and were soon lost in the darkness.

All this time the sound of big guns and the rush of rockets and flares skyward marked the Line—that wonderful heroic Line! Then we were in a street with a trench all along the canal bank on one side and a row of silent cottages on the other. Here and there a cottage had fallen from its place in the ranks, and its walls and roof lay across the roadway or pushed into a heap roughly. We reached the end and hesitated, for a road went to the right towards the rocket flares; a road went to the left round a corner. We turned leftwards—for we sought the town—and swung round the corner in the darkness into lines of men and rifles. We walked on, wondering a little, but not daring to talk, and suddenly a big figure barred our way and we were challenged. We explained our errand, and an officer appeared. These were the French lines, and he directed us to the English sailors' dressing-station, where, he said, there were wounded. A little sergeant came with us to the corner and put us on our way, and so we walked up the hill one behind the other, for a long line of soldiers was coming towards us single file. They eyed us as we passed, but the darkness veiled us from each other, though I heard one wondering voice say:

"Mother of God! are there women here?"

And one little man twisted his head round and sent after us a soft "Goodnight, *mademoiselle*, God keep you!"

Gradually a wider street lay before us, and we were stopped by a patrol of French marines, who explained our whereabouts and continued on their way.

Houses with gaping wounds in their walls were everywhere—houses with no upper floor. Heaps of loose stones and masonry had to be crossed; in places the streets were almost impassable. The stars had come out now, and there was a pale moon, and we could note our surroundings better.

One street corner I remember well. A large corner house was much broken up. The big lower rooms lay open; the floor above was a mass of stones and furniture—chairs and tables were mixed with remnants of ceiling that had crashed through, and waved protesting legs upwards. We had to pick our way across the roadway, for it was one huge mass of debris. Bits of curtains and carpets were discernible.

Once Chris saved me from walking straight into a cellar: the covering was off, and it must have been a veritable death trap! Once in another cellar we caught a glimpse of a soldier cooking his supper on a small lamp. In one street, where the upper storeys no longer stood and the lower were barred, we heard songs and merriment; and on we walked, till suddenly a great pile stood against the sky. The cathedral, I suppose. Its towers were damaged, and here and there shells had struck it, and we longed to see it by daylight. We walked on and on, but no sign of the dressing-station caught our eye.

At last we stopped. It was about 1 a.m., and an eerie feeling of unreality seemed to encircle us. We had left all buildings behind us for the moment—the last a sort of square or crescent, where every house was empty and deserted. Louder than ever echoed the sounds of battle, and the light of the flares lasted five full minutes. We could see each other's face, and we could hear more and more distinctly the snip of rifles—even, it seemed to us, we could hear the click of the triggers. The pale strange light that was on everything was weird, and we decided to go back and see if we had passed our destination.

I think it was an unspoken relief to us to return towards the houses and the presence of others. It has been an everlasting regret, all the same, that we did not explore just a little farther!

We struck a house with a light showing through the shutters and hammered on the wall, but could get no reply. And at last in a side street we saw a dull red lamp burning over a door and hurried towards it. The door bore a large red cross, so we knocked, but getting no reply, walked in. The first room was empty save for a table and chair; the second had three beds in it, but empty also; then a small room to the right had mattresses on the floor and a broken chair. That was all. A scrap of paper on the wall caught our eyes, and with an electric torch we read enough to know it was a Belgian dressing-station.

We walked on, and at last a French sailor guided us to the corner of a street and pointed to a door. We found there a large inscription that English wounded were to be brought here, and fetched from here when opportunity occurred. We walked in, calling out in English, but never a sound greeted us. We found mattresses and chairs and heaps of straw, and one or two bandages, and a chair much the worse for wear; but that was all, and no wounded nor sign of wounded. So we thoughtfully left a card with our names on the table, wondering who would find it, and if an Englishman found it if he would believe that his countrywomen had really penetrated to such a God-forsaken place at 1 a.m. in the morning.

Our errand had developed into a wild-goose chase, so we retired sadly. Going out of the town we suddenly saw two great black figures emerge so swiftly from the roadway at our sides that we jumped, startled, and hurried on breathing rather hard. Strange to say, a week later one of them was brought to Calais wounded, and recognised Chris as she helped to put him in her ambulance.

"Oh, *mademoiselle*," he cried joyously. "I saw you in Nieuport not long ago!"

But to us that early morning this figure of a *zouave* black with African suns was a sinister one, and for very little we would have taken to our heels and run!

We negotiated the sentinel easily on our return journey, picked up the "*Petit Camerade*," and got in. I lay inside on the wooden floor with my head on a biscuit tin, and knew nothing more until Chris pulled me out in the hospital yard at Calais—4.30 a.m.

"You've slept peacefully all the way," she said cheerily. "Oh, but it's cold"; and not a sign of fatigue nor strain did she display.

So ended our night in Nieuport—a city of death and desolation, one of the many that cry to God for vengeance on the Boches.

CHAPTER 7

An English Billet

Boulogne Quai was busy. Englishmen, Frenchmen, Belgians were running round, each in their own way typical of their nation. Nell drew "Unity" to a halt between a French and an English car, and proceeded to change a tyre. The French driver protested it was a hard job for a woman—the English were courageous—an Englishwoman, to change a heavy tyre like that! The English driver strolled languidly round the car, stood for an instant watching, sauntered slowly back to his own 'bus, strolled back to ours, levers in hand, and still in unbroken silence took tyre and nuts and operations generally out of Nell's capable hands. Only when the new tyre was on did he speak.

"That'll do, I'm thinkin'," he remarked wisely, and strolled off again.

Down at the quaiside a cheery, slightly rotund personage, clean-shaven and in mufti, turned to me.

"Is that your car over there—Unic Ambulance?"

I replied truthfully.

"Who are you attached to?" he asked—"English Red Cross?"

"Why do you ask?" I replied, "because I hail from the Scottish hills."

"You've got no number on the car," he returned; "you must have a number now."

"Really," I said superciliously. "In ——, where we are stationed, we don't use numbers; haven't done since October."

His eyes twinkled, and he solemnly assured me that we were then exempt from having numbers. Someone told me later he was the chief detective, or something of the sort, and a power in Boulogne. However, we always grin when we meet.

The leave-boat arrived meanwhile, and the brother with it. So we sailed off merrily towards that Mecca of the British Expeditionary Force—G.H.Q. It would be an indiscretion to name it as a town, because everyone knows, even the people in England. The Germans knew before the B.E.F.; they always do. A Canadian told me the other day how he and his comrades left England in severe ignorance of their destination. Even when they started to march from railhead to their little spot in the trenches they were in blissful ignorance, and as they "took over" and were busy settling in mud and dugouts, still not knowing where they were, a cheery Teuton from the trench opposite shouted across in the darkness:

"Shut up, you Canadians; we know you're there!"

However, that is by the way.

Nell and a gallant Scots Grey were in front, my brother and I sat behind, our legs dangling on the tailboard. We had lots to talk of—for in war-time one does not see much of one's relatives. The long hills, the wide stretches of country, the fascination of the vast views, held us too; and then the darkness came, slowly at first with a mellow golden sunset, and then—rain. Oh, that rain!—but we did not heed it much. It was an unknown road to Nell; once we overshot it and had to return, but at last we came to G.H.Q. and drew up before the hotel in the big square. The brother was proud of us, but I think his Scots Grey friend was bashful. They tried to get a sitting-room, but that was impossible, and they had to face the roomful of khaki-clad men with us, who, women-like, were hugely enjoying their embarrassment and pretending to be unconscious of it.

For ladies, even ladies who are military, are not supposed to penetrate to G.H.Q. We had a much-needed meal and started off again. This time the way was hard to find, and the rain and darkness increased. But we swung on past convoys, through sleeping villages, enjoying the astonishment of sentries at the vision of women soldiers as we swept off into the night. At last we struck Hazebrouck, and the brother wanted to send us back from there, but we wouldn't go.

We left the Scots Grey and his bags, and the brother and I got in front with Nell, and off we went again. We stumbled on an A.S.C. depot and took some petrol on board. The two sentries were Scots, and vastly overcome at hearing their own tongue spoken by a woman in the heart of that little French village. On again through a still and quiet town, devoted to staff—a town where, I have heard men say, no Englishwomen have been since the war (but Nell and I knew better). At last we reached *the* village, where the billets were, and the brother ushered us in proudly.

It was a little cottage—on one side a sitting-room, on the other a kitchen. Three mattresses were on the floor, with sleeping bags and pyjamas spread out; a door led into another room, the adjutant's, who had the privilege of a room to himself. Books, papers, chocolate boxes (empty, I regret to say) were strewn about; pipes, cigarettes, and a gorgeous English home-made cake. The orderly appeared and got us some cocoa, and we wandered out to see the brother's horses. They were stabled at the back, and very "comfy" they looked. The man who was on guard was grateful for the boxes of "Gold Flake" we showered on him, and we left lots for further distribution.

Then we had cocoa, and the brother was very worried about us going back in the darkness and rain, but we wanted to catch a boat at Calais next day. However, he sent his man with two horses to wait for him at a certain spot, and he was to come with us so far to show us the way. We ran up the road, past the little church, past an open window where floods of light streamed through (all the village was in darkness), and at a table with lamps—and, ye gods! a yellow silk lamp shade—we saw the brother's colonel, who had arrived by the same boat, having a merry meal with three French officers. The brother stopped us farther along outside a cottage and crept up the garden path followed closely by me.

He tapped on a shuttered window and called softly: "Hallo, Harry, are you asleep?"

And I, seized with the demon of mischief, laughed: "Hallo, Harry, are you asleep?"

A gasp of astonishment followed my voice, and "Harry" flung back the shutters and appeared blinking, still in wonderful pyjamas. He was delighted to see the brother and more delighted to see me—utter stranger as I was—and hastily appeared in a British warm, etc., to be formally introduced. His delight knew no bounds. It was months since he had spoken to Englishwomen, and he offered to go and sleep with the brother if we would stay till morning and have his room. But we were firm, and out in the road were chatting gaily. "Unity" was ready to start; a baby canal was on one side of the road. The brother and Harry were in the roadway, Nell on the box, and I frivolling with the headlights. Suddenly the brother shouted, seized a flashlight, and sprang to the rear of the car waving it. Then I saw him leap backwards, throw up his hands, and disappear into the baby canal.

Harry's shout of "Jump for your lives!" Nell's sudden rush—a crash—and the sudden swerve of the Unic towards me were all simultaneous, and I leapt backward—down, down into slimy, cold, horrible water. I fumbled wildly in the air; one thought alone dominated me—"I had new boots on." Why in that moment they gripped my whole mind I cannot tell. I thought for a moment I would drown. Harry's strong hands seized mine and pulled me up to firm ground, and all my gratitude said was "My new boots will be ruined." Then my senses steadied down. "Where is ——?" I shouted, for I remembered vividly his shout and the glimpse of that great car crashing into us; but my brother was beside me, so was Nell; and Harry, too, appeared.

Then a tall man in khaki hastened towards us from the other car.

"Much damage, you fellows?" he called, and I replied there seemed to be a good deal. I felt rather than saw the start of surprise, and then his eyes peered into my face as he saluted.

"I beg your pardon, I did not expect to find a lady!"

Still suffering from the shock, he walked backwards a step looking at the car, and my warning cry came too late; he disappeared over the same kilometre stone as I had and *sat* down in the water, his arms and legs waving in the air for one ludicrous moment.

"It is all right; no, I am not wet," he declared, like the sportsman he was, and we pushed old "Unity" along to a corner, and they set to work to repair her. The chauffeur of the other car was annoyed with life, and he promptly tried to drive his car on a bit; but the steering gear was smashed, and amid our howls of laughter he toppled over into a ditch, and there his car hung on one wheel—a pathetically droll object.

It was clear we could not push on over unknown country with a damaged car, so the brother set off on foot to recall his horses. The three officers (French interpreters) who had run us down were already hammering and struggling with our engine in their shirt sleeves, despite the rain. They were very gallant gentlemen, and at last we were persuaded to leave them to their task and go with Harry to his billet. Stretchers from the car made beds for Harry and the brother on the kitchen floor, whilst Nell and I were to have his room. I got off my wet boots and dried my feet at the stove, and we found some coffee and began to grind it. Then Harry's "landlady" appeared—a dear old soul, who proceeded to boil water and get us coffee and rolls and butter, though it was now 2.30 a.m. She stoutly refused to go to bed. It appears she had been an interested spectator of the smash and subsequent events, and I rather fancy she thought we ought to be chaperoned!

We had a merry meal, and a strange experience it was, for I suppose few, if any, Englishwomen have passed that way since war started and spent a night billeted in the English lines. We went to bed soon after 3, and slept peacefully till 6, when we found more coffee and rolls and eggs all ready for us. The French interpreter had returned to see the car start, and as he and Harry gathered a few flowers for us and the brother's orderly cleaned our boots we could hear the heavy booming of the guns in the distance. The sun was shining and spring was in the air: a passing regiment of English Tommies cheered us lustily; they broke their lines, terribly craning their necks to see their countrywomen. Dear lads! I suppose they had not seen one for months. We got aboard, and the interpreter turned the handle.

Harry shook our hands and bade us "*au revoir*" reluctantly. We promised to return that day week and stay a day. (We did, but only to find empty billets and the regiment gone to Ypres!) As for the brother, he stood there in the sunlight, big and strong and happy; and my heart was heavy despite the prospect of seeing him in a week. Was he, too, troubled with foreboding? I know not. For a moment he took my hands in his as we said farewell. There were gay and cheery greetings. The spring of life and hope and love seemed very full that morning, and my eyes kept turning to the big brother in the sunlight, straight and tall and fit. Was it a warning, that weight at my heart?—a knowledge that never again would I see him standing so, the sun's rays on his dark eyes and cheery smile.

Ah me! It was only a month later, within 30 miles of that sunny spot, that I knelt in silent agony by his side as he too passed into the Great Beyond!

CHAPTER 8

The Sentry and Paris in Wartime

The night was dark and chilly. All that long, rainy Sunday we had laboured over tyres by the roadside, a tiny *estaminet* providing us at length with hot coffee. Then on again into the little country town, where no amount of inquiries could produce a garage. True, there were signboards relating to automobiles on two doorways, there was a hotel that announced "Essence" and "Garage"; but everywhere, it was told us sadly, the war had taken the men and the cars; tyres were no longer in stock—not even a boy to repair. For another three hours we struggled with an inner tube of which the valve leaked, and all round us were inner tubes in various stages of senile decay, and in my heart I cursed my folly in having started with fewer than a dozen spares! But then, could one have foreseen three bursts and a wretched puncture? I decided it was unwise to indulge in Sunday travelling.

However, at last a kindly old Frenchman and his daughter came to our aid—took me with them to see their tyres and supplied us with an inner tube that did not leak, supplied me with a cup of English tea, bread, butter and jam. I felt so greedy when I returned to poor Nell, who had been struggling on with her punctures. At last we were off; the large and rather unpleasant crowd were pushed back sufficiently to let us through, and we left the village behind cheerfully. "Unity" ran like a bird, responding generously to Nell's light, sure touch. The sun set in a grey haze and the darkness descended. We ran on: kilometres flew past gaily; adventure and the song of the road was in our souls. Then we came to a barrier.

A waving lantern warned us to stop; two little blue figures shambled alongside, and I handed over the magic pink paper that was "*Open Sesame*" to towns in the war zone that one refers to with a delicious thrill as "Somewhere in France." But what was this? The signature and

278

seal we held in reverence were not known to the little "*piou-piou.*" The one who held the *laissez-passer* became voluble.

"*Pas français—des femmes—tres louches,*" were remarks that fell on our astonished ears. Indignantly—for was not the standing of my country involved?—I announced "that an English military pass was good everywhere."

"*Non, non,*" screamed our little ally; "this is France—this is not a French pass."

I turned "dour" and my remarks impressed the second sentry, who urged his comrade to let us pass. The comrade was annoyed, hesitated, and walked round our car. Then came a howl of derisive delight:

"Where is your number? You have no number! Fetch the corporal of the guard—you who would let pass these strange women."

"We do not use numbers in ——"said I firmly; "we have many cars and we have no number—no, not one, except that we keep inside the bonnet. *Regardez.*"

He found the number on the engine and nearly dropped a match inside.

"You stay here," he shouted excitedly. "Your papers are not in order; you have no number; it is night, and you are women; we shall see . . . . Go, Jacques, fetch the corporal—at once, I tell you. Ah! there are spies in France."

These last remarks were hurled at us loudly, to impress the little crowd that had gathered from nowhere. Sentry 2 hurried off to fetch his corporal. Nell and I pulled out our large khaki handkerchiefs and pretended to dry imaginary tears, and laughed. Alas! our little "*piou-piou's*" fury increased. He pulled a cartridge with a malignant gesture from his pouch; he ostentatiously inserted it in his rifle, and he glared at us malevolently.

"If you advance one step, if you retire one step," he shouted, sweeping his free arm towards heaven with a great and dramatic movement, "*I will shoot!*"

His sweeping hand came down heavily on the bonnet of the car, and alas! the radiator was boiling. A yell of pain ended his patriotic speech, and he almost overbalanced with the shock. The loud laughter of the crowd did not appease him.

"You tell me what wrong. You come for supper now. I speak English. He keep you here all night. He silly little man," said a cheery and sympathetic voice.

A woman broke through the crowd.

279

"I speak all English—dressmaker in London, me. I like English people."

She proudly carried on a conversation with us, and triumphantly translated to the crowd.

"This man is a fool," I told her; "he has been drinking, and we have an English military pass, signed by a great English general. Oh, but the silly man will be punished!"

The crowd began to advise him to let the car pass; then the corporal arrived. He accepted my explanation about the number, but not, alas! the English seal we had with much pains procured and with great pride possessed!

However, having for long formed the habit of carrying multitudinous papers about with me, I managed to find a very ancient pass issued by a certain embassy begging everyone to treat me and my car with kindness! This paper, long despised and rejected near the front, was seized on with delight by the corporal, who, alas! noted the discrepancy the issue of one and the other I had changed my name—in fact, I faltered, I had married. To me the naked truth sounded a lame explanation of a suspicious fact, but to my infinite relief the corporal chortled with joy.

"Pass, *Mesdemoiselles*" (*had* he believed the explanation?); "let these ladies pass, you ——" and reluctantly, fiercely, the little sentry removed himself from between our headlights. Muttering, growling, he stood to one side to let us through the little town. The crowd sent a joyous "*Bon voyage*" after us, and our cheery little friend, the dressmaker from London, could be heard far behind us relating to the corporal her conversation with the English miss—those strange English, whose women tour 300 miles of France in war time alone and unafraid. I have often wondered if the little sentry remembered to extract his cartridge before it did any harm.

We pressed on in the darkness along the great white roads; a moon was rising slowly, and soon the whole way lay bathed in silver light. It was cold, intensely cold, but "Unity's" engine was running well, and the night air was soothing. Our mission had been satisfactorily accomplished, and we were at peace with all the world.

The hours and the kilometres passed rapidly. Long, straight roads and stretches of fields gave place to towns, and a glimpse of the silver river and steep banks and woods around it. We arrived at Etampes late, indeed after midnight, and a friendly porter at the station suggested a hotel. We rang up the good woman, left "Unity" in the garage, and got to bed, tired, indeed, but happy. Next morning we were up betimes, and our bill was the smallest I have ever settled, owing to the dear lady of the hotel classing us as chauffeurs and showing her appreciation of our work by sparing our pockets. So on we ran this time with a blue sky and a life-giving sun overhead, winding along the river bank, loitering to admire the views, and at length through the great woods, beautiful in their solitude. What a lovely road that is from Tours to Paris; and what a happy life must be the life of a motor tramp! The approach to Paris on this early spring day seems now to memory's eye a *vista* of blossom—orchards on every side, the shimmer of snow across them, and the fresh greens of spring. The painful process of navigating miles of rough *pavé* was atoned for by the glimpse of woods and moors and river, and at length Paris herself—Paris in war time!

At first there seemed little to indicate the war. To our eyes, so long accustomed to uniforms and small shops and tents and huts, this world of wonderful shop windows and daintily-dressed women and busy scenes of traffic was novel and thrilling. But very soon we picked out the black frocks, the crepe veils, the limping soldiers, the hospitals, the subdued sorrow that seemed to hover over the city.

The crowd seemed to find us of as much interest as we found them. We found the offices we had to report at, and then ran out to Neuilly to the American Hospital. What a wonderfully organised place it is! Rows of immaculate motor cars in the courtyard, with lamps that glistened in the sunlight, burnished brass and smoothly painted bodies. Poor "Unity" jibbed self-consciously as she was drawn up to her place in the ranks; but "Unity's" dull coat and unpolished brass hid a stout heart that never failed in difficulty or danger—I, at least, was proud of her.

Inside were luxurious wards, white-clad, clever-looking doctors, beautiful women in white garments that made our weather-beaten khaki look dull and dirty. They received us most kindly and gave us a kindly send-off. Having an hour and a half to spare, we could not resist memories of Rumpelmeyers, and, despite our khaki uniforms, we were soon rejoicing over chocolate and chestnut cakes. Near us at a small table two ladies in beautifully-cut clothes talked of us and smiled in our direction, and at length one came over and said to us cordially:

"I must tell you how we admire you and your work. If I were twenty years younger I would come with you myself."

Dear, kindly Paris, roused from light-hearted frivolity; what a cheery break our little visit made!

We left Paris late in the afternoon, and were hung up with tyre trouble again and again, until, indeed, we reached our next break at 2 a.m. and found the chief hotels full and closed up. However, we managed to get shelter, and next morning took a pitiful tale to the friendly great ones near by, and borrowed money to pay our bill and speed us on our way—for my last forty *francs* had gone to buy a new inner tube at I that morning in a tiny town. And so once more to Calais, where we were greeted with new orders that our cars must be numbered henceforth.

To show our independence, I promptly submitted a list of numbers which began with F.A.N.Y. I and ended (then) with F.A.N.Y. 7. To my exceeding joy the numbers and lettering were accepted, and from that day the French sentries dubbed us the FANYS, as on the approach of a car they at once caught sight of the number and with their ready smiles exclaimed "Pass, Fany."

CHAPTER 9

Life at Ruchard

Ruchard! Does the name bring to your mind anything at all? Have you, perchance, in time of peace drifted through Tours and Azay, Angy and Amboise? Do the old historical *châteaux* of France spring up before your mind's eye, with their stately terraces and fertile gardens—their charm and grace of a long-vanished race of courtiers? In summer there are few valleys so smiling and so prosperous; in winter few places so bleak and damp and bare. And in the centre, tucked away, lies Ruchard—a vast plain, now, of huts and tents; but when first I saw it the huts were few and the tents many, and mud was everywhere.

Here, then, is the home of thousands of soldiers. I cannot, for obvious reasons, deal in figures; but we are concerned with only 700, and these are convalescents. To them the F.A.N.Y.'s have brought comfort and comradeship and an atmosphere of home for which the lonely little Belgian soldiers are intensely grateful. In April, then, of 1915 I paid my first visit to the camp, and returned from it sad of heart for the want of comfort and the monotony of life for these brave fellows. Many things intervened, and it was August before I returned. Chris drove us down in "*Le Petit Camerade*"—the good little Ford that has done so much good work. And with us went Cole Hamilton—ready for the pioneer job in front of her.

The journey was not without its amusements—*and* its trials. "*Le Petit Camerade*" started by bursting a tyre before we reached Boulogne. That was soon remedied.

The day was intensely hot, the road was long and gritty, and one tyre after another burst joyously, and soon even the two spares had gone the way of the others. Chris smiled through it all—imperturbable. I chafed and fumed, and was intensely disagreeable. And so, instead of having afternoon tea at Rouen, we were yet 12 kilometres from

RESTING BY THE WAYSIDE.

THE FIRST SOLDIERS CANTEEN IN THE BELGIAN ARMY.
RUCHARD, 1915.

that stately town at something to 11 at night. And not all the coaxing in the world would make those tyres and tubes behave. (It was more than tiresome.) Our supper was coffee and eggs in a wayside *estaminet*, and the good woman tried her best to make us partake of tinned tripe. And at length, with the sacking that contained our brand-new tent tied round the wheel with the ropes cut from that same brand new tent, we rumbled and bumped into Rouen towards midnight. All garages were closed save one, for so the French help to make munitions, and a grand thing it is that every garage becomes by night a factory of munitions.

Into the one garage we gained admittance, to find the *concierge* screaming like one possessed, and an officer—whose nationality shall remain a secret—trying to light his lamps with unsteady gait and a cheery confidence in his powers of speech. The *concierge* and the officer were quarrelling (over national customs perhaps), and the officer demanding paraffin wildly, got it (only it was petrol), and on applying his match up went his two headlights in a blaze.

At this juncture three Red Cross men offered me a seat in their car as far as the Supplies Depot, On the way they sighted a baby Peugeot racing along.

"That's the man you want," they said, and gave chase.

At the barrier a temporary check brought us level. I was hoisted unceremoniously beside the pilot of the Peugeot, and the Red Cross car sped into the darkness and vanished.

When I had recovered my breath I looked at my companion. He was young, immaculately clad in the usual khaki and Sam-Browne, and his face was quite expressionless. In fact he had the air of a man to whom such a trivial incident as the sudden shooting of a lone damsel into his car in the streets of Rouen at dead of night was quite unremarkable.

"Can I do anything for you?" he asked, without the shadow of a smile, but in a polite, friendly way.

"Yes," I answered frankly. "I want two Ford tyres and two inner tubes, and I want them tonight."

He slowed down his car, turned neatly on one wheel, and talked of general matters. So small is the world that he knew intimately friends whom I had visited in New Zealand!

"Here's our place!" He hooted at two great gates, but no reply was vouchsafed. Then he hammered on the doors, and then to my horror he scrambled up those great gates and vanished over the top. I sat in the car waiting for a shot to break the stillness, and for myself to be arrested as a spy. But the great gates creaked back. My pilot took the wheel once more, and we went into a great yard, where all was darkness and silence and long covered buildings. We drew up noisily, and a figure appeared halfway down the yard.

"Halt! Who goes there?" came a voice faltering with surprise.

And then . . . Well, the sentry hadn't much show, and I learnt the correct way to call the guard over the coals if you break into their precincts like a thief at dead of night. A sleepy corporal wandered through stacks and stacks of tyres of all sizes and makes, and at length produced what was wanted. Oh, joyous moment! The British Army is never to be found lacking in time of need.

But alas! Sleepy as was the corporal, and sympathetic for my plight, he had orders to accept only *one* signature for those tyres. My pilot proved himself a true comrade. He put me back in the car, took the wheel, and was off like a flash past barriers and pickets, and drew up in front of a great gloomy *château* on a lonely country road. This was true adventure. I chuckled to myself at the faces of the dear people at home could they see me now! Of a sudden lights flashed at all the windows; pyjama-clad figures were silhouetted; anxious voices asked what the something, something all the row was. An awful silence followed. The figures withdrew hastily; the announcement that there was a lady in the car quite overwhelmed them. In ten minutes the one possible signature was in our possession, and in half an hour the tyres and inner tubes were also in our possession and we were on our way to the garage.

A weary Chris and a weary subaltern who had stayed to offer his services were tinkering with the car. Cole Hamilton slumbered at odd moments in the seat of the landaulet. My pilot tackled the job, and after much trouble got a tube on and pinched it. What a time! He got on a new tube and a stiff new tyre at last. Cole Hamilton saved our lives and sobered the *concierge* by making Bovril on a Tommy's cooker. The final triumph was achieved when our kindly pilot took a long iron pole from the floor to hammer the new tyre in its place, tools being hard to obtain as the *concierge* was drunk. It was nearly 4 a.m. as we passed from the garage into the cold night air and made for Vendôme.

We reached Ruchard at mid-day—200 kilometres—having stopped for an hour and a half for breakfast and an hour's sleep. We reported at camp duly and fixed our appointment with the general.

Ruchard in summer, with the sun streaming over everything, is alluring. The formalities at camp settled, we were taken by the colonel to General P—— at Tours. He was courtly and kindly to a degree; his words of gratitude were eloquent, and he did not stop at words. The expenses of building a hut had weighed heavily on our minds. He gave us generously the use of two large stone huts, and ordered the dividing wall to be knocked down. And so we got our barrack.

The weeks that followed saw the barrack transformed. Tables and chairs, a large counter, a small dining-room for the staff, a kitchen with a range and a big boiler of hot water, a store-room—all these were built by the soldiers under Cole Hamilton's supervision. Then the interned men, or "*compagnie spéciale*" painted the whitewashed walls with the arms of Belgium and the Allies, and over the door painted largely the badge of the F.A.N.Y. Corps. Posters of shipping companies, advertisements that were artistic, went up as pictures; casement curtains finished off the windows; and now the stage erected by the men themselves has transformed the bare barrack into a home. The piano we pay for—12 *francs* a month; and what a big 12 *francs'* worth of happiness is ensured! The men get up concerts and acts, and draw their own programmes and posters.

Chris taught them English; one of her classes held five professors, now soldiers! How they love it all, these men! And it warms one's heart to stand at the counter pouring out tea and coffee, giving them cake and chocolate, hearing their stories, listening to the experiences they have undergone, admiring the pictures of their wives and babies. Then they love games—bagatelle, draughts, cards, chess, dominoes; and how they love to have a game with an "English miss"—a "Fany." And after midday dinner is over in camp they go out and play rounders or hockey and forget their sorrows and their exile.

All afternoon the room is crowded; then it is cleared for an hour and crowded again in the evening. Twice a week the mad and epileptic come, and how they enjoy themselves! They play at cards, and one man stakes "one million *francs*," "two million," "ten million"; and they palm cards and hide them under the table and cheat frankly and gaily and happily. They sing, too—poor madmen whose voices once drew thousands to listen. One poor lad broke into violence, and was sent "to be cured" to a neighbouring asylum. We heard after his return that he was tied with his hands above his head for *four hours* under a cold *douche*. And that was the cure!

There are huts close by for consumptives, who may not use the canteen, but they are visited by Nurse Lovell, who cares for them with the utmost devotion, which they repay tenfold! Such is Ruchard.

The work is hard and the comforts few, but the workers give their services cheerily, and do not think of themselves. Miss Crockett must miss her Australian sunshine in the long dreary days of winter, but she stays on undaunted. Miss Cole Hamilton directed it all—led it through the difficulties of the start; Chris cheered them all and taught them and sang to them, and all the staff have done their share; and it is no small thing to bring sunshine into the lives of hundreds of gallant soldiers—not only sunshine, but strength; and that is proved by the utter lack of crime, drunkenness, etc., since the F.A.N.Y. Canteen opened.

In closing, I may say that, whatever experiences people may have, the F.A.N.Y.'s have always met with respect and gratitude from all soldiers, Belgian and British and French. Their first year's work was chiefly amongst Belgians. They had Belgians as patients in hospital at Lamark, as orderlies, as comrades at the front, and as friends at Ruchard, and everywhere they have found intense gratitude from the men themselves—an appreciation of their services that has encouraged them to continue in giving them, a childlike confidence in their power to help, and a warm admiration for the trifling sacrifices of home-life and comforts that such work has entailed.

Perhaps the future generations of Belgian girls will receive broader and finer training in consequence. Certainly the chivalry of all our soldiers has been tested and proved over and over again. In that lonely world of men, where few women were found in the beginning, the F.A.N.Y.'s were as safe as in their own homes. Courtesy and consideration were the chief characteristics of the Belgian soldiers—brave and gay as they are, simple in their tastes, and simple in their pleasures. They saw with wonder how women could work, and they surrounded women henceforth with respectful devotion.

May little Belgium soon come into her own, and her people be reunited and restored to their hearths and homes where that is possible. They are plucky and uncomplaining, and deserve a great reward.

CHAPTER 10

Oddments and the End

The F.A.N.Y.'s have always prided themselves on their versatility. Among ambulance work, canteens and hospital, they still had time and place for a motor kitchen and a motor bath.

The motor kitchen first, as it came to Calais in February, 1915, and with its auburn-haired owner and pilot. It did work at the station, it went to distant troops with coffee and soup, and then one day its great adventure came. That was quite an ordinary day in May when a Belgian officer and a member of the British Intelligence Staff called to ask for the loan of the motor kitchen. It was 3 o'clock when they stated the case—that a certain Belgian battery attached to an English division would be grateful to have the kitchen with them to cook for the men. At 6 o'clock the kitchen was filled with provender, a tent on the roof; petrol and paraffin inside; Betty and Tommy on the box, with a sergeant sent by the battery to guide them. I saw them off with envy in my heart—and triumph; for here at last prejudices had been swept aside—the battery was on its way to the firing line.

It is not for me to tell fully that tale of gallantry, but at least the bare facts have been told me. The first three or four days were spent in tiny villages, and billets were found for Betty and Tommy. (This is not improper or even romantic—Tommy is a F.A.N.Y., therefore a girl.) Then—height of desire—the battery came along the rough shell-shattered road to Ypres, and through Ypres and beyond Ypres. Here was congestion of convoys and troops; but the driver never failed, nor did the gallant little Ford. Along a road rough and almost impassable the kitchen advanced, and when the battery settled for the night the two F.A.N.Y.'s, after mess, turned into rest in an ancient barn.

The booming of the guns all round lulled them to sleep—their last thoughts were of the struggle going on three miles from them. . .

. At 3 in the morning they woke to a strange, sickly smell, and wondered if the barn was on fire; then they were called, and an orderly brought them their gas masks, which were being issued to the whole battery. This, then, explained the smell, and the sick feeling that came over them. They got out into the air—no longer fresh, alas! From the direction of the trenches men were coming—weary, staggering figures—first one or two, and then a little group of five, of which the two outside figures lurched against and seemingly supported the other three; and suddenly two of them rolled over and lay on the road, gasping, spluttering, sick unto death, with grey-green faces, and eyes which mirrored the horrors of hell.

Then Betty and Tommy started to work. Man after man was helped into the barn—pulled to his feet, steadied down the road—and hot strong coffee was forced down their throats. Two Canadians had lost their masks, and the two girls handed them theirs, and soaked wads of cotton wool in soda, and tied that across their own faces. Came two men helped by comrades, themselves scarcely able to walk, and these two would yield to no treatment. The Canadian medical officer came, shrugged a sorrowful shoulder, and passed on; but the F.A.N.Y.'s blood was up. They made coffee blacker and hotter than ever coffee was made before, they forced it down the throats of the two whose lives seemed ended, and when the Canadian doctor returned his looks were more eloquent than his curt words of commendation.

That day, indeed, the kitchen justified itself, and two lives were saved for England. Then the wounded and the gassed had to be carried to a *château* half a mile down the road; and that half-mile of roadway was under fire. But Tommy, the F.A.N.Y. lance-corporal, and Betty, the chauffeur, directed the stretcher-bearers as calmly as in the hospital yard at Calais, and the barn was cleared. One fact impressed them, and that was that the men with South African ribbons held to their rifles as long as the power to stand remained in them—a small thing and yet significant.

And what was the end of this story? Well—rumours grew round it as rumours will, but it was a plain, bald ending. The British powers that were awoke amazed to the fact that two girls were in the ranks. The other fact that they bore themselves as men was of no avail—nor even that in consequence two men still lived whose breath had gone from their bodies; and so an officer came with courteous but strict injunctions to escort them to G.H.Q., and at G.H.Q. a bland and genial personage interviewed them and blandly and genially suggested that the hospital at Calais was healthier than the trenches near Ypres—and that was all.

Now for the bath. A certain Scottish and enterprising firm—the same that produced the Unic in seven days as a complete motor ambulance because it was essential—invented a bath-house fitted with large tanks to contain and boil water, and ten collapsible full-length canvas baths, and a disinfecting press to hold clothing. This bath-house they put on a motor chassis, and made taps and fitted piping, and surrounded the whole with awning that could be furled up on the outside of the bath when not in use. This, then, was a motor bath-house destined to supply baths for luckless soldiers who were not near bathing establishments. This ingenious and intricate affair was shown me by the director of the firm, and alas! it was going to the Director-General of Medical Services.

I was promised the refusal of the next one built, and wondered hopefully where the funds would come from. Then two energetic and enterprising sisters blew in at the hospital on their way from Paris to England, joined the F.A.N.Y.'s, and when they returned from England brought the bath with them. Then the bath and red tape made each other's acquaintance; but after all red tape is like barbed wire entanglements—if you can't cut it, get round it. And the bath got round. In after years, perchance, grandchildren of this generation may hear from the lips of veterans of the Great War how once upon a time were many men in khaki who had to go for long weeks without baths, until one day came two maidens attired in khaki and with them a large unwieldy-looking monster; and of how ten baths were laid out in neat rows and awnings unfurled and 250 men in a day spent fifteen minutes each in a bath . . . . and how by this means the troops refreshed themselves. And these maidens belonged to a strange corps called F.A.N.Y.'s, who seemed to get just where they were most wanted at the right moment. And not only British, but Belgian soldiers can tell this tale.

There have been other side-tracks also. The sudden arrival of two divisions from the front at a station in Northern France was coped with by the F.A.N.Y.'s, who carried on a day and night canteen and a full hospital with one staff, which required four-hour shifts for the girls.

Then another not unimportant task has been giving concerts to the men in the various camps, and highly appreciated such concerts are. Then, too, the chaplains have again and again been thankful to have a F.A.N.Y. play for the Sunday services, and perhaps sing a sacred solo at the end; and one *padre* told me his congregations were doubled in every camp after this innovation was effected.

Now, after a year's probation, the F.A.N.Y.'s are within sight of their goal,—pioneers of women's work—and a fitting ending to this volume comes with the tale of the F.A.N.Y. Convoy. As long ago as November, 1914, a certain distinguished surgeon-general at G.H.Q. courteously dismissed the idea of the F.A.N.Y.'s driving motor ambulances for the British Army. He explained regretfully that we were not yet attached to the R.A.M.C. . . . It was impossible. I grinned cheerfully and as a parting shot announced:

"We'll do it yet; wait and see."

And he smilingly replied:

"I'll back you to win hands down, so it's *au revoir.*"

In July, 1915, I wrote to the War Office on behalf of the F.A.N.Y.'s and offered a motor-ambulance convoy for Calais or any base which they might suggest. The answer to this was in the negative. "It was not considered practical."

Three or four months later my "sister-office" and I paid a flying visit to G.H.Q. and reminded our friend there of his "*au revoir*"; thence we hurried to two other "Somewheres" in France, pressing the possibilities of a woman's convoy, and at last, with a helping (and very helpful) shove from a place officially designated I.G.C.H.Q. (which he who runs may read), the F.A.N.Y. Corps was accepted for service with the British Army. On New Year's Day, 1916, a convoy of motor ambulance and motor lorries, drivers, orderlies, and cooks—all women—started work in France.

Their work is strenuous and of real service. Each girl driver keeps her car in running order; she turns out in the morning and cleans and oils her car. When the barges come down the motor ambulances are there drawn up in a straight line, each girl standing to attention beside each car. The wounded are loaded in: the driver starts off slowly and carefully through the streets, and delivers her load at the hospital indicated. Then, as need may be, she may return for other loads, or be sent on an "isolation" job—that is to say, she drives to a camp some miles out to fetch in a case of fracture or other casualty. Then she may have to stand to and drive loads of wounded from the hospital to the hospital-boats; and two or three times a week she has to take "loads" of convalescents to a neighbouring base some 20 miles away.

This is the first convoy of women, but already it is not the last.

Here is scope for hundreds of women, for this work can quite well be given to women to do. There is no danger and no untoward physical strain. If every convoy in base towns was "manned" by women, then all the men at present so employed could be given the rougher work further afield that women perhaps cannot undertake. Already, within ten months of the start, the F.A.N.Y. convoy has given such satisfaction it has been greatly increased; and I am confident it will yet increase.

Women have proved what they can do since the war broke out; and is this a mean record—for a corps that had no influence, no money, and no recognition to start with, that now, after two years' active service, it has more than doubled its membership and has five units working in France?

A few names have been mentioned more than others, but the roll-call of the F.A.N.Y.'s will one day be published and give the names and services of all who have worked with the corps. For every individual member has rendered splendid service to the world, and when the history of the corps is written full justice will be done to all.

This is more or less a record of personal happenings taken from my diary, circulated privately and published now at the request of those friends whose interest was aroused. I have omitted the exciting story of Sister White and other two F.A.N.Y.'s who received the Order of Leopold from King Albert for bravery under fire. I have not dwelt upon the steady and wonderful work done by our band of trained nurses, nor the quiet devotion displayed by probationers and ward orderlies. I have not pictured our Belgian doctors or adjutant or orderlies—not even the irresistible humour of Louis, the orderly whose vocation calls him to the priesthood, who in his proud knowledge of the English language tells visitors blandly "he is learning to be a father."

All these things and many more will be related after the war is over in the History of the F.A.N.Y. Corps.

Lightning Source UK Ltd.
Milton Keynes UK
UKOW05f2246301214

243811UK00001B/150/P